CASE STUDIES IN ECONOMICS

ECONOMIC POLICY

CASE STUDIES IN ECONOMICS

Principles of Economics
Projects and Role Playing in Teaching Economics

CASE STUDIES IN ECONOMICS

ECONOMIC POLICY

C. T. Sandford
M. S. Bradbury
and Associates

SECOND EDITION

M

First edition 1970
Second edition 1977

Published by
THE MACMILLAN PRESS LTD
London and Basingstoke
Associated companies in New York
Dublin Melbourne Johannesburg and Madras

ISBN 0 333 21478 1   (hard cover)
0 333 21480 3 (paper cover)

Printed in Great Britain by
Lowe & Brydone Printers Limited, Thetford, Norfolk

Contents

List of Cases

Preface to the First Edition

This book is one of a series on case studies in economics consisting initially of three volumes. This and a companion volume on *Principles of Economics* use case studies as illustrations and exercises and are intended to be study and workbooks. The third volume, *Projects and Role Playing in Teaching Economics*, is written specifically for teachers, and offers guidance on how to prepare case studies, along with examples of projects and role-playing case studies in a form which makes it easy for teachers to adopt them.

The main advantage of the case-study approach is its realism, for a case study is taken to be a detailed examination of an actual or closely simulated economic situation, phenomenon or development from which economic understanding can be gained.

A notable feature of the series is the extent to which the material has been tried out in the classroom or the 'field'. Thus most of the chapters in this book have been modified in the light of the comments of the teachers who tested the material with their own students. The authors gratefully acknowledge the benefit gained from discussions with teachers in a working party of the Bristol branch of the Economics Association. Some testing was undertaken by the authors in their own educational institutions, and thanks are due to students of Bath University, the City of London Polytechnic, Jordanhill College of Education, Glasgow, and the North Staffordshire Polytechnic. More specifically the authors wish to thank the teachers listed below, all of whom tested copies of one or more draft chapters and made helpful comments. We are most grateful to them and their students:

D. J. Burningham of Brunel University.
C. L. Davies of Rodway School, Mangotsfield.
P. N. Dean, formerly of Bristol College of Commerce
    (now Bristol Polytechnic).
E. F. Dyson of Bristol Grammar School.
Mrs W. B. Gillman, formerly of Hartcliffe Comprehensive School, Bristol.
D. J. Hancock and D. P. Gabriel of Madeley College of Education.
G. N. Lang of Redland College of Education, Bristol.
D. Lee of Rolle College, Exmouth.
E. R. Savage of St Luke's College, Exeter.
N. A. Shute, formerly of Withywood Comprehensive School, Bristol.

The authors wish to thank Messrs Sweet & Maxwell Ltd for permission to reprint the extract from *British Tax Review* (1957), by Professor G. F. Break.

C. T. S.
M. S. B.

Preface to the Second Edition

This second edition differs from the first in three ways. First, it contains much new matter; the background material has been rewritten where there have been new developments to take into account: over half the cases in this edition are completely new; and where the earlier cases have been retained they have been extended and updated as appropriate. Second, we were dissatisfied with the very short cases (consisting of little more than a table and a few questions) that appeared in the first edition, and these have been dropped. Third, with Britain securely a part of the European Community, we have felt it desirable to include some cases on aspects of E.E.C. policy – in particular on agriculture, competition policy and tax harmonisation.

Whilst there have been these very considerable changes in content, we have not felt any need to change the purpose or structure of the book; the basic approach remains the same.

C. T. S.
M. S. B.

M. S. Bradbury is a civil servant who has contributed to this book on a personal basis. Any news expressed in his contributions should not, therefore, be attributed to the Department of Industry.

Introduction

Economic Policy and the companion volume *Principles of Economics* are both designed as study and work books which can be used to complement and supplement any good textbook. The case studies, which illustrate the topics in this volume, consist of detailed examinations of situations, events or developments by means of which economic principles or concepts can be learnt, or significant contemporary happenings in the economy made more meaningful. We believe that the study of economics can gain in reality and vividness by the consideration in some detail of actual economic phenomena. The approach also serves to bring together in convenient form much material not otherwise readily accessible to students; and many of the cases and exercises help to familiarise the student with statistical sources and give needed practice in handling elementary statistics.

If these are the very real merits of case studies, the users must also be aware of the limitations and pitfalls. Because many of the case studies contain a considerable degree of detail, the coverage of any one topic must necessarily be limited. Because the coverage of a topic is limited, there exists a very real danger that the unwary student may generalise too hastily from the one or two examples presented to him. Reality in depth may be obtained at the expense of reality in breadth. The authors hope they have sufficiently guarded against this danger by the background material to the studies of each chapter, which tries to put the cases in perspective and endeavours to indicate how far the cases included can be regarded as representative. Moreover, the volume is not a 'do-it-yourself kit'. It is assumed that the user will have the assistance of a textbook and, still more important, a teacher.

The layout of each chapter has been standardised to facilitate use. Each begins with a *summary of background material*. The selection of material has proved far from easy, and the teachers who have tested the draft chapters in the classroom have expressed divergent views on these introductions: some would like them shorter, other longer; some with more theory and others with more history. The authors have tried to follow certain principles. Because it is assumed that students will have a good text, the background is primarily intended as a revision exercise to bring to the student's mind what he has already met – to provide, that is to say, a comprehensible but essentially concise summary. Where, however, it is felt that textbook coverage may be inadequate because the subject (e.g. developing countries) is often scantily treated in introductory texts, or because of very recent developments which have yet to penetrate the textbooks, a fuller treatment is provided. Another consideration has been the coverage of the companion volume in *Principles of Economics*; where that contains a summary of the economic theory relevant to topics in this book, a treatment emphasising recent legislation and history has seemed appropriate for *Economic Policy*.

The *exercises* which follow the cases have a designed pattern; they are arranged in order of difficulty, the simplest first. Also, in general, the earlier questions can be answered briefly, by means of a paragraph, a list or a simple calculation; the later ones are more complex and suitable for an extended essay or a class discussion. A distinction is drawn between the questions after each case and the *supplementary exercises* at the end of each chapter. The former are capable of being answered from the material in the case (plus a certain minimum of general economic knowledge and understanding); the supplementary questions span more than one case and/or draw on material not wholly contained within the volume. A list of *sources and references* for more extended reading concludes each chapter, but these do not include references to standard textbooks; the teacher can best supply his own according to which text he uses. Answers to numerical questions are listed at the end of the book.

The book, so arranged, can be used in several ways. It can provide material for private study and class work in parallel with a course in applied economics. The background summaries and different method of approach make it useful as a form of pre-examination revision. Or it has particular value for students such as third-year sixth-formers who already have a grounding in economics and who, whilst having access to a teacher, are spending much of their time in private study, broadening and deepening their grasp of the subject.

The level of the book is roughly that of the good A-level/first-year university student. Because this is not a textbook and the chapters and cases can be used individually, the editors have not felt it necessary to impose a rigorously uniform level. Whilst the majority of the cases are appropriate to the average sixth-former, there are some which all but the best sixth-formers will find difficult; similarly with the questions. These divergencies in level of both cases and questions enable the volume to be used in courses of slightly differing levels and purposes and provide an opportunity for teachers to give to students on the same course assignments which vary according to individual student capacity. Besides A-level and first-year degree courses, we hope that students preparing for the finals of professional examinations and for diplomas in business studies will find the book useful. Not least, we hope that, as the series embodies a relatively new approach to the teaching and learning of economics in this country, it may prove acceptable to teachers and students of economics in the growing number of colleges of education which are introducing economic studies.

The subjects chosen for inclusion in this volume are some of the more important topics which might be expected to figure in a course on applied economics or on economic policy. The selection is to some extent governed by the suitability of the topic for case-study treatment. It is also conditioned by the need to avoid duplicating material in the companion volume, *Principles of Economics*; for there is no clear-cut division between 'principles' and 'applied', and a few of the chapters in either volume could fit almost equally well into the other. The same problem arises in the allocation of material between the parts and, indeed, the chapters of the present volume; there is an element of arbitrariness in the arrangement. Thus the study of overpopulation in Mauritius, included in Part 1, 'The Population Framework', could have appeared in Part Four on 'Developing Countries and World Trade', and Case 3 on internal migration in Great Britian could equally well have appeared as part of Case 5 on regional economic and social indicators. We have sought to indicate these relationships by cross-referencing and by a contents list of cases as well as chapters at the beginning of the book. Interrelationships are also indicated in the short introductions to parts, which are included where they can be helpful.

The title, *Economic Policy,* has been interpreted broadly. We have felt it right to include a few cases which pose problems for the community on which governments have not yet formulated policies or have decided to leave the solution to 'natural forces'.

A difficulty in economics, particularly acute in treating economic policy, is that the authors' value judgements and personal bias intrude. Some of the matters considered, like the value of a prices and incomes policy or indicative planning, are highly controversial. The authors have sought to be 'positive' in their assessments and to let the facts or documents speak for themselves as far as possible. But the very process of selecting material – deciding which facts to include and which to exclude – inevitably allows personal bias to enter; as the contributors do not all share the same political convictions, at least if personal bias has crept in it will not all be one way!

Doubtless reviewers will not be slow to tell us how far we have fallen short of our objectives. The gap between aims and achievements, like the gap between teaching and learning, is often very wide, and we are concerned to reduce both.

We therefore invite and welcome comments from teachers who use the series. In the Preface we acknowledged our debt to the many teachers and students who tested material before publication and who gave us the benefit of their advice. This has certainly eliminated some of the blemishes; but we do not doubt that many remain, and we shall be grateful to those who take the trouble to tell us of imperfections and how we may set about removing them.

C. T. Sandford
M. S. Bradbury

Part 1

The Population Framework

CHAPTER 1

Population Growth and Structure

T. K. Robinson

Summary of Background Material

Divergent Views on the Economics of Population

Changes in population are important to an economy in two respects: from the standpoint of production, they affect the combination of labour and other productive factors; and from the standpoint of consumption, they influence the level of effective demand within the economy.

Population theory is noteworthy for its diversity. Those economists who have expressed fears of overpopulation have usually been concerned for the living standards of the individual, believing that a restriction in numbers in the community will lead to a higher real income per head of population. The alternative view is that population expansion, by providing a greater market, is the stimulus and challenge needed for economic growth in a society.

Population theory pre-dates Malthus. It is found in some medieval economic writings, and in the late seventeenth century William Petty provided a surprisingly thorough analysis of the advantages and problems of the very high population density of the Netherlands at a time of its great commercial achievement. He argued that the development of trading and manufacturing activities and of an efficient system of internal and external communications would not have been economical without the increase in population and the corresponding rise in production.

This idea of 'indivisibilities', which are more fully utilised as an economy grows, became the basis of a theory of increasing returns related to the Industrial Revolution, when both population and general living standards were rising. It was further developed by Marshall and, more spectacularly, by Allyn Young, who contended, in 1928, that an industrial country would directly benefit from an enlargement of its population and that British industry needed a domestic market of 100 million people if the economies of scale, both internal and external, were to be realised. Everatt Hagen has pursued this line of thought by showing that densely populated countries required considerably less capital per unit of product than sparsely peopled areas; existing population density and the rate of population increase are both important factors in reducing the net burden of capital requirement in an economy as the risks of loss from acts of

investment are reduced owing to the greater range of alternative uses available
for capital.

It has also been argued that population growth has a positive effect upon
savings because a stationary or declining population has a higher proportion of
older people who consume capital instead of creating it, whereas the lowering
of the average age, usually associated with an expanding population, leads to
more positive concern about the future. Hence an economy with a growing
population tends to be dynamic both in the supply and the use made of capital.

This optimistic view of the economic effects of rising population has been
recently and persuasively expressed by Colin Clark, who contends that the
challenge of an increased number of producers and consumers leads to increased
scientific and technological innovation.

The more traditional Malthusian statement about population growth and
change is quite different. In the famous *Essay* of 1798, he argued that man's
power to produce population is greater than his capacity to produce subsistence
and that, if left unchecked, a population could double itself in twenty-five years.
This chronic tendency would automatically lead to vice and misery unless held
in check by a moderate postponement of marriage, by moral restraint and
perhaps by emigration. His fears of the consequences of the accelerating rate of
growth of the British population at the time were due to his acceptance of the
current economic view that successive applications of units of labour to a fixed
supply of land in agriculture would inevitably lead to diminishing returns, but he
can be criticised for failing to perceive that increased application of capital in
agriculture and industry would lead to increased food production at home and
to increased trade in manufactures overseas. His view of population increasing
beyond the means of subsistence and being brought back by preventive or
positive checks suggested an oscillation which has certainly not occurred in
Britain. Indeed, the rapid growth of the population throughout the nineteenth
century, coupled with a general rise in living standards, seemed to refute his
gloomy forebodings, and when the slowing-down in the rate of growth occurred
it resulted mainly from family limitation by birth control rather than by moral
restraint which he had advocated. Although living standards continued to rise,
changes in economic and social attitudes, ranging from the effects of factory
legislation to the growing emancipation of women in society, tended to reduce
the average family size. By the 1920s some economists, including Keynes, were
arguing that population growth in industrialised countries was coming to an end
and that the economics of a stationary or even a declining population would need
to be studied more closely, but majority opinion favoured a continuation of the
increase of population because it would provide the incentive necessary for the
workings of the free market and for private investment.

The debatable logic of Malthusian views in relation to British population expansion does not mean that they lack relevance elsewhere. Many of the less developed countries of the world are currently passing through the same phase of

population growth associated with a marked increase in the survival rate which Britain experienced in the nineteenth century, and this has placed a heavy burden upon the means of subsistence in these areas. The poverty of many rural areas in Asia, Latin America and parts of Africa leaves us in no doubt about the reality of Malthusian checks for them. Industrialisation and improved agriculture which these countries are struggling to achieve may bring higher living standards which may in turn lead to a fall in the birth rate – but this may not come soon enough to avert a catastrophe, hence the urgent need for programmes of family planning.

More recently, in Britain and other advanced industrial countries, there has been a tendency to favour a smaller population on environmental grounds.

Optimum Population

Is it possible to define the optimum population of a country? Edwin Cannan in the late nineteenth century described it as that population which for a given age distribution and given technology produces the maximum output per head. He readily agreed that it is extremely difficult to know at a given moment of time what the sum total of the resources of a country are and how they are being used, and, in fact, it is only possible to look back over a period of time and suggest evidence of either under- or overpopulation in relation to changes in the real income per head of the community. Perhaps the greatest value of this concept is that it establishes some criterion for determining the relationship between the growth of resources and the growth of population. The terms under- and overpopulation – especially the latter – are often loosely used without any attempt being made to conduct an analysis of this kind.

No entirely satisfactory theory of population fluctuations either as cause or effect of other economic variables has yet been produced; and changes in total population cannot be explained by economic factors alone, but require a multi-disciplinary treatment.

Illustration by Case Studies

The first case examines the problems of the island of Mauritius, with one of the fastest growing populations in the world. The second case is concerned with the fluctuations in the birth rate of the United Kingdom since 1945 and also with projections of future birth and fertility rates and their possible implications for education policy.

CASE 1. A STUDY IN POPULATION EXPLOSION: MAURITIUS*

World population is expanding at an unprecedented rate. The 1970 figure of just over 3600 million was reached in something like a million years of human development; according to the most recent estimates prepared by the United Nations, world population will double by the end of the century, mainly because of a vast increase in the survival rate (birth rate minus death rate) in the less developed areas of the world.

Mauritius in the Indian Ocean represents in microcosm the present population growth of these areas. It is a small island (about the size of Surrey) which has been influenced over the centuries by colonists from a great variety of European

TABLE 1.1

Group	Per cent of total population	Economic position	Background influences
1. Franco-Mauritian	5	Rich landowners, professional occupations (lawyers, doctors, architects, etc.).	French-speaking, Roman Catholic, conservative.
2. Creole	25	Artisans, minor government officials.	Descendants of African and Malagasy slaves. Some intermarriage with French settlers. Speak 'pidgin-French'.
3. Indian	66	Labour force on sugar estates. A few wealthy merchants.	Mainly Hindu, but a substantial Moslem minority.
4. Chinese	4	Retail traders (almost a monopoly).	Very frugal and enterprising. Large families.
5. British	Negligible	Official positions. A single sugar estate owner.	No links with other groups through marriage.

Population structure of Mauritius

*The main source for this case study is J. E. Meade, 'Population Explosion, the Standard of Living and Social Conflict', *Economic Journal* (June 1967).

countries (Portugal, Holland, France and Britain) and by the influx of African slaves and Indian indentured labour, so that its population structure is very complex.

The island depends to a remarkable extent on a single crop – sugar – which in the 1960s was responsible for around a third of G.D.P. and nearly 100 per cent of all exports. There are big inequalities in the distribution of wealth and income, marked political divisions, language barriers and educational backwardness; the Roman Catholic Church, which is very influential, has been opposed to family planning.

TABLE 1.2
Birth and death rates (per thousand of the population) in Mauritius

	Total population (thousands)	Birth rate	Death rate	Natural increase
1931 – 5*	401	31.1	29.6	1.5
1944 – 8*	429	41.5	27.2	14.3
1949 – 53*	484	47.4	15.2	32.2
1954 – 8*	575	41.6	12.9	28.7
1962	686	38.5	9.3	29.2
1966	759	36.0	8.9	27.1
1970	819	26.7	7.8	18.9

*average

TABLE 1.3
Age distribution of Mauritius population (compared with a sample of European countries)

	Percentage of total population				
	Mauritius				European countries
	1944	1952	1962	1970	1960
Under 15	35	40	46	44	26
15 – 64	62	57	51	52	64
65 and over	3	3	3	4	10
	100	100	100	100	100

SOURCE: *United Nations Demographic Year Book, 1971.*

Since 1945 British policy has sought (*a*) to introduce measures of preventive medicine and to remove such scourges as malaria, and (*b*) to establish greater social and political freedom as a prelude to independence.

The generally low standard of education, the attitude of the Church and the reduction in death rates have combined to produce the present population growth in Mauritius of nearly 3 per cent per annum.

There is no doubt that the heavy population growth has reduced real income per head below what it would otherwise have been. Although Mauritian standards are high compared with the poorest countries of the world, the value of output per head in 1970 was less than one-fifth of that of the United Kingdom.

In order to cope with the increase in population on the basis of even the lower projection indicated in Table 1.4, a big programme of economic development would be necessary as well as a reduction in the dependence of the economy on sugar. But the backwardness in technical education, the lack of enterprise and good management, the inflexibilities of racial traditions and divisions all impede structural change.

TABLE 1.4

Projected population of Mauritius in age groups, 1977 and 1987

	Actual	*Projection A (thousands)*		*Projection B (thousands)*	
	1962	*1977*	*1987*	*1977*	*1987*
Under 15	313	514	776	356	385
15 – 64	351	579	813	579	757
65 and over	22	37	51	37	51
Total	686	1130	1640	972	1193

Basis of Projections

A. Continuation of average of 1961 – 3 rates of fertility.
B. Fertility rates rapidly reduced between 1966 and 1972 so that no family has more than three children by the latter date.
Both projections assume an annual gain of one-half a year in life expectancy.

The Clash of Economic Efficiency and Social Justice

A wage rate is both the price of a factor of production and an income. The low wage rate necessary to encourage the widespread use of the abundant factor of production in an overpopulated country, labour, also results in widening the income gap between rich and poor. Mauritius has a very high rate of unemployment. There are many ways in which a low wage might have an effect in encouraging a more economic use of resources. For example: (1) weeding sugar plantations by hand instead of using imported herbicides; (2) loading sugar on to ships by hand; (3) growing labour-intensive tea instead of land-intensive sugar; (4) the development of labour-intensive manufactures like textiles to compete with textiles from similarly overpopulated areas like Hong Kong. 'But', as Professor Meade sums up, 'a wage rate which is low enough to make these activities worthwhile may lead to a quite unacceptable inequality in the distribution of income.'

Exercises

(1.1) What features in the society and recent history of Mauritius have particularly promoted population growth?

(1.2) Why may rapid population growth in Mauritius be expected to reduce real income below what it would otherwise have been?

(1.3) What do the figures in Tables 1.3 and 1.4 tell us about the 'burden of dependency' in a situation of rapidly growing population?

(1.4) How far do trends in the birth and death rate in Mauritius between 1962 and 1970 support or refute (*a*) Projection A and (*b*) Projection B (Table 1.4)?

(1.5) What features of Mauritian society exacerbate the problems raised by the rapid population growth?

(1.6) Why may there be a conflict between 'economic efficiency' and 'justice' in the determination of wages in an overpopulated country?

CASE 2. BIRTH-RATE TRENDS IN GREAT BRITAIN AND THEIR EFFECT ON EDUCATION PROVISION*

Of the three influences affecting the growth of a population – birth rate, death rate and migration flow – the first has been much the most important in causing changes in the population of Britain in the post-war period and also in affecting the projections of population growth for the remainder of the present century and beyond.

Since 1945 there have been four distinct phases in the birth rate:

(*a*)   1945 – 9: a period of birth rate increase in the immediate aftermath of the war, similar to that experienced for a short time after 1918;

(*b*)   1949 – 55: a period of birth rate decrease, again following a similar pattern to that in the comparable period after the First World War;

(*c*)   1955 – 64: a second period of birth rate increase – an unexpected tendency caused partly because people were marrying younger and having children earlier and perhaps because of the general improvement in the standard of living; and

(*d*)   Since 1964: a second period of birth rate decline which has coincided with a slowing down in the reduction in the average age of marriage; those married in the past ten years also appear to be having fewer children in the first years of their married life than those married in the previous decade.

Any meaningful analysis of births must relate them to the size and characteristics of the population as a whole. Table 1.5 shows the main annual measures which are used:

(*a*)   The birth rate represents the number of births per thousand of the population of all ages. It is sometimes referred to as the 'crude' birth rate.

(*b*)   The general fertility rate is the number of births related to the population of women of reproductive ages (conventionally taken as 15 – 44 years).

(*c*)   The gross reproduction rate is the number of daughters a woman would produce if she survived to the end of her reproductive period, and if throughout her life she was subject to the fertility rates of the year for which the gross reproduction rate is calculated.

(*d*)   The net reproduction rate is the gross reproduction rate adjusted for the effects of mortality on women until the end of the reproductive age range. It is a measure of the extent to which a generation of women, subject to the fertility and mortality rates of a particular period, would replace themselves by the next generation of women. It is usually regarded as the most useful single indication of the trend of fertility, but it has the disadvantage that it is related to the fertility and mortality experience of a single year.

*The main source of this case study is P. Venning, 'Falling Birth Rate May Upset all the Plans for Schools and Staffing', *Times Educational Supplement* (9 Feb 1973).

(*e*) The total period fertility rate takes account of both male and female births and is calculated in the same manner as the gross reproduction rate. As approximately 106 boys are born for every 100 girls, this rate is roughly equivalent to 2.06 times the gross reproduction rate.

TABLE 1.5

Births: numbers and rates, 1955 – 74 (Great Britain)

Year	Live births (thousands)	Birth rate per 1000 population of all ages	General fertility rate per 1000 women aged 15 – 44	Reproduction rate		Total period fertility rate
				Gross	Net	
1955	760	15.3	74.1	1.09	1.05	2.24
1956	796	16.0	78.2	1.16	1.12	2.38
1957	821	16.4	81.2	1.21	1.16	2.47
1958	840	16.7	83.3	1.24	1.19	2.53
1959	848	16.8	84.0	1.24	1.20	2.56
1960	886	17.4	87.7	1.30	1.26	2.69
1961	912	17.8	89.9	1.35	1.31	2.78
1962	943	18.2	91.3	1.38	1.34	2.84
1963	957	18.3	91.6	1.39	1.35	2.86
1964	980	18.7	93.2	1.41	1.37	2.91
1965	963	18.2	91.7	1.37	1.34	2.83
1966	946	17.8	90.5	1.34	1.30	2.76
1967	928	17.4	89.0	1.29	1.25	2.65
1968	914	17.0	87.7	1.25	1.21	2.57
1969	888	16.4	85.2	1.20	1.17	2.47
1970	872	16.1	83.6	1.16	1.13	2.40
1971	870	16.1	83.8	1.16	1.13	2.39
1972	810	15.0	78.0	1.08	1.05	2.25
1973	750	13.8	71.9	0.98	0.96	2.03
1974	710	13.0	67.6	0.93	0.90	1.91

SOURCE: Office of Population Censuses and Surveys.

Thus, in 1955, when the birth rate had reached one of its lowest post-war points, a net reproduction rate of 1.05 indicated that the population would be likely to rise by 5 per cent in the next generation (usually estimated as 27 years), with an average completed family size of 2.24 children. In 1964, when the birth rate had almost returned to the high level of the late 1940s, the population seemed likely to rise by 37 per cent in the next generation with an average completed family size of 2.9 children.

It is clear from this that projections of population growth based on these data may vary even from year to year and they have to be considerably adjusted if there is a continuous upward or downward trend in the birth rate lasting over five years or more. In 1963, the Registrar General anticipated that the U.K. population would reach 65 million by 1990; the 1974-based estimate is of a U.K. population of only 58 million at that date.

One vital factor in determining fertility trends is clearly the average age of marriage. In the 1930s fewer than one in ten women were married before the age of 20; by the early 1950s, two in ten were married by this age, and by 1972 almost three in ten were married by this age. In the 1930s, 25 per cent of women aged 20 – 4 years were married; now almost 60 per cent of this age group are married. The effect of this has been generally to lead to an earlier pattern of child bearing and has reduced the average generation length by $1\frac{1}{2}$ - 2 years since 1945. But there is some indication in the early 1970s that newly married women are deferring the birth of their first child beyond the first two years of marriage, and this is an important factor in accounting for the present lower birth rate and fertility trends. The higher birth rate of the early 1960s was probably due mainly to the coincidence of one marriage group or cohort with a high fertility in the 25 – 9 age range and another with a high fertility in the 20 – 4 age range; it was also affected by the considerable influx of young immigrants with a high fertility rate. The present low birth rate is due to a reversal of all these tendencies.

The crucial factor determining the birth rate in the next decade and more is how far the marriage groups now in the early stages of child bearing intend to have similar family sizes to those now nearing the end of the reproductive cycle. If their intentions are similar, then the birth rate must rise substantially within the next decade. Some recent surveys, for example the *General Household Survey* and John Peel's *Survey in Hull* suggest that women who married recently tend to have rather smaller families than their counterparts ten years previously. In the short term this would still leave average completed family size above replacement level, but, if it continued over a period of a decade or more, it might well lead to a situation in which a stationary population became a real possibility.

The conclusion of this general analysis is that the margin for error in extrapolating trends in the birth and reproduction rates is wide, and this is disturbing when the planning of future economic and social policy depends on a reasonably accurate forecast of population growth. This is particularly true of the education service, which has been forced into frequent changes of policy, many of them short-term expedients, to cope with the changing estimates of school, college and university populations in the post-war period.

Thus, in the 1960s, the service was under continual pressure to provide additional accommodation for the considerably increased primary school population produced by the birth rate increase of the late 1950s, and also the greatly increased population in the later stages of the secondary school and in further and higher education produced by the even larger increase in the birth rate of the late

1940s; also a higher priority was given to these forms of education.

The fall in the birth rate since 1964 has opened up a number of new possibilities in education, some expansionist and others more restrictive in scope – raising the school-leaving age, expanding nursery education (advocated in the 1972 Government White Paper), improving pupil – teacher ratios, reducing expenditure on teacher training, reducing the school-building programme (or making it more flexible). But the latest projections of the Registrar General's office, which take into account marriage rates, births to married women, illegitimate births and the effect of assumed migration estimates, suggest that the birth rate in Britain may start rising again soon, and continue on an upward trend in the remainder of the decade (with an average of 930,000 births per year between 1971 and 1981), mainly because of an increase in the number of women of child-bearing age rather than an increase in the anticipated completed family size. If this projection is correct, then educational planning will have to make yet another rapid adjustment, but it will not be clear that it is correct for at least another two to three years.

Exercises

(1.7) Summarise the reasons given in the case for the changing trends in the U.K. birth rate since 1955.

(1.8) Why is the net reproduction rate a more reliable indicator than the birth rate of the likely future growth of the population of a country?

(1.9) From Table 1.5 explain what the figures for net reproduction rate and total period fertility rate for the following years imply for population growth in the subsequent generation: 1957; 1962; 1967.

Supplementary exercises

(1.10) Consider the view that Great Britain overcame the Malthusian devil only at the cost of a heavy dependence on international trade.

(1.11) Figure 1.1 shows the approximate percentage rates of growth at current prices in the different branches of the educational system between 1960 and 1970 using the financial year 1960–1 as a 'base'. Expenditure includes all public spending, both by local authorities and by the central government, current as well as capital, but not private spending by individuals. How far can changes in expenditure on education in the period 1960 to 1970 be explained by fluctuations in the birth rate referred to in Case 2? Indicate some of the other factors which influence expenditure on particular forms of education. Consider how the pattern of education expenditure is likely to be affected by the birth-rate trend of the period 1970 -4, as shown in Table 1.5.

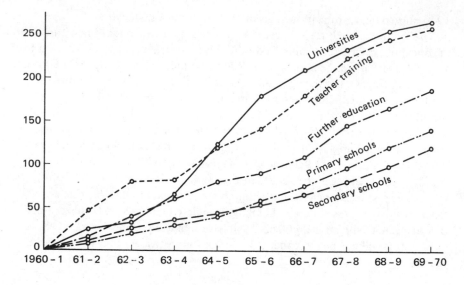

FIG. 1.1

Public expenditure on education

Sources and References

COLIN CLARK, *Population Growth and Land Use* (London: Allen & Unwin, 1967) chs iii and vii.

JOHN I. CLARKE, *Population Geography* (Oxford: Pergamon, 1965) chs vi and x.

P. K. KELSALL , *Population* (London: Longmans, 1967) ch. xii.

Population Projections: mid 1974 based, Office of Population Censuses and Surveys.

R. M. WILLIAMS, *British Population* (London: Heinemann, 1972).

Report of the Population Panel, Cmnd. 5258 (London: H.M.S.O., 1973).

CHAPTER 2

Population Movement

M. S. Bradbury and T. K. Robinson*

Summary of Background Material

Emigration and Immigration

Three factors determine the rate of population growth of a country – birth rate, death rate and rate of migration (emigration and immigration). Of these, the rate of migration is the most difficult to measure as so much depends on the reliability of the information obtained from different countries. It is only possible to assess the effect of migration on population structure if the data from both sending and receiving countries at least distinguish between long-term and short-term migrants and indicate the extend of reflux (the difference between gross and net emigration or immigration). Net migration is best recorded as the difference between the recorded inter-censal population change and the natural increase of the population (birth rate minus death rate).

Since 1801, when population censuses began to be taken, migration has played a relatively small part in the population growth of Great Britain compared with natural increase. The general movement has been outwards, but from 1931 to 1941 and again from 1956 to 1961 there was net immigration. The experience of Ireland (all of which was part of the United Kingdom in the nineteenth century) has been quite different, with net emigration exceeding the natural increase of the population throughout the second half of the nineteenth century. Most of this movement was to the United States, which attracted settlers from almost every part of the world at this time, and although this trend has been reduced in scale since the 1920s, when selective restrictions on immigration were introduced, it has had a profound influence on the present population of the country. Brinley Thomas has argued that migration from Europe to the United States occurred in long cycles of years (1845 – 54, 1863 – 73, 1881 – 8, 1903 – 13) and that these were all periods of rapid growth not only in the American economy but also in most of the sending countries. The reduction in the rate of growth of the labour force of these countries may have increased the earning power of the remaining workers and checked the tendency to emigrate in the interval periods.

Yet all statements about the economic motives for international migration have to be qualified. If contrasting living standards between sending and receiving countries were a major factor, then it might be expected that the poorest countries

*T. K. Robinson wrote the summary of Background Material and Case 4; M. S. Bradbury wrote Case 3.

would provide a steady stream of willing emigrants; but this is not generally so. The outward movement usually begins when previously rural communities are in transition and exposed to urban and commercial influences which provide more knowledge of comparable living standards elsewhere. It is equally difficult to generalise about the importance of employment opportunities and variations in relative real wages as economic motives for movement. There does seem to be a strong relationship between Irish and West Indian immigration to Britain and relative employment opportunities, but this does not seem to be so marked for British emigration to Canada, and a detailed study of trends in emigration from Britain to Australia does not reveal any significant correlation between the extent of migration and levels of real wages in the two countries.

Most emigration is from countries where there is some pressure of population on existing resources. This seems to account for the large-scale Irish emigration, which began after the potato famine of the 1840s, and it also explains the even more remarkable case of Puerto Rico, where in a single year, 1953, the gross emigration from the area was 12 per cent of the entire population. Other small countries and islands (e.g. Malta, Corsica, Lebanon), which have experienced population pressure at home, also appear to specialise in emigration as a possible solution to their problems.

Demographic factors also affect migration policies. A few major countries, e.g. Britain, Italy and Japan, have at times actively encouraged emigration, but many more nations have attempted to restrict it because of fears that they might lose the youngest and most active and enterprising sections of their population. Immigration controls, which were relatively insignificant in the last century, have now become increasingly common, and have usually been designed to restrict the entry of certain ethnic groups considered undesirable for a variety of reasons, only some of which can be regarded as strictly economic. The White Australia policy, the limitation on Chinese entry into South-east Asian countries and the restrictions on coloured immigration to Britain since 1962 are a few of the most outstanding examples of these controls.

Internal Migration

Movement of population within a country is easier to measure than international migration, but again there is no general economic theory which can deal with all the varying motives for movement. Migrations from rural to urban areas are the most important form of internal migration in countries experiencing industrialisation and technological change, and this was the pattern in Britain in the nineteenth century; but more recently the rural – urban movement has been less important than inter-urban migration.

It has been customary to examine these movements in terms of the 'pull' influence of better employment opportunities and working and living conditions in the areas of reception and the 'push' elements of population pressure and fears

of unemployment due to decline of basic industries in the areas of departure.
Most economists have concluded that these changes have been beneficial in that
they have assisted economic growth and development and have secured a higher
average standard of living in a community.

Colin Clark has analysed the economic potential of different locations in terms
of the sum of regional incomes around them, and has distinguished between macro-
location (the location of population and industry between regions and groupings
of industrial towns) and micro-location (the location of population and industry
within such areas). He argues that macro-location tends towards an ever-increasing
concentration in a limited number of areas whilst micro-location tends towards an
ever-increasing diffusion or sprawl.

It might be thought that the operation of free-market forces would reverse these
tendencies because a greater supply of labour in the reception area would reduce
its earning power and hence its attraction for further movement, whilst the opposite would occur in the area of departure. In practice, however, national collective-
bargaining pressures prevent this flexibility in earnings, and the areas attracting
population and industry gain many external economies through concentration,
and achieve rates of growth, vigour of enterprise and quality of infrastructure
which sustain the movement. In a modern economy which is becoming increasingly
service-orientated, the important factors of location are markets and environment
rather than raw materials and power sources, and so there is a cumulative effect of
migration; the additional supply of labour is readily absorbed through the increase
in the scale of the economy in the more favoured areas, whilst the reduced supply
of labour in the less fortunate regions may cause them to experience a higher rate
of unemployment because of the general decline in demand for labour through the
contraction of production. Hirschmann has referred to the polarisation effects of
migration, whereby it causes interregional differences to widen rather than narrow.
The drift of population to the south in the United Kingdom, to the west in
Germany and to the north-east in the United States in the past generation would
seem to bear out this contention.

This presents a formidable problem to modern governments. Should they
leave redistribution of population to market forces, which may tend to accentuate
interregional distinctions, or should they seek to influence migration movements
within their economies by a mixture of negative constraints and positive induce-
ments affecting the mobility of capital and labour?

Illustration by Case Studies

Case 3 illustrates migration between and within the standard regions of Great
Britain, 1966–71. The implications of population growth and movement for a
single region are considered in Case 4, which examines population movement in
the South-east of England since 1951.

The geographical mobility of a group of redundant workers is examined in
Case 6, p. 47.

FIG. 2.1 *The Regions of Great Britain**

*Source: *Census 1971, Great Britain: Migration Tables* (London: H.M.S.O., 1974) pt I, p. xxiii. .

CASE 3.   INTERNAL MIGRATION IN GREAT BRITAIN, 1966 – 71

This case is concerned with migration between and within the standard regions of Great Britain (see Figure 2.1). Overseas migration and migration between Great Britain and Northern Ireland, the Irish Republic, the Channel Islands and the Isle of Man is excluded. The case shows that the geographical mobility of population is considerably greater over short distances, that is within a region, than over long distances, that is between regions (particularly where regions are not adjacent).

TABLE 2.1
Regional Population Changes in Great Britain, 1966 – 71

	1966 (thousands)	1971 (thousands)	Percentage increase (1966 – 71)
Great Britain	52303	53979	3.2
North	3261	3296	1.1
Yorkshire and Humberside	4704	4799	2.0
East Midlands	3230	3390	5.0
East Anglia	1540	1669	8.4
South-east	16652	17230	3.5
South-west	3560	3781	6.2
West Midlands	4909	5110	4.1
North-west	6615	6743	1.9
England	44472	46019	3.5
Wales	2663	2731	2.6
Scotland	5168	5229	1.2

SOURCE: *Abstract of Regional Statistics, 1974* (London: H.M.S.O.) table 3.

It will be seen from Table 2.1 that some regions have increased their population at a faster rate than others. Differences between the 1966 and 1971 populations for each region are the net outcome of three factors:

(i) Natural change (births and deaths within the region currently tend to increase population in all cases);

(ii) Civilian migration both between regions and between each region and elsewhere leading to net gains or losses of population;

(iii) Other adjustments (a small statistical adjustment reflecting changes in armed forces, residential, educational establishments and prisons).

TABLE 2.2

Interregional Migrations in Great Britain, 1966 – 71 (10 per cent sample)

Movement to	Movement from										SAMPLE TOTAL GAIN	SAMPLE TOTAL NET GAIN OR LOSS	TOTAL NET GAIN OR LOSS
	North	Yorkshire and Humberside	East Midlands	East Anglia	South-east	South-west	West Midlands	North-west	Wales	Scotland			
North	—	3630	957	339	3372	801	1023	1874	361	1611	13968	−2571	−25710
Yorkshire and Humberside	3246	—	3501	782	4760	1025	1523	3485	559	1360	20241	−4237	−42370
East Midlands	1446	4046	—	1282	7343	1224	3566	1906	674	1415	22902	3495	34950
East Anglia	648	1081	1618	—	10992	917	854	854	347	587	17898	7368	73680
South east	4753	6257	5737	5337	—	13395	7635	8427	4279	6415	62235	−4663	−46630
South-west	1066	1736	1932	1002	19399	—	4072	2710	2040	1326	35283	11635	116350
West Midlands	1325	1876	2585	551	6275	2284	—	2952	1845	1382	21075	−3899	−38990
North-west	2188	4022	1628	522	6489	1493	3211	—	1779	2164	23496	−3545	−35450
Wales	385	703	604	312	3654	1429	2112	3362	—	399	12960	642	6420
Scotland	1482	1127	845	403	4614	1080	978	1471	434	—	12434	−4225	−42250
SAMPLE TOTAL LOSS	16539	24478	19407	10530	66898	23648	24974	27041	12318	16659	242492	0	0

SOURCE: *Census 1971 Great Britain: Migration Tables* (London: H.M.S.O., 1974) pt I, table 1B.

Information about migration is obtained from censuses of population. When measuring migration between and within the standard regions of Great Britain, migrants are defined as 'persons who stated that their usual address five years before the date of the 1971 Census was different from their usual address at the date of the Census'. This definition tends to understate such migration in at least two respects. First, it excludes migration by children born after 25 April 1966. Second, the intermediate moves of persons making several successive moves are excluded, that is a previous move is tabulated as a migration from his usual address five years before census date direct to his usual address at census date.

Table 2.2 shows in matrix form the interregional migration experienced between 1966 and 1971, of a 10 per cent random sample of respondents to the 1971 population census for Great Britain. It will be seen that the sample total gain or loss of population experienced by a region reflects the balancing of much larger inward and outward population movements. The final column of Table 2.2 'Total net gain or loss' is obtained by multiplying the preceding column 'sample total net gain or loss' by ten, on the assumption that the 10 per cent sample is representative of the whole population.

TABLE 2.3

Migration within individual regions of Great Britain, 1966 – 71
(10 per cent sample)

Great Britain	1,501,925*
North	94,735
Yorkshire and Humberside	136,300
East Midlands	82,174
East Anglia	37,436
South-east	502,965
South-west	93,115
West Midlands	140,053
North-west	186,513
England	1,273,297*
Wales	64,253
Scotland	164,375

*Excludes migration between regions.

SOURCE: As Table 2.2.

Exercises

(2.1) In respect of each region, express the total net gain or loss of population due to migration between regions during 1966 – 71 as a percentage of the corresponding population in 1966. Comment on the results and compare them with the percentage increase in population in each region during 1966 – 71.

(2.2) 'The South-east of England is the largest origin for and destination of migrants for most regions.' Comment.

(2.3) For each region, express migration within the region as a percentage of its population in 1966 (see Table 2.3). Comment on the results and contrast them with the corresponding data for gross migration (movements in plus movements out) between regions (see Table 2.2).

CASE 4. POPULATION MOVEMENTS IN SOUTH-EAST ENGLAND*

The present population of the South-east of England is over 17 million (more than one third of the total population of England and Wales), and the region provides employment for over 8 million workers, mainly in the faster-growing industries of the economy. It is the only region in England and Wales where the rate of population growth has been consistently above the national average since 1801, although this growth has not been spread evenly throughout the region (see Table 2.4).

TABLE 2.4
Total Population, 1801 – 1969 (millions)

	England and Wales	*South-east region*	*Rest of England and Wales*	*South-east Region as a percentage of England and Wales*
1801	8.9	2.5	6.4	28.1
1851	18.0	5.1	12.9	28.5
1901	32.5	10.5	22.0	32.4
1951	43.8	15.2	28.6	34.7
1961	46.1	16.3	29.8	35.4
1969	48.8	17.3	31.5	35.4

In the period 1951 – 61, the South-east gained nearly $1\frac{1}{4}$ million population by natural increase and more than $\frac{1}{4}$ million by net migration, and during the 1960s the natural increase in population was at least ten times as great as the net migration flow, despite the fact that gross migration flows were large and increasing. The trend to the south from the north of England, Scotland and Wales continued, despite policies designed to secure economic growth in these regions, but there was also a considerable increase in the number of people moving from the South-east region especially to East Anglia and the South-west as desire to move away completely from the congestion of the South-east was matched by considerable improvements in facilities for commuting by rail. In terms of internal migration flows, the South-east is already losing population; this is a significant contrast to the predictions of population change made as recently as 1964.

*The main sources of this case study are: *South-east Area Study 1961–81* (London: H.M.S.O., 1964) and *Strategic Plan for the South-east* (London: H.M.S.O., 1970).

Migration from overseas to the region has been particularly important. Between 1961 and 1966, migration to Great Britain from all countries was 940,000 people, and of these just over 500,000 settled in the South-east region, mainly in the London area. Another special feature of the migration flow into the region is that it contains a high proportion of young adults. As a result, the population of the South-east includes a higher proportion of working-age adults and a lower proportion of dependants than elsewhere in England and Wales (62.2 per cent in 1966 compared with a national average of 61.2 per cent). The South-east is the only region which gained in the proportion of economically active in its population, and the total number in employment grew more rapidly than the growth of total population between 1961 and 1966 from 7.6 million to 8.2 million. The increase was especially marked in employment of women in service occupations.

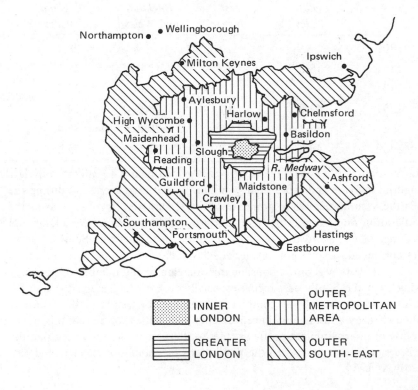

FIG. 2.2 *The South-east region*

TABLE 2.5
Distribution of population and availability of employment

Of the 17.3 million population of the South-east region in 1969:

45 per cent lived in Inner and Greater London	(7.7 million)
30 per cent lived in the Outer Metropolitan area	(5.25 million)
25 per cent lived in the Outer South-east	(4.3 million)

Population Movements in South-east England

In the period 1951–68 Inner and Greater London lost about 450,000 population (an annual average decrease of approximately 26,000) whilst the Outer Metropolitan Area (O.M.A.) increased its population by nearly 1.7 million (annual average increase of approximately 98,000). The major places of growth in the Outer Metropolitan Area were in Guildford, Reading, Slough, Maidenhead, High Wycombe, Crawley and the new towns of Basildon and Harlow. Meanwhile, the population of the Outer South-east (O.S.E.) increased by over 780,000 (annual average increase of approximately 46,000) with the main areas of advance in South Hampshire and Oxfordshire (see Figure 2.2).

In terms of employment in the same period the number of jobs in the Greater London Area increased slightly despite the loss of population; the Outer Metropolitan Area showed a marked increase in employment opportunities, though with some slowing down towards the end of the 1960s; the Outer South-east saw a steady increase in the growth rate of employment opportunities.

It is estimated that by the end of the century an additional 5 million people may have to be accommodated within the South-east region, outside the Greater London Area. Assuming an over-all density of twelve persons per acre, this increase will require a further 600–700 of the region's 10,500 square miles for urban development. In addition, roads, airports, electricity-generating facilities, reservoirs and similar demands will place additional burdens on land utilisation.

This population and accompanying employment growth might be provided for either in a number of towns scattered throughout the South-east region or in a smaller number of much larger growth points. The *Strategic Plan for the South-east*, after investigating similar urban regions in Europe and the United States, has concluded that there are strong advantages in concentration rather than dispersal. The main reasons for these conclusions are:

(1) concentration provides large labour markets which allow the growth of a labour force with diverse skills and a wide range of job opportunities;

(2) concentration provides an industrial base large enough to support specialist sub-contracting and also service activities;

(3) concentration encourages the provision of more effective public transport;

(4) concentration allows for the preservation of more extensive areas of open countryside; and

(5) concentration offers a wider range of social and recreational services than

scattered dispersed communities can provide - this is of particular importance for
the less privileged groups within society.

There are some dangers in a policy of concentration - for example, it might
reproduce London's congestion problems on a smaller scale - but the city regions
envisaged would, wherever possible, be based on already urbanised areas with
considerable economic activity, and this should avoid the problem of urban
sprawl. Where new city regions are created (e.g. at Milton Keynes) there are
opportunities to develop a variety of urban forms which should be compact and
self-contained.

The strategy set out for the region in the remainder of the century envisages
the development of a limited number of growth areas within the O.M.A. and
O.S.E. areas, mainly established along the principal radial and communication
routes from London and providing diversity of employment opportunities. There
would obviously be some invasion of the existing green belt but the aim of the
plan is to preserve as much countryside as possible within the road and rail network, and the planners considered carefully both the physical and cultural
environment of the area as a whole before deciding on the most suitable growth
points.

The population of Inner and Greater London is estimated to fall to 7 million by
the end of the century, and this should provide an opportunity for much more extensive redevelopment and rehabilitation of the area for the benefit of those who remain.
The O.M.A. is likely to experience slow population growth, mainly concentrated
around Reading and Crawley and in South Essex. The major growth points for
population and employment in the O.S.E. and outside the region will be in South
Hampshire (Southampton - Portsmouth), the Milton Keynes - Northampton -
Wellingborough area and with smaller increases in the vicinity of Ashford, East-
bourne - Hastings, Bournemouth - Poole, Aylesbury, Basildon - Harlow, Chelmsford
and Ipswich. The *Strategic Plan for the South-east* estimated that the population
of the South-east region would expand by 4.2 million by the end of the century.

Exercises

(2.4) Explain the variation between the population growth (a) of the South-east
between 1951 and 1961, and since 1961; (b) of the different areas of the South-
east (Inner and Greater London, Outer Metropolitan Area and Outer South-east)
between 1951 and 1968.

(2.5) The study discussed above sets out arguments in favour of concentration
rather than dispersion as a means of dealing with the anticipated population
increase in the South-east by the end of the century. How far do you find these
arguments convincing?

(2.6) Some of the major growth points for population and employment are outside the South-east area as normally defined. Does this contradict the view that development should be concentrated rather than dispersed?

(2.7) Since 1970, there has been some slowing-down in the rate of movement into the South-east of England. How would you expect this to affect the projections outlined in this case?

Supplementary exercises

(2.8) How far does Case 4 support Colin Clark's distinction between macro-location and micro-location?

(2.9) Can the following properly be described as economic regions: (*a*) Inner and Greater London; (*b*) the Outer Metropolitan Area; (*c*) the Outer South-east Area?

Sources and References

Additional to those for Chapter 1 and those mentioned in the text of this chapter.

COLIN CLARK, 'Industrial Location and Economic Potential', *Lloyds Bank Review* (Oct 1966).

Part 2

Aspects of Government Industrial Policy in the
United Kingdom and the European Economic
Community

Introduction

M. S. Bradbury

In Part 2 of this volume we are concerned with those aspects of government economic policy which impinge directly on the behaviour and performance of individual firms and industries, and into which useful insights can be gained by using microeconomic analysis: location of industry, competition, selective intervention, agriculture and nationalised industry.

Interrelationships

Part 3 of this volume emphasises macroeconomic policy. The distinction between microeconomic and macroeconomic policies should not be over-stressed. Almost any government economic policy has implications for individual firms and industries. For example, the framework of aggregate demand for goods and services in the economy as a whole is influenced by the government's fiscal and monetary policies. These, in turn, influence, amongst other things, the demand for the products of individual industries and firms, the prices at which goods can be sold and the prices and availability of the factors of production. Likewise, it is often suggested that national economic growth may be retarded by widespread defects in the structures of individual markets. It follows, that the distinction between microeconomic and macroeconomic policies and hence between Parts 2 and 3 of this volume is one of analytical and expositional convenience rather than practical realities. Chapters 11 and 12 ('Prices and Incomes Policy' and 'Indicative Planning') could have appeared logically in either of Parts 2 and 3.

Likewise, within Part 2, because of the need to concentrate attention on manageable areas of learning for teaching purposes, we talk of 'location policy' or 'selective intervention' as if they were independent of each other. This is not so; as illustrated for example by Case 16, in practice a particular problem may carry implications for several industrial policies.

Economic Analysis

The common feature of most chapters in Part 2 is the attempt by the state to modify the decisions of firms. A necessary preliminary to their consideration therefore is a sound grasp of the theory of the firm and a thorough conversance with the arguments for and against state intervention in individual markets.

The Value of the Theory of the Firm

In the theory of the firm, economists try to predict the price of a firm's product and its output, given a set of cost and revenue conditions and a closely defined market environment. For example, in an elementary model of monopoly, we assume that the firm is the sole producer of a good for which there is no close substitute and that other producers are unable to enter the market. We then predict the price and output decision which would be made under given cost and demand conditions, if the firm wished to maximise its profits. Notice that the model does *not* predict how a monopolist will behave; it predicts the outcome of the behaviour needed to achieve a given objective under the conditions specified. It follows that great care is needed in applying the models of elementary theory to behaviour in an actual market. There are many reasons why a market may only approximately correspond to our models. For instance, firms may pursue multiple or vague objectives, operate in a market which is difficult to define, or have cost structures which show wide variations between firms producing similar outputs. This does not mean that the elementary theory of the firm tells us nothing about the real world. From the theory we can obtain, first, some idea of which variables have an important influence on the behaviour of firms and hence on the economy, and second, a method of approaching the analysis of individual markets.

State Intervention in Individual Markets

The general arguments for and against state intervention in individual markets are discussed in most introductory textbooks.* Where appropriate, these general arguments are related to specific aspects of government economic policy in the 'Summary of Background Material' which accompanies each chapter. Positive economics suggests two major grounds for government intervention in individual markets, to counter the exercise of monopoly power and to correct for the failure of market forces to take account of externalities (costs and benefits which stem from the actions of firms but which are not reflected in their profits). However, it must be remembered that government intervention in individual markets may be motivated by non-economic considerations, e.g. desires expressed through the ballot box that a person has a right to a job close to his home or that the private ownership of the firms is 'wrong'. Although positive economics often gives insights into the potential consequences of such motives, it must be recognised that the acceptance or rejection of such motives involves value judgements. Whilst economists have some expertise in recognising value judgements, their resolution is outside the competence of positive economics.

*See, for example, R. G. Lipsey, *An Introduction to Positive Economics*, 4th edn (London: Weidenfeld & Nicolson, 1975) ch. 32.

The Legislative and Administrative Framework

The 'Summary of Background Material' in most of the chapters in Part 2 outlines the legislative framework within which government economic policy operates. For economists, interest lies not in the legal detail of legislation, but its motivation and in the extent to which it either reflects or impinges on the operation of economic concepts.

In recent years there have been frequent changes in the organisation of relevant government departments. For example, the Board of Trade's powers in relation to competition policy passed to the Department of Trade and Industry and subsequently to the Department of Prices and Consumer Protection and the Office of Fair Trading. It is likely that further such changes will occur during the life of this volume.

CHAPTER 3

Location of Industry

M. S. Bradbury

Summary of Background Material

The Location Decision

In principle, finding the optimum location for a profit-maximising firm requires consideration of both the supply (cost) and demand (revenue) conditions facing the firm. However, research has found that whilst some types of industry are tied to particular locations by the nature of their operations, the production costs of a substantial proportion of manufacturing and service industries in the United Kingdom are, within wide limits, insensitive to the precise choice of location. Likewise, it seems probable that in many industries revenue is less sensitive to location in the United Kingdom than in more dispersed markets such as the United States. It follows that there exists in the United Kingdom a significant range of industries whose profitability (pre-tax and subsidies) is relatively insensitive to location; such industries are said to be 'foot-loose'.

Changes in the Distribution of Industry

In the absence of government intervention the following are some of the more important forces which will tend over a period of several decades to cause fundamental changes in the distribution of industry:

(1) Changes in the relative prices and the availability of factors of production (e.g. a firm requiring large inputs of unskilled labour may find that the expansion of other firms in the area has made labour both difficult to obtain and more expensive; to resume expansion and perhaps cut costs, such a firm may move to an area where unemployment is higher).

(2) Improvements in the transport network may make a previously unattractive location viable (e.g. the building of the North Circular Road in London during the inter-war years attracted a significant amount of light industry to the area).

(3) Changes in technology may lead to new processes requiring different combinations of factor inputs (e.g. the relative decline in the importance of fuel as a location influence in the steel industry) or to a change in the scale of production (e.g. the closure of small electricity power stations and their replacement by a reduced number of larger stations linked by the national grid).

(4) The emergence of new products and changes in the pattern of demand, which with other factors will lead to variations in the growth rates of different industries (e.g. the expansion of the computer industry and the contraction of the cotton textile industry), hence changing the relative importance of different industries in the geographical distribution of employment.

In the absence of expansion a firm will rarely move to a new location when some of the above changes occur. Instead, it may find it more profitable to invest to reduce the disadvantage of its existing location. This is particularly likely where a firm's variable costs are small and it has substantial specific plant and equipment with a long physical life expectancy.

In practice major changes in the distribution of industry are not caused by the movement of production from one location to another, but by the failure of industries to grow in one area, and the tendency for the newer and more rapidly expanding industries to locate elsewhere.

Since the First World War, these forces have led to a redistribution of industry in the United Kingdom, in which the newer industries have expanded in the South-east and Midlands of England and in which the stagnation of the older and the failure to attract the newer growth industries has led to the relative decline of the traditional industrial areas, e.g. South Wales, North-west and North-east England and Lowland Scotland. There are signs that this trend may now be ending.

Should the State Intervene in the Location of Industry, and if so how?

State intervention in location decisions is a controversial topic, involving value judgements which cannot be resolved solely by reference to economics. The economist can point out that in making its location decision, a profit-maximising firm will only consider the private costs and benefits which influence its profits, not the social costs and benefits which flow from its location decision, such as the legacy of surplus housing, schools and roads in the area it leaves and the need to create such assets in the area in which the firm chooses to expand. Likewise, if the level of employment could be increased in the depressed areas and the pressures of over-employment reduced elsewhere, it might be possible to achieve a modest increase in national product without creating additional pressures on the balance of payments or the general level of prices. However, the economist cannot say that a desire for a job close to the individual's present place of residence is wrong; he can merely point out the economic consequences.

If it is accepted that the state should intervene in the location of industry, we are still left with the problems of method. A fundamental issue is whether to encourage a greater geographical mobility of labour or of capital or to attempt both. Given the reluctance of people to move in sufficient numbers over long distances, the problems of wasted social assets in declining areas and over-crowding in expanding areas, and the existence of foot-loose industries, the tendency in the United Kingdom has been to lay more stress on moving work to the worker than on moving the worker to the work.

It is possible to envisage a whole range of 'carrot and stick' measures which can be used to move industry to the area required. One measure would be to prevent firms from expanding in areas of overemployment, e.g. the Industrial Development Certificate procedure used in the United Kingdom. To be effective, such a procedure presupposes the existence of a pool of foot-loose industries and a way of exempting cases where movement imposes unrealistic additional production costs. Alternatively the state could give subsidies to compensate firms for any reduction in their profits caused by choosing different locations from those indicated by the market. Except to the extent that discrepancies between private and social costs are eliminated, such subsidies do not eliminate higher real costs which may (but need not) exist in the new location; rather they transfer the burden of increased costs from the firm to the community as a whole. Similarly, the state may use taxes to increase a firm's costs in an area of over-full employment. Lastly, the state may attempt to make an area more attractive to industry by investment which will reduce real costs, e.g. by improving its transport infrastructure.

The precise way in which the above measures are used will depend upon the objectives of the government's location policy. If its primary aim is to minimise unemployment, then industry will be encouraged to move to areas of high unemployment. On the other hand, if the government believes that labour is mobile over short distances, as seems to be the case in the United Kingdom, it may be prepared to accept that some areas shall decline and that industry will instead be encouraged to move to near-by growth points, where conditions are felt to be more favourable.

Location of Industry Policy in the United Kingdom

Location of industry policy in the United Kingdom has been implemented by a wide and frequently changing flow of legislation. Major legislation has included the *Special Areas Act* of 1934, the *Distribution of Industry* and *Town and Country Planning Acts* since 1945 and 1947 respectively, the *Local Employment Acts* since 1960, various *Finance Acts* and the *Industry Act* of 1972 (the core of current legislation).

Four aspects of location of industry policy in the United Kingdom are discussed below:

(1) the criteria used to designate areas receiving assistance;

(2) the incentives offered to firms providing employment in assisted areas;

(3) the operation of negative constraints on the provision of employment in non-assisted areas; and

(4) the interaction between location policy, regional policy and devolution.

Assisted areas

Until recently location of industry policy in the United Kingdom has tended to concentrate on the relatively slow-growing manufacturing sector of the economy, rather than on the more rapidly expanding service sector. Consequently, the local impact of location of industry policy on the problems of any particular area will partly depend on whether foot-loose sectors of manufacturing industry are encouraged to move to narrowly or widely defined areas.

Early legislation diffused assistance over a few extensive geographical areas, which often included significant sub-areas with both above- and below-average unemployment. However, the *Local Employment Act* of 1960 concentrated assistance on 165 smaller development districts based on local employment exchange areas; district status was tied to unemployment rates, causing frequent boundary changes and the inclusion of districts in the otherwise prosperous South-east of England.

The Industrial Development Act of 1966 made two major changes in the approach to designating assisted areas. First, the designation of assisted areas was based on wider criteria, that is, 'all the circumstances actual and expected including the state of employment and unemployment, population changes, migration and the objectives of regional policy'. Second, the five 'development areas' created by the Act included about a fifth of the country's insured population. This later change reflected a belief that, given good local communications and the greater mobility of population over short rather than long distances, it might be better to exploit the growth potential of nearby areas, rather than to move industry to potentially unsuitable problem areas.

Fearing that the rapid contraction of the coal-mining industry might lead to severe local unemployment, the government introduced additional incentives in November 1967 to encourage the establishment of new industry in selected parts of the development areas, called 'special development areas'. Further special development areas were created in 1971.

When the *Industrial Development Act* of 1966 came into force, the Economic Planning Councils for the North-west, Yorkshire and Humberside and the South-west argued that its measures could have an adverse effect on the prosperity of their regions, by attracting a higher proportion of new industry to the development areas. These fears were particularly strong in towns close to the development areas, where unemployment was often somewhat above the national average. Such areas became known as *intermediate* or *grey* areas. In June 1969, following the publication of the *Hunt Report*, which advocated assistance to such areas, the government, whilst rejecting many of its recommendations, announced that it would introduce legislation to extend limited assistance to intermediate areas.

The division of the United Kingdom into assisted and non-assisted areas is shown in Figure 3.1.

Incentives for industry in assisted areas

Two aspects of the *Industry Act* of 1972 provided major incentives for industry in assisted areas.

(1) As shown in Table 3.1 cash grants towards specified investment in assisted areas were provided at differential rates over and above the generous tax allowances provided under the *Finance Act* of 1972 for investment anywhere in the country.

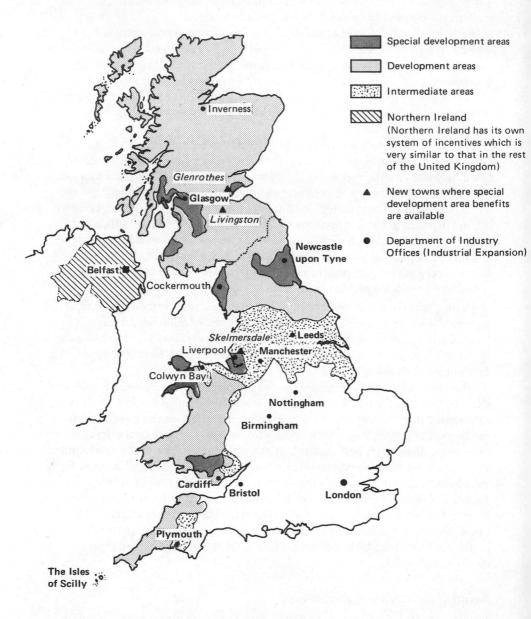

Special development areas

Development areas

Intermediate areas

Northern Ireland
(Northern Ireland has its own
system of incentives which is
very similar to that in the rest
of the United Kingdom)

▲ New towns where special
development area benefits
are available

● Department of Industry
Offices (Industrial Expansion)

Inverness

Glenrothes
Glasgow
Livingston

Newcastle
upon Tyne

Belfast

Cockermouth

Skelmersdale   Leeds
Liverpool   Manchester

Colwyn Bay

Nottingham

Birmingham

Cardiff
Bristol   London

Plymouth

The Isles
of Scilly

FIG. 3.1*

*Areas for Expansion (Department of Industry, 1975).

TABLE 3.1
Regional development grants

	Special development areas	Development areas	Intermediate areas
New machinery, plant and mining works	22 per cent	20 per cent	NIL
Building and works (other than mining works)	22 per cent	20 per cent	20 per cent

Note: In July 1976 it was announced that from April 1977 eligibility for regional development grants would be confined to manufacturing investment, thus excluding investment in the construction and mining industries.

SOURCE: *Incentives for Industry in the Areas for Expansion* (Department of Industry, 1975) p. 6.

(2) Selective financial assistance was made available to mining, manufacturing and construction industry projects which provide, maintain or safeguard employment in assisted areas. Where projects create new employment loans at concessionary rates, interest-relief grants and removal grants are available. Modernisation and rationalisation projects which do not create additional employment can be assisted by loans at commercial interest rates where these are not available from normal market sources.

Since 1967 a *regional employment premium* has been paid in respect of all employees in manufacturing establishments in special development and development areas (currently £2 per week per full-time adult employee and less for other employees). The regional employment premium benefits existing as well as new employment.

In June 1973 it was announced that, to encourage the movement of service industries to assisted areas, help under the *Industry Act* of 1972 was to be made available in two ways. First, a grant to the employer of £800 for each employee moved with his work, up to a limit of 50 per cent of the number of additional jobs created in the assisted area. Second, a grant would be paid towards the rent of premises for up to three years in intermediate areas and five years in development and special areas. Comparable grants would be paid where premises were bought.

Lastly, there are a wide range of miscellaneous forms of assistance provided under a variety of legislation, e.g. rent-free periods in government-built factories, training assistance, help for transferred workers and preference for firms in assisted areas when placing government contracts.

Controls on employment creation

Under the terms of the *Distribution of Industry Act* of 1945 firms had to notify the Board of Trade of their intention to erect buildings of more than 10,000 square feet, thus enabling the government to use the granting of building licenses to divert industry to areas of high unemployment. This measure was strengthened by the *Town and Country Planning Act* of 1947, which provided that any application for planning permission to erect prescribed industrial buildings was of no effect, unless accompanied by an Industrial Development Certificate (I.D.C.) from the Board of Trade (now the Department of Industry), stating that the proposed building could be carried out 'consistently with the proper distribution of industry'.

The intensity with which I.D.C. controls were implemented has varied considerably since their introduction. I.D.C.s have not been required in the development areas since July 1972 and never were required in Northern Ireland. Currently I.D.C.s are required for all developments exceeding 12,500 square feet in the South-east of England and 15,000 square feet elsewhere in England.

The *Control of Office and Industrial Development Act* of 1965 provides for the control of office development in parallel with the I.D.C. control on industrial development. Following changes in policy in June 1975, Office Development Permits (O.D.P.s) are only required for offices exceeding 15,000 square feet in the South-east of England.

Apart from potential flexibility of application, the major benefit of I.D.C. and O.D.P. controls is that they encourage firms to consider locations which might otherwise escape their attention.

Location policy, regional planning and devolution

Between late 1964 and early 1966 the government created a range of consultative bodies and administrative arrangements to further regional planning, as part of its wider exercise in indicative planning (see Chapter 12). At the time it was expected that this would lead to fundamental changes in the nature of location policy; this has not happened, but these bodies have had two significant effects on location policy. First, their research work has improved our knowledge of the environment within which location policy operates; second, they have acted as regional pressure groups advocating particular changes in location policy, e.g. assistance for intermediate areas. During 1976 constitutional changes leading to a devolution of power from the central government to Scottish and Welsh Assemblies were under consideration. It is as yet too early to evaluate the impact of devolution on location of industry policy.

Regional Policy and the European Community

The origins of European Community regional policy can be found in the Preamble to the Treaty of Rome, which refers to 'reducing the differences existing between the various regions and the backwardness of the less favoured regions'. Even before the Paris summit meeting of October 1972 the work of many Community institutions had significant regional implications. For example, nearly 85 per cent of the funds allocated by the European Investment Bank between 1958 and 1972 were spent on regional development schemes. It has been estimated that reconversion and re-adaptation financing under Article 56 of the European Coal and Steel Community Treaty helped to create 110,000 jobs within the E.E.C. and made re-adaptation possible for nearly 500,000 workers, mostly in declining coalmining areas. The Social Fund and Common Agricultural Policy also had significant regional repercussions.

However, the present phase in the Community's regional policy began when the Paris summit meeting of October 1972 declared:

> The Heads of State or of Government agreed that a high priority should be given to the aim of correcting, in the Community, the structural and regional imbalances which might effect the realisation of Economic and Monetary Union.

Economic and monetary union aimed to create a Community economy and hence involved much closer integration of the economies of member states. With the achievement of economic and monetary union, the fiscal, monetary and exchange rate instruments used by member states in the macroeconomic management of their economies would tend to become more constrained by 'Community' requirements, and hence be less able to meet the needs of individual national economies. A successful regional policy was therefore seen as a way of ensuring that economic and monetary union did not leave significant parts of the Community unable to adjust adequately to changing economic conditions.

On 18 March 1975, after lengthy negotiations, the Council of Ministers formally adopted the regulation creating the Regional Development Fund. The Fund was allocated 1300 million units of account (about £540 million) over the three years 1975-7. Net beneficiaries relative to their contribution are Italy, Ireland and the United Kingdom with 40, 6 and 28 per cent of the Fund respectively. There are detailed provisions on the areas to qualify for assistance, the types of project eligible for assistance, the number of jobs to be created or maintained, the proportions of each investment which the Fund can assist and the control of Fund expenditure which is administered by the Fund Management Committee on which all member states are represented. Member states are also required to prepare regional development programmes which provide a background description of the regional problems and national aid measures against which the significance of the individual applications for Fund aid may be seen. Only the governments of member states can apply for a contribution from the Fund towards the cost of certain industrial, service (including tourism) and infrastructure projects, and these projects must already be assisted or financed from public funds. The receipt of contributions from the Fund will enable more resources to be devoted to regional problems than would otherwise be the case.

The Community has not attempted to standardise the various measures of assistance available within member countries but it has tried to co-ordinate the levels of assistance in different regions to ensure that the least favoured areas of the Community are eligible for the most help and that they are further protected by restricting the aid which governments may give in the most prosperous areas. However, as part of the decision to create the Regional Development Fund, a Regional Policy Committee was established, consisting of representatives from member states and the Commission to study regional problems in the Community, the progress made towards solving them and the measures needed to further the achievement of the Community's regional objectives.

Illustration by Case Studies

The first case in this chapter illustrates the use of regional indicators to give a 'snap-shot' of regional differences in the United Kingdom during 1973. Of particular interest in the case is the way in which a relatively wide range of indicators tend to show broadly similar patterns of regional differences. Further insights can also be obtained by considering the trend of regional indicators over time. Reference should also be made to Case 3, as net migration can be regarded as an important regional indicator.

The second case illustrates in human terms the reality behind the re-allocation of factors of production in response to economic change. Data of the kind derived from the U.C.S. survey on which the case is based, is essential for cost – benefit studies which would make possible a more informed and rational choice between alternative policies on redundancy.

It is a mistake to think that location problems are only relevant to manufacturing industry. As office location is not discussed in most textbooks, the third case deals with the dispersal of government office work as an instrument of regional policy.

Reference may also be made to Case 16, which describes the creation of a U.K. aluminium-smelting industry located entirely in assisted areas, and to Case 14, in which I.R.C. intervention in the paper industry assisted regional policy.

CASE 5. REGIONAL ECONOMIC AND SOCIAL INDICATORS: THE UNITED KINGDOM, 1973

There is no single indicator of the economic and social health of a region. Instead, there are a wide range of indicators each dealing with different aspects of human activity in a regional context. When considering the extent to which a particular region differs from 'average' conditions in the country as a whole, it is often possible to fault specific indicators. For example, high car ownership per head of population in a region may indicate above-average income, a dispersed settlement pattern or inadequate public transport. Similarly, a high proportion of home owner-occupiers may be expected in an area which is favoured for retirement, such as the South-west. What matters is the extent to which many indicators show similar patterns of regional experience.

TABLE 3.2

Selected employment indicators for regions of the United Kingdom

Region	Average unemployment rates (per cent) 1973 (males and females)	Percentage of unemployed males unemployed for over a year at 9 July 1973	Female economic activity rates 1971*
United Kingdom	2.7	29.2	46.5
North	4.7	35.7	43.7
Yorkshire and Humberside	2.9	33.3	45.4
East Midlands	2.1	33.9	46.7
East Anglia	1.9	30.4	42.3
South-east	1.5	20.7	48.8
South-west	2.4	28.9	41.3
West Midlands	2.2	28.6	49.0
North-west	3.6	29.1	48.1
England	2.4	28.7	47.0
Wales	3.5	30.8	39.8
Scotland	4.6	31.4	46.7
Northern Ireland	6.4	28.4	41.5

*Civilian labour force plus armed forces plus students as a percentage of female population aged 15 and over and enumerated in the 1971 *Census of Population.*

SOURCE: *Abstract of Regional Statistics, 1974* (London: H.M.S.O.) tables 42, 44 and 45.

The case concentrates on showing regional differences in the United Kingdom at as near to a single year (1973) as readily available statistics allow. Indicators have been selected to illustrate three aspects of regional activity: employment, income and wealth, and social infrastructure. Each indicator is an 'average' for the region in question and does in some cases mask considerable variations in experience between different parts of the region. For example, the South-west of England includes both the prosperous Bristol area and assisted areas in Cornwall and Devon.

Employment

By comparing the first two columns of Table 3.2 it will be seen that those regions which had above-average unemployment rates in 1973 tended also to have above average long-term male unemployment. Unemployment statistics do not show the full extent to which labour is under-employed, partly because married women tend not to register as unemployed when difficult labour-market conditions lead them to become economically inactive.* It will be seen from the third column of Table 3.2 that regions with above-average unemployment rates tend to have below-average female economic activity rates (the broad pattern of average unemployment rates in 1971 was similar to that in 1973). Table 3.2 does not show the variation of employment indicators during the year.

Income and Wealth

It will be seen from Table 3.3 that, except for the ownership of television sets (which does not vary significantly between regions of Great Britain), the broad pattern of differences in income and wealth is similar to that shown in Table 3.2 in respect of employment.

Social Infrastructure

Table 3.4 shows selected social indicators for regions of the United Kingdom. Excluding Wales, the number of pupils in public-sector schools aged 18, expressed as a percentage of 13 year-olds five years earlier, shows a similar pattern of regional differences to those found in Tables 3.2 and 3.3, implying that education beyond the statutory school-leaving age may suffer when employment and hence income are in doubt. Although the percentage of dwellings built before 1919 broadly corresponds to the pattern shown in Tables 3.2 and 3.3, this is less true of the number of persons per doctor, which can perhaps best be explained in terms of the age and urban/rural distribution of a region's population.

*Unemployment statistics have to be interpreted with considerable care. For example, they do not indicate the amount of overtime or short-time worked, but do include some workers whose poor health makes them unlikely candidates for employment.

TABLE 3.3

Selected indicators of income and wealth for regions of the United Kingdom

Region	G.D.P. per head (factor cost: current prices) £s 1972	Average household income £s per week 1972–3*	Percentage of households with (1973)						Percentage of households owning or buying home (December 1973)
			Car	Central heating	Refrigerator	Television	Telephone	Washing machine	
United Kingdom	964	46.16	53.9	38.5	77.6	93.4	43.3	66.6	52
North	819	40.54	41.8	40.6	65.9	94.6	32.6	75.7	44
Yorkshire and Humberside	903	41.39	46.2	32.4	68.5	94.4	32.2	78.8	52
East Midlands	928	44.68	54.7	39.6	77.5	93.7	39.0	76.6	54
East Anglia	919	43.30	65.5	44.7	75.7	94.9	34.5	70.2	55
South-east	1117	52.91	58.7	44.5	89.5	92.1	58.0	57.1	54
South-west	932	44.84	63.3	43.5	85.8	92.9	40.6	65.0	60
West Midlands	984	46.39	57.5	37.2	77.1	93.8	41.2	64.9	54
North-west	900	43.88	50.2	33.9	73.5	93.6	42.8	69.7	57
England	991	46.94	55.0	40.1	79.8	93.3	45.2	66.4	54
Wales	843	42.24	52.4	27.4	69.3	94.7	24.7	65.9	58
Scotland	880	43.20	45.5	33.8	67.6	95.3	41.5	73.9	32
Northern Ireland	678	37.61	52.9	23.9	54.6	86.5	25.2	47.7	47

*Average of 1972 and 1973.

SOURCE: Abstract of Regional Statistics, 1974 (London: H.M.S.O.) tables 29, 77, 87 and 94.

Aspects of Government Industrial Policy

TABLE 3.4

Selected social indicators for regions of the United Kingdom

Region	General medical practitioners (persons per doctor 1973)	Percentage of dwellings built before 1919 (December 1973)	No. of pupils in public-sector schools aged 18 on 1 Jan 1973 as % of 13 year-olds five years earlier
North	2465	33.0	5.4
Yorkshire and Humberside	2513	35.0	6.1
East Midlands	2510	32.0	5.2
East Anglia	2309	36.0	4.6
South-east	2339	33.0	7.2
South-west	2211	36.0	5.4
West Midlands	2473	28.0	5.4
North-west	2481	37.0	5.0
England	2398	33.0	6.0
Wales	2207	46.0	8.4
Scotland	1928	33.0	2.9
Northern Ireland	2102	—	5.0

Note: corresponding data for the U.K. as a whole are not available.

SOURCE: *Abstract of Regional Statistics, 1974* (London: H.M.S.O.) tables 23, 29 and 35.

Exercises

(3.1) How would you explain the high proportion of car-owning households and low proportion of households with a telephone in East Anglia?

(3.2) On the basis of the regional indicators used in the case, which region of the United Kingdom do you regard as (*a*) the most prosperous, and (*b*) the least prosperous? Give reasons for your answer.

(3.3) On the basis of the regional indicators used in the case, comment on the broad pattern of regional differences in the United Kingdom and on the relative experience of your own region.

CASE 6. THE REDEPLOYMENT OF REDUNDANT SHIPYARD WORKERS FROM UPPER CLYDE SHIPBUILDERS, 1969–71

This case is based on a survey, 'Redundancy and Redeployment from U.C.S. 1969–71', carried out by F. Herron in 1971 and published in the *Scottish Journal of Political Economy* (November 1972). The study was primarily concerned with four aspects of redundancy and redeployment: the impact of age and skill on employment status; the duration of transitional unemployment; mobility (geographical, industrial and occupational); and the 'quality' of the first jobs held compared with those at U.C.S.*

The U.C.S. Redundancies

Following the recommendations of the *Geddes Report* for improving efficiency in British Shipbuilding, Upper Clyde Shipbuilders Ltd (U.C.S.) was established in February 1968 by merging all the five yards still building ships on the upper reaches of the river. In 1969 a shortage of working capital forced U.C.S. to ask the Shipbuilding Industry Board (S.I.B.) for further financial assistance, a request which was granted on condition that steps were taken to reduce overmanning. Consequently, between August 1969 and December 1970, in addition to natural wastage, just over 2000 workers were made redundant by U.C.S. Although about a fifth of the redundancies occurred in August 1969, the majority of redundancies occurred between June and December 1970. Volunteers for redundancy were offered from four to eight weeks tax-free pay over and above their entitlement under the *Redundancy Payments Act* of 1965. To control the nature and cost of the redundancies, U.C.S. limited volunteers to workers with less than five-years service, reserved the right to refuse volunteers and determined the date of discharge.

The Glasgow Labour Market

In June 1969 about 6 per cent of the male labour force of Glasgow was directly employed in shipbuilding and marine engineering, compared with about 1 per cent in Great Britain as a whole. An unquantified, but thought to be significant, proportion of the Glasgow workforce was also indirectly involved in shipbuilding as producers of bought-in parts.

Male unemployment in Glasgow was just over 6 per cent in late 1969, rising to 6.7 per cent in June 1970, 8 per cent at the end of 1970 and over 10 per cent by

*The paper in the *Scottish Journal of Political Economy* also contrasted the results of the U.C.S. survey with those obtained in earlier studies of engineering and railway workshop redundancies. A more comprehensive discussion can be found in F. Herron, *Labour Market in Crisis: Redundancy at Upper Clyde Shipbuilders* (London: Macmillan, 1975).

mid-1971. The trend of unfilled vacancies was even worse, deteriorating from
about 3000 vacancies for nearly 21,000 unemployed men in Glasgow at the end
of 1969 to 642 vacancies for 35,000 unemployed men in June 1970.

The Sample

A random sample of 400 redundant male U.C.S. workers stratified by occupation
was interviewed via a household survey in June and July 1971. From the sample
327 effective interviews were available for analysis. The redundant workers were
on average both younger and more skilled than either the remainder of U.C.S.
labour force, or workers in the British shipbuilding industry as a whole, characteristics which would normally be regarded as advantageous in the labour market.
Due to retirement or continuous sickness, twenty-seven redundant workers never
actively participated in the labour market after leaving U.C.S. Consequently, the
analysis is based on the experience of the remaining 300 workers.

TABLE 3.5
Employment experience since leaving U.C.S. by skill

Skill at U.C.S.	Been in employment (per cent)	Been continuously unemployed (per cent)	Numbers
Unskilled	88	12	24
Semi-skilled	71	29	42
Skilled	91	9	220
Staff	86	14	14
TOTAL	88	12	300

TABLE 3.6
Employment experience since leaving U.C.S. by age

Age	Been in employment (per cent)	Been continuously unemployed (per cent)	Numbers
< 29	97	3	101
30 – 9	94	6	71
40 – 9	89	11	63
50 – 9	71	29	40
60+	58	42	24
Not known	—	—	1
TOTAL	88	12	300

The Impact of Age and Skill on Employment Status

It will be seen from Tables 3.5 and 3.6 that the people who experienced the greatest difficulty in finding employment were the semi-skilled and those over 50 years of age.

Duration of Transitional Unemployment

It will be seen from Table 3.7 that although the majority of workers gained alternative employment within three months of redundancy, a significant minority experienced prolonged unemployment.

TABLE 3.7

Duration of transitional enemployment after leaving U.C.S. (per cent)

	Weeks unemployed						Numbers involved
Under 1 week	1 – 2	2 – 4	4 – 8	8 – 16	16 – 26	26 and over	
11	15	13	18	15	10	17	300

Geographical Mobility

Table 3.8 shows that relatively little geographical dispersion resulted from the first stage of redeployment, that is only 10 per cent of the workers in the sample had moved out of the West of Scotland. Further analysis showed that three-quarters of the emigrants were skilled workers. Herron argued that these results were consistent with the well-established trend for out-migration from Scotland to rise and fall in conjunction with the difference between the Scottish and Great Britain unemployment rates, that is, the outcome reflected the depressed state of the U.K. economy as a whole at the time of the redundancies.

TABLE 3.8

Percentage distribution of first jobs by location

Glasgow – Paisley	57	Rest of Scotland	2
Clydebank – Dumbarton	16	England and Wales	6
Greenock – Port Glasgow	6	Ireland and abroad	2
Rest of West of Scotland	11		

Numbers involved   264 (300 – 36 unemployed)

Industrial Mobility

The U.C.S. redundancies were biased towards the finishing trades, that is towards skills which were less specific to shipbuilding than, for example, those of the steel-making trades. Consequently, the transfer of redundant U.C.S. workers into a wide range of industries, shown in Table 3.9 was in line with expectations.

TABLE 3.9

Industrial distribution of U.C.S. workers in their first jobs

Industry	(Per cent)
Shipbuilding, etc.	23
Other engineering	23
Other manufacturing	8
Construction	29
Services	17
Numbers involved	264

Occupational Mobility

It will be seen from Table 3.10 that on re-employment more people moved out of the ranks of skilled and staff workers than moved into them, that is over-all occupational mobility was slightly downwards. However, Herron points out that of 200 skilled job seekers from U.C.S. 85 per cent found new jobs of similar status, indicating much stronger 'craft consciousness' than exhibited by other tradesmen whose redundancy had been investigated.

TABLE 3.10

Occupational distribution (per cent) in first job and job from which made redundant

Occupation	U.C.S.	1st Job
Unskilled	8	13
Semi-skilled	11	13
Skilled	76	69
Staff	5	3
Self-employed	—	1
Numbers involved	264	264

Job Quality

Tables 3.11 and 3.12 compare the take-home pay and working hours of workers at U.C.S. and at their first post-redundancy job. Although a significant minority of workers obtained better pay and working hours than at U.C.S., it is clear that average earnings fell and average hours worked increased on redeployment. The survey also found that the alternative employment was relatively risky, in that sixty-eight of the men who had left their first job after U.C.S. did so through redundancy yet again.

TABLE 3.11

*Difference in usual take-home pay between former job
and first post-redundancy job (per cent)*

Lower by (£s)				Same	Higher by (£s)				Numbers involved
6 or more	4 but under 6	2 but under 4	Under 2		Under 2	2 but under 4	4 but under 6	6 or more	
23	9	13	5	16	3	10	7	15	264

TABLE 3.12

*Difference in hours of work between U.C.S. and
first job after (per cent)*

Lower by (hrs)				Hours the same	Higher by (hrs)				Numbers involved
10 or more	6 but under 10	3 but under 6	Under 3		Under 3	3 but under 6	6 but under 10	10 or more	
14	5	6	3	31	8	9	4	19	264

Exercises

(3.4) How was the re-employment experience of redundant U.C.S. workers related to age and skill? Suggest reasons for such relationships.

(3.5) What relationship would you expect to exist between the transitional unemployment experience of redundant U.C.S. workers and male unemployment in the Glasgow labour market?

(3.6) Why did relatively few redundant U.C.S. workers seek alternative employment outside of West Scotland?

(3.7) Comment on the industrial and occupational mobility of redundant U.C.S. workers.

(3.8) Suggest reasons for the lower earnings, higher working hours and reduced job security experienced by U.C.S. workers in their first post-redundancy employment.

CASE 7. THE DISPERSAL OF GOVERNMENT WORK FROM LONDON

In October 1970 it was announced that the location of government work was to be reviewed to see whether more of it could be dispersed from London. The case summarises the economic aspects of the review and the resulting changes in government policy.*

Past Dispersal

The 'Hardman Report' had been preceded by two major dispersal initiatives in the previous thirty-five years. First, anticipating attacks on London, government work was moved in 1940 to such places as Bath, Blackpool, Colwyn Bay and Harrogate, where empty hotels often provided rapidly available accommodation. The dispersal of 'staff close to the very centre of Government activity'† was also contemplated but rejected by the Prime Minister because of its damaging effects on efficiency and morale.

Second, in 1963 Sir Gilbert Fleming reviewed 95,000 headquarters posts. The review identified self-contained units of executive work, which could be separated relatively easily from other government work and dispersed with little loss of efficiency. Sir Gilbert Fleming recommended the dispersal of about 14,000 posts from the London area, the movement of 5500 posts to the outskirts of London and unquantified dispersal from Defence Departments. Subsequently the government decided in 1965 that new public organisations should if possible be located outside London and, in 1967, that wherever feasible dispersal should be to assisted areas.

The 'Hardman Report' estimated that during 1963–73 about 50,225 posts had been affected by dispersal, excluding the Post Office and movements within London (defined as within sixteen miles of Charing Cross). These posts were made up as follows:

(1) 22,525 existing posts dispersed;
(2) 7840 existing posts awaiting dispersal;
(3) 9490 new posts set up outside London; and
(4) 10,370 new posts to be set up outside London.‡

The Dispersal of Government Work from London, Cmnd. 5322 (London: H.M.S.O., June 1973). Often called the 'Hardman Report' after the leader of the review, Sir Henry Hardman.

†Minute to Sir Edward Bridges, 14 September 1940, in W. S. Churchill, *The Second World War* (London: Cassell, 1949) vol. 2, ch. XVII.

‡ *The Dispersal of Government Work from London*, p. 22.

The Situation

In October 1972 there were about 690,000 civil servants, of whom 500,200 were in the non-industrial civil service. About 70 per cent (356,500) of the non-industrial civil servants worked outside London, and 47,800 of the 143,700 working in London were employed in regional or local offices. Excluding work which could not be moved from London, e.g. in the Cabinet Office and some museums, about 86,000 posts remained to be reviewed (78,000 headquarters, 3000 military and 5000 in publicly financed bodies). Given the earlier dispersal of much routine work and the direct and indirect involvement of many head-quarters staff in giving advice to and doing work for Ministers, dispersal was expected to be more difficult than hitherto. Furthermore, it was necessary to balance two conflicting aspects of dispersal, the efficiency of government operations and the needs of regional policy.

The Economics of Dispersal

The 'Hardman Report' considered three economic aspects of dispersal: resource effects; changes in government expenditure (exchequer cash flow); and impact on civil service numbers.

Resource effects

In principle, the maximum resource saving from employing staff in alternative locations can be measured by the total cost of employing somebody who would otherwise be unemployed. If recruitment of the unemployed were restricted to Clerical Officer level and below, a maximum saving of about £1400 per job per annum would occur (the average earnings, including pension provisions, of a Clerical Officer at the time of the Report). In practice, such resources benefits will be reduced by the relatively high proportion of staff transferred from London. In addition, many workers recruited will not have been registered as unemployed both because of the recruitment of people already in employment and the suitability of much civil service work for married women, many of whom do not register as unemployed. It was concluded that on balance staff-resource costs might fall by about £300 – 400 per annum per job dispersed.

At 1971 price levels, it was estimated that central London offices occupied by the government were worth about £5 – 7 per square foot of letting space, compared with about £1 in provincial locations. Allowing a saving of about £5 per square foot and 150 square feet per employee, accommodation savings of about £750 per annum per job dispersed were available.

Other items considered were the cost of moving staff, differentials in local-authority rates, working wives' loss of income and possible employment, and local income multiplier effects. It is often thought that the local income multiplier effects of dispersal are substantial. However, the 'Hardman Report' argued that two factors moderated the local income multiplier effects of dispersal. First, taxation and the 'import' of goods from other parts of the country means that only a small proportion of the resulting expenditure creates value-added locally. Second, as the economic case for dispersal rests on the net gain to the whole nation, credit can only be taken for local value-added from resources which were previously unemployed or were cheaper than in London.

The 'Hardman Report' assumed that dispersal would start in 1975 and be spread in equal stages until 1984. Over this period the discounted gain in resources per job removed from London varied between £3000 and £8000. The range mostly reflected variations in office rents between different parts of London, research having shown that costs did not differ significantly between provincial locations.* It was estimated that if 31,000 jobs were dispersed, the resource gain to the nation as a whole would be about £170 million (£5,500 per job).

Government expenditure

Dispersal affects government expenditure directly via its impact on such items as accommodation costs, transfer grants to staff and salary differentials. It was estimated that if the recommendations of the 'Hardman Report' were implemented, direct government expenditure would rise by about $£2 - 8\frac{1}{2}$ million per annum initially (reflecting the provision of accommodation), break even by 1980 and be about £24 million per annum lower by 1984. Indirect effects of dispersal on government expenditure, such as the reduced social-security payments which it was hoped would follow from lower unemployment, were not evaluated. Changes in government expenditure are part of the redistribution of income which flows from the resource gains to the nation created by dispersal, that is they are a transfer payment. It follows that savings in government expenditure cannot be added to resource gains when evaluating the benefits of dispersal.

Civil service manpower

Dispersal is likely to result in a need for extra staff to manage the dispersal move, recruit and train staff at the new location, 'double-bank' during the hand-over period and provide liaison with London. Much of the increased manpower requirement would be temporary, and the 'Hardman Report' suggested that the permanent staff increase in departments subject to dispersal would be less than an average of 1.5 per cent of their present London headquarters staff.

The Communications Study

The 'Hardman Report' was concerned primarily with the headquarters offices of government departments where policy work predominated. Such work involves close contact between Ministers, civil servants and representatives of many out-

*J. Rhodes and A. Kan, *Office Dispersal and Regional Policy* (Cambridge University Press, 1971).

side organisations. To the extent that dispersal makes such contact more difficult
to sustain, it may impair the efficiency of government decision-making. To help
determine the extent to which the need for face-to-face contact constrained
dispersal, a communications study was undertaken. The communications study
measured the frequency with which staff met, and evaluated the need for such
meetings. The results of the communications study were used to isolate apparently
self-contained blocks of work, whose dispersal was then discussed with the
departments concerned.

Receiving Locations

Choice of location was influenced by two considerations, efficiency of operation
and regional policy.

Efficiency of operation

The 'Hardman Report' considered the following aspects of efficiency:

(a) Distance from London: What effect would increasing distance from
London have on the conduct of business which required the presence of dispersed staff in London?
(b) Capacity: What is the capacity of the location in relation to existing or
potential office accommodation and the ability of the Government to get and
keep staff for local recruitment posts?
(c) Attractiveness to staff: What is the likely effect on staff dispersed from
London in relation to such amenities as housing and educational facilities, the
general environment (including journey to work) and job opportunities for
dependants?*

Regional policy

About half of the 31,000 posts recommended for dispersal were in grades filled by
local rather than national recruitment. Allowing for the possibility that some
existing job-holders in local recruitment grades would move with their work, it
was clear that dispersal would make little impact on unemployment in assisted
areas unless concentrated on a few locations. However, the 'Hardman Report'
argued that dispersal had two other beneficial effects on regional policy. First,
there were wide variations between regions in the proportion of workers employed
in offices, e.g. Greater London 25.4 per cent, the Northern Region 13.4 per cent
and Wales 13.1 per cent (1966 Sample Census). Dispersal would help to provide a
greater diversity of employment opportunities in regions with below-average
office employment. Second, there were wide variations between regions in employment opportunities for women (see Table 3.2, p. 43). As about half of all

The Dispersal of Government Work from London, p. 55

TABLE 3.13

Recommended dispersal

Department	Number of posts in blocks of work to be dispersed	Suggested receiving location
Ministry of Agriculture, Fisheries and Food	1250	Manchester
Agricultural Research Council	140	Manchester
Civil Service Department	707	
	comprising	
	357	Norwich
	300	Basingstoke
	50	Sunningdale
Her Majesty's Customs and Excise	500	Southend
Ministry of Defence	10890	Milton Keynes
Department of Employment	1540	
	comprising	
	1400	Liverpool
	140	Plymouth (with Home Office)
Department of the Environment (D.O.E.)	1248	Bristol
D.O.E. (Property Services Agency)	4100	Cardiff
Foreign and Commonwealth Office (F.C.O.)	986	Central Lancashire New Town (Preston – Leyland – Chorley)
F.C.O. (Overseas Development Administration)	1177	Glasgow
Department of Health and Social Security	1480	
	comprising	
	500	Newcastle
	980	Central Lancashire New Town
Home Office	1437	Plymouth
Criminal Injuries Compensation Board	83	Plymouth
Board of Inland Revenue	1610	Teesside
Natural Environment Research Council	191	Swindon
Office of Population Censuses and Surveys	920	Central Lancashire New Town
Science Research Council	388	Swindon
Her Majesty's Stationery Office	380	Norwich
Department of Trade and Industry	1800	
	comprising	
	1442	Cardiff/Newport
(Laboratory of the Government Chemist)	358	Teddington
Export Credits Guarantee Department	600	Liverpool
Total	31427	

SOURCE: *The Dispersal of Government Work from London*, p. 12.

clerical work in the civil service is done by women, dispersal would provide greater employment opportunities for women in regions with 'hidden reserves' of female labour. Lastly, dispersal would relieve pressure on resources in the London area.

Selection of locations. The 'efficiency' criterion pointed towards two types of location, major centres of communication and places to which departments had already dispersed work (or planned to do so). Studies were then made of the capacity of each area to absorb civil service employment and a short list of twenty-one locations prepared, which included locations in both assisted and non-assisted areas.

Recommendations. After considering the trade-off between resource savings and the results of the communications study the 'Hardman Report' recommended the dispersal shown in Table 3.13. The recommendations envisaged the dispersal of a little over half of the posts to assisted areas and over a third to locations in the South-east of England. Alternative solutions which dispersed the same number or posts with biases towards the efficiency and regional criteria were considered but not recommended.

Postscript

When the 'Hardman Report' was published in June 1973 the government announced that, whilst in principle it endorsed the view that few rather than many locations should be selected, it wished to consider the matter further before making final decisions. In particular, the government wished to consult representatives of the staff affected by dispersal. Following the change of government, it was announced in July 1974 that ultimately slightly more jobs would be dispersed than recommended in the 'Hardman Report', and that the government accepted the principle that few rather than many locations should be selected (thus improving the career prospects of dispersed staff). However, the recommended distribution of posts between assisted areas and the South-east of England was unacceptable to the government, who announced that about 90 per cent of the posts dispersed from London were to be located in assisted areas.

Exercises

(3.9) How did the dispersal of government work from London considered in the 'Hardman Report' differ from earlier dispersal exercises?

(3.10) (i) What major savings in (*a*) resources and (*b*) government expenditure were expected to result from dispersal? (ii) Why would it be wrong to add savings in resources and savings in government expenditure when considering the benefits of dispersal?

(3.11) (i) How was regional policy expected to benefit from dispersal? (ii) Why did the 'Hardman Report' recommend the concentration of dispersal on few rather than many receiving locations? (iii) What criteria were used to select receiving locations for dispersed work?

(3.12) What considerations constrained the dispersal of government work from London?

Supplementary exercises

(3.13) Suggest regional indicators additional to those in Case 5 which you would find useful when comparing the *economic* well-being of different regions.

(3.14) Why might it be to the advantage of an employer such as U.C.S. to reserve the right to refuse some workers who volunteer for redundancy?

(3.15) Table 3.14 indicates the distance that clients of the Location of Offices Bureau have moved or are moving. Contrast such private-sector moves with the findings of the 'Hardman Report' on the dispersal of government work from London. Suggest reasons for the different patterns of private-sector and government dispersal.

TABLE 3.14

*Distance that clients of the Location of
Offices Bureau have moved or are moving*

Distance from central London	No. of firms	Percentage of firms	No. of jobs	Percentage of jobs
Inside G.L.C. area	535	45	35884	37
Beyond G.L.C. area				
19 miles	140	12	7853	8
20 – 39 miles	269	22	20368	21
40 – 59 miles	67	6	5731	6
60 – 79 miles	73	6	12588	13
Over 80 miles	114	9	15260	15
TOTAL	1198	100	97684	100

SOURCE: Location of Offices Bureau, *Annual Report 1971 – 72*, table 10, p. 37.

(3.16) What impact on the dispersal of government work from London would you expect from: (i) The increase in salary differentials between London and the provinces from £175 per annum to £410 per annum in 1974? (ii) The devolution of power from the central government to Scottish and Welsh Assemblies?

Sources and References

A. J. BROWN, 'Regional Economics with Special Reference to the United Kingdom', *Economic Journal* (Dec 1969); reprinted in *Surveys of Applied Economics*, vol. I (London: Macmillan, 1973 for the Royal Economic Society and the Social Science Research Council).

'European Regional Development Fund: Council Adopts RDF Regulation', *Trade and Industry* (25 Apr 1975) pp. 238 - 9.

Incentives for Industry in the Areas for Expansion (Department of Industry, updated regularly).

Sources of Funds Available from the European Community: A Brief Guide for Local Authorities, Trade Unions, Industry and Agriculture (Commission of the European Communities, 1975).

CHAPTER 4

Competition Policy

M. S. Bradbury

Summary of Background Material

Policy in the United Kingdom – Economic Background

Competition policy in the United Kingdom is primarily concerned with three interrelated situations, the abuse of dominant positions, restrictive trade practices and mergers.*

A *dominant position* occurs when a firm's market share is large enough to enable it to behave like a monopolist. Where the remaining producers are relatively small, a market share of as little as 25 per cent may give a firm a dominant position. In a U.K. context, *restrictive trade practices* refer primarily to two activities. First, agreements between firms in an industry which impose restrictions on such things as the prices to be charged, conditions of sale or quantities to be supplied. Second, the stipulation by firms of a price, at or above which the retailer must resell the product (called resale price maintenance – R.P.M.). *Mergers* occur when previously independent firms become subject to sufficient common ownership to make common control or material influence possible. Such a definition includes not only the total integration of the ownership and control of previously independent firms, but also the exercise of effective control of or material influence over another firm via a minority ownership interest and the common ownership of firms over which unified control is not, but could be, exercised.

Common to the three situations is the existence, strengthening or potential creation of *market power*, that is control by firms of the environment in which they operate. Except under highly restrictive conditions we cannot say that all such departures from competition will necessarily have an 'adverse' effect on resource allocation. Instead, assessing the consequences of a given market situation involves a complex comparison of costs and benefits.† For example, a merger

---

*Competition policy in the United Kingdom is also concerned with *complex monopoly*, that is oligopoly situations where a group of firms conduct their affairs so as to restrict, prevent or distort competition other than by registrable agreements.

†Discussions of the 'competition' versus 'monopoly' controversy can be found in most introductory textbooks. See, for example R.G. Lipsey, *An Introduction to Positive Economics*, 4th edn (London: Weidenfeld & Nicolson, 1975) ch. 24.

aimed at creating a dominant firm may lead to the introduction of monopoly prices and the earning of abnormal profits in the long run. Alternatively, if the firm is not a profit maximiser, induced mediocrity, that is toleration of high costs, slowness in adjusting to changing patterns of demand, a lack of innovation and low accounting profits, may result. Conversely, a merger might ultimately enable economies of scale beyond those available under competition to be exploited, or create the resources and security needed for expensive high-risk research and development to be undertaken. In the last report the balance of advantage in such trade-off situations is largely an empirical matter.

In principle, competition policy may operate against either the existence or the abuse of market power. Both approaches can be found in U.K. competition policy. For both monopoly and merger policies the critical issue is not the existence, but the abuse or potential future abuse of market power. Conversely, market power derived from restrictive trade practices is presumed to act against the public interest unless the firms concerned can prove otherwise.

Policy in the United Kingdom – Legislation

The evolution of current U.K. competition policy can be traced through four major legislative stages:

(1) tentative first steps – *The Monopolies and Restrictive Practices (Inquiry and Control) Act* of 1948;

(2) the effective control of restrictive trade practices – *The Restrictive Trade Practices Acts* of 1956 and 1968 and *The Resale Prices Act* of 1964;

(3) the extension and strengthening of monopoly policy and the beginning of merger control – *The Monopolies and Mergers Act* of 1965; and

(4) co-ordination, extension and partial consolidation – *The Fair Trading Act* of 1973.

Each of these major legislative measures is summarised below. Three features particularly stand out:

(1) the gradual extension of the market situations to which competition policy applies;

(2) the changing attitudes towards specific business practices as experience increases; and

(3) the evolution of the institutional framework within which competition policy operates.

The Monopolies and Restrictive Practices (Inquiry and Control) Act, 1948

The 1948 Act was the first step towards the continuing investigation and control of monopoly situations in the United Kingdom. Three features of the Act are of interest: the situations to which its terms applied; the investigation and control procedure used; and the tentative nature of the legislation.

The provisions of the 1948 Act applied where at least one-third of a class of goods was supplied in the United Kingdom by a single firm, or a group of firms acting together so as to restrict competition. Thus the legislation recognised that a firm could effectively control a market even though it was not the sole producer, and that in some markets firms could obtain similar advantages by agreeing between themselves to reduce competition.

Initiative in selecting monopoly situations for investigation lay with the Board of Trade. It could ask the Monopolies and Restrictive Practices Commission, which had been established by the Act, to investigate potential monopoly situations and report:

(1) whether the conditions to which the Act applied prevailed in the market concerned;

(2) what things were done by the parties concerned as a result of, or for the purpose of, preserving these conditions; and

(3) whether the conditions in question, or the things done, operated, or could be expected to operate, in the public interest.

Where the Commission found practices which it considered contrary to the public interest, it usually recommended remedies. The Board of Trade could then make an Order declaring the practices unlawful and requiring the parties to end them, or it could negotiate a voluntary compromise agreement. The basis of this procedure of inquiry and control was the acceptance of the view that it was not the existence but the abuse of monopoly power that was contrary to the public interest.

The tentative nature of the 1948 Act was indicated by:

(1) the exclusion of significant sectors of the economy from the provisions of the Act; e.g. nationalised industries and the supply of services;

(2) the extremely wide definition of the 'public interest';

(3) the absence of any acceptance or rejection of specific types of monopoly abuse; and

(4) the political veto on the activities of the Commission which the Board of Trade could exercise both by its selection of markets for investigation and right to implement, modify or ignore the Commission's recommendations.

It should, however, be recalled that very little was known at the time about the actual, as opposed to the predicted, effects of monopoly and restrictive trade practices in the United Kingdom.

The Restrictive Trade Practices Act, 1956

Initially, the Commission devoted much of its efforts to investigating restrictive trade practices, its findings leading to the *Restrictive Trade Practices Act* of 1956. The Act established a Registrar of Restrictive Trading Agreements and a Restrictive Practices Court. Restrictive trading agreements* have to be registered with the

*Such agreements include formal and informal agreements, written and unwritten.

Registrar. An industry wanting to continue an agreement has either to amend those parts considered contrary to the Act by the Registrar, or obtain a ruling from the Restrictive Practices Court that the agreement is positively in the public interest (the onus of proof is on the parties to the agreement).

To prove that an agreement is not contrary to the public interest, it has to be established that one or more of the following circumstances applies (often called the 'gateways' to the public interest):

(*a*) the restriction is reasonably necessary to prevent injury to persons or premises;

(*b*) the removal of the restriction would deny to the public specific and substantial benefits which result from the agreement;

(*c*) the agreement is needed to protect the parties against restrictive behaviour by a competitor(s);

(*d*) the agreement is needed to protect the parties against the use of monopsony power (a monopsonist is a sole buyer);

(*e*) ending the agreement will cause serious and persistent unemployment in areas where the industry is located;

(*f*) ending the agreement would have an adverse effect on export earnings, which is substantial either in relation to total U.K. exports, or to the total output of the industry;

(*g*) the restriction is reasonably required in order to maintain an agreement which has been approved by the Court; and

(*h*) the restriction does not directly or indirectly restrict or discourage competition to any material degree in any relevant trade or industry and is not likely to do so. (This gateway was added by the *Restrictive Trade Practices Act* of 1968.)

If successful in establishing that one or more of the above circumstances apply, the parties to the agreement must then prove that these circumstances outweight any detriment to the public resulting from the agreement (sometimes called the 'balancing act').

The 1956 Act changed the name of the Monopolies and Restrictive Practices Commission to the Monopolies Commission, reduced its size and changed its functions. The Monopolies Commission was concerned with the following:

(1) the dominant supplier or processor (market share of at least one-third);

(2) agreements relating exclusively to the export trade; and

(3) markets in which companies which accounted for at least one-third of the supply of a good adopted policies which restricted competition, other than by an agreement which was registrable with the Registrar of Restrictive Trading Agreements.

The less tentative approach of the 1956 Act towards restrictive trading agreements reflected the widespread evidence from early Commission Reports of the variety and effects of restrictive practices.

The Resale Prices Act, 1964

There are two ways in which manufacturers have attempted to enforce R.P.M. agreements. First, a retailer who failed to charge the maintained price for *one firm's goods* might face a withdrawal of supplies by *all producers of similar goods*, e.g. car tyres, and would only have supplies restored after a trade court had received assurances about future conduct and in some cases after a fine had been paid. Second, an individual firm might enforce the agreement by withholding supplies from a retailer or, if the retailer could acquire the goods from other sources, by obtaining an injunction prohibiting a breach of the R.P.M. agreement.

Although the collective enforcement of R.P.M. was prohibited by the *Restrictive Trade Practices Act* of 1956, the same Act strengthened individually enforced R.P.M. The enforcement of minimum resale prices by individual manufacturers was, except under certain conditions, prohibited by the *Resale Prices Act* of 1964. Under the Act, a manufacturer can withhold supplies from a firm using its product as a loss leader, that is a good sold not with a view to profit, but as an advertisement, or as a way of attracting customers, who it is hoped will then buy other goods.

Exemption from the *Resale Prices Act* can be obtained if it can be proved to the Restrictive Practices Court that the continuation of R.P.M. for a particular class of goods is in the public interest. To do this manufacturers must first establish that one or more of the following five consequences will follow in the absence of R.P.M.:

(1) the quality and variety of goods available for sale would be substantially reduced to the detriment of the public;

(2) the number of establishments in which the goods are sold would be substantially reduced to the detriment of the public;

(3) retail prices would increase to the detriment of the public;

(4) goods would be sold by retail under conditions likely to cause danger to health in consequence of their misuse by the public;

(5) any necessary services actually provided in connection with, or after the sale of, the goods by retail, would cease to be provided or would be substantially reduced to the detriment of the public.

Having established a detriment to the public, the manufacturers must then prove that this detriment outweighs any detriments resulting from the maintenance of minimum resale prices.

The Monopolies and Mergers Act, 1965

During the late 1950s and early 1960s there was growing criticism of monopolies legislation. Investigations took several years, and often the resulting recommendations were only partly acted upon (sometimes because the Board of Trade doubted its legal ability to implement some of the Commission's recommendations). Legislation applied to the supply of goods, thus excluding from consideration the increasingly important service industries, for example, banking, insurance, entertainment and the professions. It also seemed to be an anomaly that, whilst a dominant supplier or processor could be investigated, nothing could be done to investigate and, if necessary, prevent a takeover bid or merger, which might lead to the creation of a dominant firm where none existed before or to the strengthening of an existing monopoly situation. These criticisms led to the *Monopolies and Mergers Act* of 1965. The principal changes made by the Act were:

(1) The maximum membership of the Monopolies Commission was increased.

(2) On reference from the Board of Trade, the Commission was empowered to investigate restrictive practices and monopoly situations (as described in the 1948 Act) in the service industries.

(3) The powers of the Board of Trade to act on the Commission's report were extended. For example, they now had the power to require the publication of price lists, regulate prices and prohibit or impose conditions on acquisitions.

(4) Where a merger created or strengthened a monopoly situation, or involved gross assets in excess of £5 million, the Board of Trade could, if it wished, refer the merger to the Commission for investigation and report. To minimise uncertainty, such references must normally have been made within six months of the merger being completed, and the Commission was normally to report within six months of the reference being made. If the Commission decided that the merger was against the public interest, the Board could prohibit it, or dissolve it if it had already taken place.

(5) Special conditions applied to newspaper mergers where a wider definition of the public interest applied, that is the Commission had to 'take into account all matters which appear in the particular circumstances to be relevant, and having regard amongst other things to the need for accurate presentation of news and free expression of opinion'.

The Restrictive Trade Practices Act, 1968

Following criticism of the 1956 Act, the *Restrictive Trade Practices Act* of 1968 was passed, primarily to make the operation of the 1956 Act more flexible and to improve its enforcement. Two features were of particular importance.* First, the Board of Trade was empowered to exempt from registration agreements promoting the carrying-out of projects of substantial importance to the national economy or those aiding prices and incomes policy. Second, the Board of Trade was empowered to require the registration of information agreements. (Under information agreements, firms exchange information of the type which may be contrary to the public interest under the 1956 Act, e.g. members of a price ring declared contrary to the public interest may exchange details of forthcoming price changes 'for information only'.)

*As mentioned on p. 63, the Act also added a new gateway (*h*) to the public interest.

The Fair Trading Act, 1973

The Act replaces the 1948 and 1965 Acts and amends the *Restrictive Trade Practices Acts*. The Act extended the scope of consumer protection policy (not discussed below) and revised the institutional framework through which competition policy operates.

The Act created a Director General of Fair Trading and an Office of Fair Trading. The Director General has the duty of collecting information about market structures and the behaviour of firms, a task previously undertaken within the Board of Trade and subsequently the Department of Trade and Industry. References (other than mergers, nationalised industries, other statutory bodies and restrictive labour practices) to the renamed Monopolies and Mergers Commission can be initiated by the Director General, who also advises the Minister on any follow-up action resulting from the Commission's report. Ministers retain parallel rights to initiate investigations and can veto a reference to the Commission made by the Director General. Although the Director General is the Minister's adviser on mergers (other than newspapers) only the Secretary of State for Prices and Consumer Protection can initiate a merger reference to the Commission. Lastly, the functions of the Registrar of Restrictive Trading Agreements are transferred to the Director General.

Non-institutional changes made by the *Fair Trading Act* of 1973 included:

(1) Amended guidance to the Monopolies and Mergers Commission on what matters to take into account when considering the public interest, including specific reference to the benefits of promoting competition.

(2) A major extension of the situations which can be referred to the Monopolies and Mergers Commission. The qualifying market share for both monopolies and mergers was cut from one-third to one-quarter, and purely local monopolies (but not mergers) were included for the first time, as also were uncompetitive practices adopted by firms acting in their capacity as employers. Ministers (but not the Director General) were also empowered to refer nationalised industries, other statutory bodies and restrictive labour practices to the Monopolies and Mergers Commission (in the latter case there is no power to make orders based on the Commission's findings).

(3) Agreements in the services sector (other than professions) were transferred from the Commission to the restrictive practices part of the machinery.*

(4) The requirement that references specify a period (subject to extension) within which the Commission must report; and clarification of the power to confine references to specific aspects of a monopoly or merger.

Competition Policy in the European Community

When the Treaty of Rome was signed in 1957 it was thought that many of the economic benefits from reducing tariff and quota barriers to trade between member states might be lost unless action was taken to limit the potential abuse

---

*An order has since been made requiring registration of restrictive agreements in the service sector by 16 June 1976.

of market power by cartels and dominant firms. For example, potential rival firms located in different member states might agree not to compete in each other's home markets, even though tariffs or quotas which had previously limited competition had been eliminated.

The core of Community competition policy derives from Articles 85 and 86 of the Treaty of Rome.* Article 85 prohibits agreements between firms which distort competition in the E.E.C. and Article 86 prohibits the abuse of a dominant position within the E.E.C. or a substantial part thereof. In both cases, trade between member states must be affected actually or potentially, that is Articles 85 and 86 do not apply to market abuses whose effects are strictly confined to the internal trade of a member state or trade with third countries. In this respect, Community competition policy currently complements the legislation of individual member states. However, Community law overrides U.K. law if they conflict.

Article 85 prohibits agreements which distort competition. Exemption can be gained by agreements which improve the production and distribution of goods or promote technical progress provided:

(1) the customer receives a fair share of the resulting benefits;

(2) the agreement does not contain restrictions which are unnecessary to the achievement of its objectives; and

(3) the agreement does not enable the firms concerned to eliminate competition in respect of a substantial part of the goods involved.

The regulations and directives needed to make operational the principles set out in Articles 85 and 86 are made by the Council of Ministers (who must consult the Assembly and vote unanimously). The European Commission is responsible for implementing competition policy subject to a right of appeal on points of law to the European Court of Justice at Luxembourg. Agreements covered by Article 85 have to be notified to the Commission. Parties to such agreements may then request 'negative clearance' – a statement by the Commission that, according to the information available, there are no grounds for it to intervene in the agreement or that the requirements for exemption are met. Cases may be initiated by the Commission either on its own or at the request of member states or interested parties. To date, competition policy has concentrated on reducing uncertainty by rulings on a sample of representative agreements thought likely to distort competition. So far the Commission has taken action under Article 86 in only a handful of cases, but nearly all of them have been complex and raised major issues of principle.

A major weakness of Community competition policy is the lack of strong powers for dealing with mergers. The Treaty of Rome did not specifically mention mergers, and Article 86 is of limited value in this context as its use is confined to mergers where at least one of the firms is already in a dominant position. Consequently there is no mechanism for preventing the use of mergers to create domin-

---

*Special provisions apply to public undertakings, fiscal monopolies, agriculture and transport. Competition in the steel and coal industry is regulated by the Treaty of Paris, which established the European Coal and Steel Community.

ant positions. In July 1973 the Commission proposed a draft regulation on mergers, the key features of which were the following:

(1) the prohibition of mergers which hindered 'effective competition' (unless indispensable to the attainment of a Community objective, e.g. regional policy);

(2) the power to break up a merger which has already taken place or take other actions needed to restore 'effective competition';

(3) a 'prior notification' obligation in respect of large mergers (annual aggregate turnover more than 1000 million units of account);*

(4) exemption for small mergers (annual aggregate turnover of less than 200 million units of account and less than a 25 per cent share of any of the national markets); and

(5) a time limit on all but the most complex decisions (up to three months to decide whether an investigation is needed and a further nine months for investigations).

These proposals have been severely criticised, mainly on the grounds that the uncertainty caused by the potential delay in reaching a decision could prevent desirable mergers taking place. At the time of writing the Council of Ministers had not reached a decision on the draft regulation.

Illustration by Case Studies

Case 8, on the supply and processing of colour film, illustrates the investigation of a 'dominant position' by the Monopolies and Mergers Commission. Particular attention should be paid to the factors which influenced the Commission's decision and to the problems of implementing its recommendations.

Case 9, on rival bids for the Glaxo Group, illustrates the operation of merger control in the United Kingdom. As many merger proposals are based on the belief that only very large firms can undertake effective research programmes, particular attention should be paid to the reasons given for rejecting the argument in this instance.

Case 10, on the Permanent Magnet Association's agreement, and Case 11, on collusive tendering in the contracting industry, illustrate the application of the *Restrictive Trade Practices Act* of 1956.

Case 12, on chocolate and sugar confectionery, shows how an application for exemption from the general ban on R.P.M. contained in the *Resale Prices Act* of 1964 is considered by the Restrictive Practices Court.

Case 13, on the International Quinine Cartel, illustrates the use of competition policy within the European Community to counter restrictive practices which affect trade between member states.

Case 14 illustrates the use of the *Restrictive Trade Practices Act* of 1968 to exempt restrictive agreements from registration.

*At the time of writing, there were 2.4 units of account to the £ sterling for the purposes of competition policy.

CASE 8. MONOPOLY: THE SUPPLY AND PROCESSING OF COLOUR FILM, 1963 – 9

On 14 May 1963 the Board of Trade asked the Monopolies Commission to investigate and report on the supply and processing of colour film. We begin with a description of the Commission's findings on the existence of monopoly conditions, then summarise its conclusions regarding the public interest, and its proposals for remedying practices found contrary to the public interest, and conclude with a discussion of the implementation of the Commission's recommendations.

The Existence of Monopoly Conditions in the Supply and Processing of Colour Film

The Commission had first to report on whether the conditions to which monopolies legislation applied existed in the supply and processing of colour film. Monopoly conditions would exist if either (*a*) at least one-third of all colour film was either supplied or processed by one firm, or (*b*) two or more firms (other than by an agreement which is required to be registered with the Registrar of Restrictive Trading Agreements), who together supply or process more than one-third of all colour films, conducted their respective affairs so as to prevent or restrict competition.

The supply of colour film

Ignoring Japan and the Eastern bloc, the world market for colour film was largely supplied by three American, one German – Belgian and one British firm. These were, respectively, the Eastman Kodak group, the 3M group (Ferrania and Dynacolor), the General Aniline group (Ansco), the Agfa – Gevaert group and Ilford (which had links with I.C.I. and CIBA). Most of these firms also supplied other photographic materials and goods, colour films representing a small proportion of their total activities.

Kodak Ltd (a subsidiary of Eastman Kodak) and Ilford were the only producers of colour film in the United Kingdom. In spite of a high tariff barrier (20 per cent in most cases), other firms competed in the U.K. market by means of agents or subsidiaries who imported film. The market shares of the various suppliers can be deduced from Table 4.1.

Another feature of the supply of colour film was that every manufacturer and importer individually prescribed and maintained the minimum retail prices at which their colour films could be sold and the discounts to be given to intermediate suppliers. This practice prevented price competition between distributors in selling any one make of film.

TABLE 4.1
*Total net sale of colour film in the United Kingdom
by net sales value* and by area in 1964*

	£ (thousands)	sq. ft. (thousands)
Kodak	4334	6911
Ilford	203	445
Agfa†	547	773
Gevaert†	121	264
Gratispool (Dynachrome)	185	532
Rank (Ferraniacolor)	85	121
Hanimex† (Perutz)	113	92
David Williams (Ansochrome)	27	18
Other	31	35
TOTAL	5646	9191

*Manufacturers' and importers' selling prices were exclusive of purchase tax, but the prices for imported films took import duty into account. Where films were sold at a price inclusive of a charge for processing, a portion of the price attributed to this charge was excluded.

†In 1964 Agfa and Gevaert amalgamated their photographic interests by setting up jointly owned operating subsidiaries in Germany and Belgium. At about the same time Agfa acquired the sole ownership of Perutz.

SOURCE: Monopolies Commission, *A Report on the Supply and Processing of Colour Film* (London: H.M.S.O., 1966) p. 4.

The Commission held that the supply of colour film was subject to monopoly conditions since (*a*) Kodak had for many years supplied more than one-third of all colour films, and (*b*) the fixing of minimum retail prices and discounts to be given to intermediate suppliers amounted to conduct which restricted or prevented competition.

The processing of colour film

The Commission had to decide what constituted a 'process'. At one extreme it could have decided that only one process existed, e.g. developing. At the other extreme, since no two brands of colour film were identical, or could be success-fully developed in the same chemical solutions, it could have decided that each brand was subject to a separate process. Instead, the Commission decided to group films according to one of the three processes: negative – positive; substantive reversal; and non-substantive reversal. It was held that monopoly conditions prevailed in the application of substantive and non-substantive reversal processes to colour films since:

(1) All non-substantive reversal and 60 per cent of substantive reversal colour film was sold 'process paid', that is at a price which included a charge for the developing of the film by the manufacturer, importer or their appointee. This amounted to conduct which restricted or prevented competition.

(2) Agfa processed more than one-third of all substantive reversal film and Kodak processed more than one-third of all non-substantive reversal film.

In the case of negative – positive film, independent processors accounted for at least one-half of all processing; Kodak's share of processing was probably about one-third, but this could not be confirmed, and 'process-paid' films accounted for less than one-third of all films sold. It was therefore concluded that monopoly conditions did not exist in this instance.

The public interest

The Commission accepted that for economic reasons (the high cost of research and development and the economies of scale in production and processing) the bulk of the colour-film trade in Britain was likely in any event to fall into the hands of two or three firms. It believed that Kodak's dominant position (about three-quarters of film sales and two-thirds of processing) was primarily due to 'the strength of its already established position in the photographic industry which was reinforced in the years during and after the war, to the support of its American parent and to the technical and commercial skills with which it had exploited these advantages'. This position was stronger than it would otherwise have been because of the weakness of British-based competition, namely Ilford, and the existence of import duties which had prevented imported films from competing on equal terms.

In view of the economies of scale and the company's general efficiency, the Commission decided that Kodak's monopoly position did not in itself operate against the public interest. They did, however, decide that certain of Kodak's commercial policies were contrary to the public interest and should be changed. The Commission then examined four particular aspects of Kodak's commercial policies: pricing; retail margins; the limiting of the retail distribution of its colour film to certain appointed outlets; and the practice of selling some colour films only at process-paid prices (this was also considered in relation to other manu- facturers). R.P.M. would have been considered but for the fact that a ruling on the issue was to be given by the Restrictive Practices Court, under the terms of the *Resale Prices Act* of 1964.

Pricing

After analysing prices, costs and profits, the Commission concluded that Kodak's pricing policy resulted in disproportionately high profits on its colour films, compared with both its other activities and the average for manufacturing industry in general. In 1963, for example, Kodak's profits on its colour-film business, expressed as a percentage of capital employed (based on historical cost), amounted to 51.7 per cent compared with 16.2 per cent on its other business, and 13.4 per cent on average in manufacturing industry. The Commission estimated that, on the basis of Kodak's results for 1964, an average reduction of 20 per cent in the company's selling price would still have left Kodak with a profit of 20 per cent on capital employed, *even if the cut price did not increase sales.*

Retail margins

The Commission concluded that Kodak's commercial policy led to excessively high retail margins. In general, the retailer's discount was 30 per cent of sales revenue (minus tax) on the sales of colour film, and $33\frac{1}{3}$ per cent on processing (some large multiples being given larger discounts). These margins were based on those given on black-and-white films. Hence retailers were earning two or three times as much by selling a colour film as by the almost identical transaction of selling a black-and-white film (see Table 4.2).

TABLE 4.2
Breakdown of retail price of Kodachrome,* 1965

Kodak's net selling price	Retailer's margin	Purchase tax	Total retail price
23s. 9d.	10s. 2d.	2s. 10d.	36s. 9d.
(119p)	(51p)	(14p)	(184p)

*Kodachrome II, 35-mm, 36-exposure film and processing.

SOURCE: *Report on the Supply and Processing of Colour Film*, p. 65.

Retail outlets

Kodak restricted the sale of its colour film to appointed outlets, the majority of these being chemists' shops and photographic retail shops. They refused to sell colour film to Woolworths or to mail-order houses. It was argued that this was justified by the need to ensure that retailers gave advice to customers on the use of colour films, and by the fear that if the number of outlets was increased sales per outlet would fall, leading to higher distribution costs and to demands for larger retail margins. The Commission believed that Kodak, though able to reduce margins, had not done so because of pressure from the Photographic Dealers'

Association (P.D.A.). In the absence of a lead from the dominant supplier, other manufacturers then felt unable either to cut retail margins or to widen the basis of distribution. (Ilford gave details of pressure applied by the P.D.A. when it received a request for supplies from Woolworths.)

The sale of colour films at 'process-paid' prices

The suppliers of colour film argued that the practice of selling some films exclusively at prices which included a charge for processing was justified since:

(1) the economies of scale in processing were such that a brand with a small share of the market could only justify one processing plant;

(2) processing methods were subject to continual improvements which were easier to introduce when the supplier had control of the processing;

(3) if an independent processor made a poor-quality transparency, the customer would tend to assume that the cause was a poor film and then switch to another brand.

The Commission concluded that the practice was contrary to the public interest since it eliminated price, quality and service competition in the processing of colour films.

Remedies

The Commission recommended the following remedies:

(1) The import duty on colour films should be abolished.

(2) Significant reductions should be made in Kodak's own selling prices for colour film and in its charges for processing, the extent of such reductions to be decided by the Board of Trade after consultation with Kodak.

(3) Kodak should reduce the normal retailer's discount on the sale of its colour film to yield an amount not substantially more than the amount received on comparable black-and-white films, the amount of this reduction to be decided by the Board of Trade after consultation with Kodak.

(4) Kodak should permit its colour films to be stocked and sold by any retailer who wished to deal in them (subject only to normal commercial considerations), and should supply without discrimination (other than granting quantity discounts).

(5) The retailer should be free to sell film process-paid or not, as the customer might require. Processors should not maintain or recommend a retail price to be charged for processing. Suppliers should be prepared to consider giving technical help to independent processors seeking to process films previously sold exclusively on a 'process-paid' basis.

Subsequent events

The Commission completed its report on 27 January 1966. On 8 August 1966 the President of the Board of Trade announced that an agreement had been reached with Kodak and the other main suppliers for the voluntary implementation of the

Commission's recommendations. The agreement provided for:

(1) an average reduction of $12\frac{1}{2}$ per cent in the price of Kodak colour films to retailers;

(2) the abandonment by Kodak of any restrictions on the supply of colour films to retail outlets (subject only to normal commercial considerations);

(3) the introduction by all suppliers of arrangements which would enable retailers to sell reversal colour films either inclusive of a charge for processing, or not, at the customer's choice; and

(4) the provision by all suppliers of technical help for independent processors who wished to process their colour film.

The President of the Board of Trade also announced that, following an inquiry into the import duty on colour films, he had decided that a change in the tariff at the present time would not be in the public interest. At the same time it was announced that discussion with Kodak on the level of retail margins were continuing. In October 1966 the Board of Trade announced that since Kodak had decided to abandon R.P.M. and to reduce by 20 per cent the level of their retail prices, no further action would be taken on the level of retail margins.

During 1968 Ilford announced that because of intense competition it was ceasing to sell colour film under its own brand name. It would, however, continue to produce colour film for sale under retailers' own brand names. In October 1969 it was announced that I.C.I. was selling its interest in Ilford to the Swiss firm CIBA; consequently there is now no British-owned colour-film manufacturer.

Exercises

(4.1) Use the net sales value figures in Table 4.1 (p. 70) to calculate the share of the market held by (*a*) the two largest suppliers combined, and (*b*) the three largest suppliers combined.

(4.2) What reason did the Commission give for Kodak's dominant position in the market?

(4.3) Why were retailers' margins on colour films not reduced (*a*) by Kodak, and (*b*) by other producers?

(4.4) (i) What do you understand by the sale of film 'process-paid'? (ii) Why did manufacturers support the sale of film on a 'process-paid' basis? (iii) Why did the Commission consider the 'process-paid' practice to be contrary to the public interest?

(4.5) What reasons can you suggest for the recommendation that the import duty on colour films be abolished?

(4.6) 'The implementation of the Commission's recommendations strengthened Kodak's position by driving Ilford out of the colour-film market.' Discuss.

(4.7) How do you explain Kodak's ability to charge a slightly higher price for its colour films than most of its competitors, and yet at the same time dominate the market?

CASE 9. RIVAL MERGER PROPOSALS – BIDS BY BEECHAM AND BOOTS FOR GLAXO

On 2 December 1971, Beecham announced that it intended to bid for control of Glaxo. Following strong opposition to the bid by Glaxo, it was announced on 12 January 1972 that Boots and Glaxo intended to merge by means of a bid from Boots for the Glaxo share capital. Each of the three companies was engaged to varying degrees in the pharmaceuticals industry. On 4 February, the Secretary of State for Trade and Industry referred both bids to the Monopolies Commission.

The Structure of the Pharmaceuticals Industry in 1970

At manufacturers' prices, the U.K. pharmaceuticals market was valued at £280 million in 1970 – about 4 per cent of the non-communist world market. Sales were divided amongst a vast range of drugs, reflecting both the diversity of medical requirements and the varying potential for substitution between the differentiated products of rival suppliers. Consequently the pharmaceuticals market should be viewed as an agglomeration of sub-markets of varying size and competitive structure.

In common with the pharmaceuticals industry in other countries, the U.K. industry consisted of many small-, some medium- and a few large-sized producers (the 1968 *Census of Production* listed 283 enterprises in the pharmaceuticals industry). About 64 per cent (by value) of the U.K. market was supplied by foreign-controlled firms. Of the forty companies in the world with a pharmaceuticals turnover exceeding $50 million in 1970, only four, Glaxo, Wellcome, Beecham and I.C.I., were British-owned.

Research, Innovation and Competition in the Pharmaceuticals Industry

Large pharmaceuticals companies spend about 7 – 12 per cent of their turnover on research and development (R and D). An important objective of such R and D is the discovery and development of new drugs which can be patented on a world-wide basis. The patent grants a statutory monopoly for a limited period. Ultimately, the potential ability to earn monopoly profits which results from the protection given by the patent will be eroded, either by the expiration of the patent – enabling other producers to enter the market – or by competition from new or improved drugs. Another objective of R and D is to prolong the commercial life of a successful drug, by product improvement and the development of less expensive production processes. Producers maximise the benefits to themselves from such temporary monopoly situations by marketing new drugs on a world-wide basis by means of either direct export sales or overseas production by subsidiaries or licensees.

The Companies involved in the Rival Merger Proposals

It will be seen from Table 4.3 that, unlike Glaxo, Beecham and Boots obtained only a minority of their revenue from the manufacture of pharmaceuticals and related products. However, a significant proportion of Boots other revenue resulted from it being the largest retail chemists in the United Kingdom. Although each company had a record of successful research-based product innovation, Glaxo's research programme was the most diversified. Most research took place in the United Kingdom. Each company possessed extensive overseas production and marketing facilities and had for several years earned profits significantly above the average rates achieved by U.K. manufacturing industry, whether expressed as a percentage of sales or of capital employed.

TABLE 4.3

Sales and research expenditure, 1970 – 1 (£m.)

| | Sales | | Pharmaceutical research expenditure |
	Total	Pharmaceuticals	
Glaxo	134.0[1]	119.2[2]	5.50[3]
Beecham	181.8	55.1[4]	4.60[5]
Boots	257.4	40.5[6]	0.75

1. Excludes wholesaling.
2. Includes related foods.
3. Estimated (89 per cent of £6.2m.).
4. Includes veterinary products.
5. Ethical pharmaceutical research.
6. Manufacturing only, i.e. excludes retail sales.

SOURCE: Monopolies Commission, *Beecham Group Ltd. and Glaxo Group Ltd., The Boots Company Ltd. and Glaxo Group Ltd., A Report on the Proposed Mergers* (London: H.M.S.O., 1972).

Submissions by the Companies to the Monopolies Commission

Although other matters were discussed, the two key issues in the submissions by the companies for and against each merger were their impact on R and D and international marketing.

Beecham argued that if merged with Glaxo, the combined groups could sustain economically a larger R and D effort than each could achieve separately, thus strengthening their ability to compete with the larger overseas-based companies. It would also be possible to redeploy resources currently devoted to duplicated research. In reply, Glaxo argued that it was already big enough to compete successfully with large foreign companies, that Beecham's R and D programme was too narrowly based, and that the merger would damage the morale of their

R and D staff, who did not regard the philosophy appropriate to selling consumer goods as applicable to ethical pharmaceuticals.* Boots and Glaxo regarded a merger between themselves as a means of strengthening largely complementary R and D programmes.

Both Beecham and Boots argued that a merger with Glaxo would significantly strengthen overseas production and marketing facilities, thus increasing turnover and benefiting the U.K. balance of payments. Glaxo considered that Beecham had exaggerated such benefits, but agreed that, as its own overseas facilities were more extensive than Boots, significant balance-of-payments benefits would accrue from a merger between Glaxo and Boots.

The Commission's Findings

International marketing ability

Although the Commission thought that Beecham had exaggerated the likely gains from increased overseas sales, they accepted that either merger might strengthen overseas operations to the potential benefit of both the new group and the U.K. balance of payments. However, the Commission regarded the key issue as being the balance of effects of either merger on R and D.

R and D

The argument that it was necessary to match the research programme of vastly larger overseas producers rested on the relationship between size of firm, R and D expenditure and innovative output in the pharmaceutical industry. The Commission carried out two limited investigations of these relationships. First, the world-wide ethical pharmaceutical sales and relevant R and D expenditure in 1970 of fifteen major British and foreign companies which sold pharmaceuticals in the United Kingdom were compared. Research intensity, that is the ratio of R and D expenditure to sales of pharmaceutical products to third parties, reached a peak when a firm's world-wide sales of ethical pharmaceuticals reached about £120 million. Second, firm size and the number of major pharmaceutical innovations obtained during 1950 – 71 were compared for a sample of thirty-six internationally operating pharmaceutical companies. It was found that 'the very largest firms had been responsible for a less than proportionate number of the major innovations relative to their share of sales. Conversely several of the smaller firms had a more than proportionate number of innovations relative to their share of sales.' The results of both investigations were compatible with the findings of independent studies. On this basis the Commission concluded that all three companies were 'well above the minimum size necessary to engage effectively in costly and risky research for new products or processes'.

*Ethical pharmaceuticals are products advertised only within the medical and allied professions, and supplied, in general, by pharmaceutical chemists on prescription only.

The Commission accepted that more stringent official requirements for the safety of drugs was likely to increase the real costs of R and D in the future. Consequently, the Commission thought that, in principle, the larger enterprise resulting from either merger might gain three R and D advantages:

(*a*) the ability to undertake R and D projects which either company would regard as too risky or expensive to undertake alone;

(*b*) some resource savings where R and D effort is currently duplicated; and

(*c*) to the extent that more effective overseas marketing facilities increased the rewards of successful innovation, the incentive to devote resources to R and D might be increased.

However, the Commission distinguished between size achieved by growth within a company and that due to a merger. In particular, it was thought that a merger could have three adverse effects on R and D:

(*a*) Not only was there no reason to expect a merged group to generate more 'novel ideas' than its previously independent member companies, but Beecham or Boots would no longer have an incentive to widen the scope of their R and D.

(*b*) Either merger would eliminate an independent centre from which expenditure on research could be authorised and research policy determined. As there were very few such centres in the United Kingdom, the elimination of one of them was likely to impair the British-owned industry's prospects of finding and developing new products. In particular, the Commission considered that Boots as an independent company had the potential to become a major centre for research decision making.

(*c*) A merger between Glaxo and Beecham was likely to have an adverse effect on the morale of the Glaxo research staff, thus damaging the effectiveness of their research.

Conclusion

The Commission concluded that any international marketing and R and D advantages resulting from either merger would be outweighed by the above R and D disadvantages. On 13 July 1972 the Government announced its acceptance of the Commission's recommendation that neither of the proposed mergers should be allowed.

Exercises

(4.8) Why do pharmaceutical companies spend a significant proportion of their turnover on R and D?

(4.9) Why do many pharmaceutical companies tend to operate on an international basis?

(4.10) Contrast Glaxo's attitude towards a merger with Boots with its reactions to a merger with Beecham.

(4.11) Why might either merger reduce the incentive of either Boots or Beecham to widen the scope of their R and D?

(4.12) 'We are satisfied that the fact that the British-owned pharmaceutical industry contains no companies of the size of the largest foreign owned companies does not put it at a material disadvantage in research and development.' Discuss this comment made by the Monopolies Commission.

CASE 10. RESTRICTIVE TRADING AGREEMENTS: THE PERMANENT MAGNET ASSOCIATION

On 8 January 1959 the Registrar of Restrictive Trading Agreements referred the Permanent Magnet Association's agreement to the Restrictive Practices Court. Hearings in November and December 1961 were followed on 7 June 1962 by the judgement of the Court.

The Permanent Magnet Association consisted of twelve of the fifteen producers of magnets in the United Kingdom. Members made about three-quarters of the industry's output, and with one exception were all located in the Sheffield area. The total value of magnets produced by members in 1960 was £2,721,000, of which four members contributed 72 per cent. All but one member made other goods as well as magnets. The maximum number of different types of magnet made by any one member was about 500, but over 1400 types were in production. Magnets were not usually sold from stock, but were produced on a jobbing basis to meet the diverse needs of the industry's many customers. The total number of magnets sold was increasing, and advances in technology led not only to changes in costs and product specifications, but also to the creation of new markets – e.g. loudspeakers – and the contraction of existing markets – e.g. magnetos for motor-cars. Members of the Association faced competition from overseas producers and their U.K. subsidiaries or associates. Overseas producers were large relative to the members of the Association, individually having sales equal to or greater than those of the Association, and were backed by the research facilities of major electrical firms such as General Electric of America and Philips of Eindhoven.

The Agreement

Under the terms of its price agreement, the Association fixed the minimum prices at which its members could sell magnets in the home market. It also established various supporting restrictions. For the more simple magnets, which accounted for over one-half of those sold, prices were fixed by reference to a schedule prepared by a costing and prices committee. The committee obtained from members details of the cost of materials, labour and overheads, based on the production under optimum conditions of various simple magnets. To obtain a price, which was expressed as a price per ounce weight, the committee added 25 per cent to the average of the cost data obtained from members. For more complex magnets, inquiries were reported to the Association's secretaries, who notified members. Prices were then fixed by negotiations between members interested in the inquiry (usually two or three, but sometimes as many as five to seven members), or by arbitration if a dispute occurred. Over-all, a slightly lower accounting profit was obtained than that implied by the mark-up on costs because production rarely took place under optimal conditions. Minimum prices were rarely exceeded in practice.

There were two supporting restrictions of particular interest. An aggregate rebate scheme was operated, under which a rebate of 5 per cent was given to buyers whose aggregate annual purchases from members exceeded £50,000 and there was a sparingly applied provision which prevented the release of new magnetic materials to the market except on terms approved by the Association.

The Association's technical agreement established:

(1) A technical committee to which members reported the results of their research experiments, or development work, on permanent magnets. Together with all patents granted to members for such work, this information was made available for use by all members on terms and conditions determined by the Association.

(2) A central research laboratory which was financed by a levy on members and whose findings were made available to members without charge.

In addition to the price and technical agreements, there was a continuous and unrestricted exchange of 'know-how' between members.

The Case for the Agreement

The foundation of the Association's case was its belief that if the prices agreement was ended, the technical agreement would collapse. In support of this, it argued that the abolition of the price agreement would lead to the emergence of price competition, which would make firms more reluctant to impart 'know-how' to competitors, who might use it to undercut them.

The Association claimed that because of the technical agreement, more efficient and better-designed magnets were available more rapidly and cheaply than would otherwise be the case, consumers had a greater choice of suppliers and the manufacturing costs of magnets were lower, resulting in savings to both consumers and producers of magnets. If the price agreement continued, these benefits would still be available in the future. On the other hand, if the price agreement ended, the public would be deprived of them. Using gateway (*b*) (see p. 63), it was then argued that these benefits were specific and substantial, and accrued to the public as purchasers and users of magnets.

It was also predicted that the break-up of the technical agreement would cause a decline in the quality of magnets produced by members relative to those made by other manufacturers. The Association then claimed, under gateway (*f*) (see p. 63), that ending the restrictions would have an adverse effect on export earnings, which would be substantial, relative to the total business of both the Association and the U.K. magnet industry as a whole. (In 1960, members exported over 17 per cent of their output.)

The supporting restrictions were defended under gateway (g) (see p. 63), that it is to say, it was argued that they were reasonably necessary to the maintenance of the agreement. In defending the aggregate rebate scheme, the Association claimed that it was not a loyalty rebate, that is a rebate given to induce customers to buy from members instead of from other suppliers. Rather it reflected the cost savings resulting from large orders and the desire of customers to place repeat orders and to place orders with more than one member so as to have an alternative source of supply. In support of these claims it was pointed out that no publicity was given to the scheme. The justifications advanced for the restrictions on the release of new magnetic material to the market, except on terms and conditions agreed by the Association, was first that all new materials had to be disclosed to members, and second that such limited withholding as had occurred took place so as to ensure that the new material was as efficient as claimed.

Finally, the Association argued that the benefits claimed under gateway (b), (f) and (g) outweighed any detriments which might result from the restrictions.

The Decision

On the basis of various specific examples, the Court accepted that the technical agreement had resulted in the benefits claimed, and agreed that such benefits were likely to continue in the future. It also accepted that in the absence of the price agreement the technical agreement was likely to end. The fact that a price agreement preceded technical co-operation by several years was considered particularly significant in this connection. The Association thus succeeded in establishing a benefit under gateway (b).

The Court was impressed by the Association's success at selling magnets in developed countries which had magnet industries of their own, and accepted that in such markets the fall in quality caused by ending the technical agreement would reduce exports. However, it held that the Association had failed to establish a benefit under gateway (f), as it had not shown that the fall in exports would be substantial in relation to the total business of the Association or to the U.K. magnet industry as a whole.

Consideration of the supporting restrictions was limited to those attacked by the Registrar. It was held that the price schedule established by the agreement satisfied gateway (g), since 'granted a case for minimum prices, customers prefer to know where they are in relation to prices, and we think it important to them that there should be an orderly progression'. The Court also argued that the schedule saved time and expense when inquiries were received and quotations required. Similarly, the price-fixing procedure for magnets outside the schedule was held to be reasonably required within the meaning of gateway (g), even when only one member was interested. It believed that in such cases the fact that the price was known to other members was a safeguard against the quoting of a 'fancy price'. The procedure was reasonably needed as part of a minimum prices scheme to prevent one member from manipulating prices to 'suit his own pocket or a favoured customer'. The Court did not accept that the aggregate rebate scheme and the restriction on the release of new magnetic materials were reasonably required to justify these restrictions, and declared them to be against the public interest.

The Court then had to balance the benefits established under gateway (*b*) against any detriments which resulted from the agreement (ignoring the two restrictions already rejected). The principal detriment claimed by the Registrar, namely that without the agreement the prices of some magnets would be lower, was considered to be unimportant, unless the minimum price charged by the Association was, taken as a whole, unreasonable. To determine the reasonableness of the Association's prices, the Court applied the following tests:

(1) *The rate of profit.* Over the previous four years, members had obtained an average accounting profit, expressed as a percentage of the capital employed, of 15.5. (Capital employed was found by using the current value of assets, other than land, which was valued at historical cost; goodwill and 'know-how' were excluded.) These profits compared favourably with those earned by a sample of engineering firms analysed by *The Economist*, but were not held to be excessive.

(2) *The level of imports.* Magnet imports had been negligible for many years, indicating that, other things being equal, prices in the United Kingdom were not significantly higher than those charged elsewhere.

(3) *Entry to the industry.* Given that the market was expanding, overcharging would encourage new producers to enter the industry. Since the war, only one new producer had entered the market.

(4) *Customers' opinions of the reasonableness of prices.* None of the trade witnesses established a case of unreasonably high prices.

(5) *The reaction of members of the Association to changes in the techniques of production and the prices of factor inputs.* Statistics of the average selling prices of magnets indicated that allowance had been made for falls in the price of materials and for cost reductions due to technical advances.

(6) *Export prices.* The Court was impressed by the success of members in selling magnets in overseas markets, where the competition from other producers was substantial and the tariff barriers high, particularly since even though the restrictions did not apply to export orders, members charged the same price in both the home and export markets.

The Court concluded that the prices charged were not unreasonable, and that so long as this continued to be so, the restrictions, except for the two mentioned earlier, were justified.

Exercises

(4.13) Explain, with the aid of a numerical example, how the price of a 25 ounce magnet, of relatively simple design, would be fixed under the price agreement. Assume values for data of the type provided by the Association's cost and prices committee.

(4.14) (i) What, other things being equal, would be the impact on the Association's sales of charging the minimum prices fixed by the schedule if there was a substantial reduction in demand due to the emergence of better substitutes for magnets?

(ii) To what extent might the consequences of (i) endanger the continuation of the agreement?

(iii) Why, other things being equal, might members tend to ignore the prices fixed by the schedule if there was a significant increase in the demand for magnets?

(4.15) Which features of the structure of the U.K. magnet industry and the environment in which it operated encouraged collusion between producers?

(4.16) How do you explain the survival of very small producers in the U.K. magnet industry?

(4.17) What would be the effects on the structure of the U.K. magnet industry of a substantial reduction in the variety of different magnets produced, given no change in the total demand for magnets?

(4.18) 'The agreement was against the public interest, as it prevented the emergence, via process of mergers induced by market forces, of a smaller number of producers, able to survive without the price restrictions.' Discuss in the light of the fact that all but one producer also made other goods as well as magnets.

(4.19) Write a critical assessment of the tests used by the Court to determine whether or not the Association's prices, taken as a whole, were reasonable.

CASE 11. COLLUSIVE TENDERING IN THE CONTRACTING INDUSTRY

Following widespread complaints, the Registrar of Restrictive Trading Agreements investigated collusive tendering in the contracting industry. As a result, between 1 July 1969 and 30 June 1972, eighty-nine agreements between contractors were registered, of which sixty-seven were referred to the Restrictive Practices Court and injunctions were obtained against ninety-nine firms.

The Registrar found that the agreements all included one or more of the following features:*

(1) *Tabling prices.* All firms intending to submit competitive tenders agreed to meet and table (disclose) their proposed bids. A prearranged number of the lowest bids were then excluded and the lowest of the remaining bids was the lowest sent to the customer. The excluded bidders, and any firm which had notified the others that it wished to take a cover price (see below), would tender above that bid.

(2) *Payments to unsuccessful tenderers.* It was agreed that whichever firm received the contract would pay a prearranged sum to each of the unsuccessful tenderers in respect of their tendering expenses.

(3) *Cover prices.* It was agreed that one firm would disclose to another firm(s) a price above which it would not tender (the cover price). The latter firm(s) would not then tender below the cover price.

Table 4.4 outlines the terms of a representative selection of collusive tendering agreements. Commenting on such agreements, the Registrar claimed that tabling agreements raised the price paid by the buyer, as they excluded the lowest bids and induced firms who wanted the contract to submit tenders which were unlikely to be amongst the lowest priced. Payments to unsuccessful tenderers had ranged between £25 and £7000 and in some cases totalled 7 per cent or more of the value of the contract. In defence of such payments, it had been argued that where the cost of tendering was very high, it was 'fairer that the costs of the unsuccessful firms should be borne by the particular customer rather than spread as an over-head over all the work of the firm'. Many firms which took cover prices had done so because, having accepted an invitation to tender, they subsequently obtained too heavy a work load, or, having discovered which other firms had been invited to tender, decided that their bid was unlikely to succeed. The Registrar argued that fear of bidders resorting to cover prices was likely to prejudice the use of selective tendering, under which tenders are only invited from the minimum number of firms needed to ensure effective competition. In the ultimate, if all

*Restrictive Trading Agreements: Report of the Registrar 1 July 1969 to 30 June 1972, Cmnd. 5195 (London: H.M.S.O., 1972).

TABLE 4.4
Typical collusive tendering agreements

Agreement relating to electrical installations in the B.O.A.C. Overhaul Complex at London Airport. No. 3324.	Five firms invited to tender agreed that each would estimate and tender on the basis that the successful tenderer would pay £5000 to each of the others in respect of their tendering expenses.
Agreement relating to the provision of mechanical services at H.M.S. Dryad. No. 3649.	Eight firms invited to tender agreed that estimates prepared by each would be tabled at a meeting; that an estimate other than the lowest would be determined the selected price; and that those of them submitting a tender (other than the firm whose estimate was the selected price) would do so at a price above the selected price. Another firm invited to tender took a cover price from one of the eight.
Agreement relating to electrical installations at the St Albans Civic Centre. No. 3334.	Six firms invited to tender agreed that estimates prepared by each would be tabled at a meeting; that the middle one would be the lowest tender; that firms whose estimates were lower than the middle would tender at prices above it; and that estimates would be made on the basis that the successful tenderer would pay £1000 to each of the others in respect of their tendering expenses.
Agreement relating to electrical installations for the Chemistry Block at the University of Essex. No. 3499.	Seven firms invited to tender agreed that 'A' and 'B' would estimate and tender on the basis that the successful tenderer would pay £200 to each of the others in respect of their tendering expenses; that each of the others would take a cover price from 'A' or 'B'.
Agreement relating to electrical installations at the Central Market Lorry Park, Smithfield. No. 3359.	Of three firms invited to tender, 'A' severally agreed with each of the others that 'A' would quote the lowest price and would accordingly give the others cover prices.

SOURCE: *Restrictive Trading Agreements.*

but one firm took a cover price, that firm knew that it faced no competition for the contract.

Exercises

(4.20) Discuss the economic case for and against:

  (i) tabling prices;

  (ii) payments to unsuccessful tenderers by the successful tenderer; and

  (iii) the taking of cover prices.

(4.21) What circumstances are likely to encourage collusion in the contracting industry? Discuss the advantages and disadvantages of selective tendering as a means of countering such collusion.

CASE 12. R.P.M. – CHOCOLATE AND SUGAR CONFECTIONERY

When the 1964 *Resale Prices Act* came into force the leading manufacturers of chocolate and sugar confectionery registered an application for exemption from the general ban on R.P.M. As a result, the individual firms concerned were able to continue enforcing R.P.M. until a decision on the application was given by the Restrictive Practices Court. For example, on 13 March 1965 Cadburys obtained an injunction preventing Tesco from ignoring enforced list prices at its 450 stores. On 10 April 1967 the Court hearing of the application for exemption made by the registered suppliers began. Since the application was the first to be defended before the Court, the result would have important consequences. If the chocolate and sugar confectionery producers were successful, other firms would be encouraged to defend their applications when they came up for consideration; if they were unsuccessful, many firms would probably decide to do what a large number of manufacturers had already done – that is, withdraw their applications or offer no defence when their application came to be considered by the Court.

The Case for the Registered Suppliers

Exemption was claimed on the grounds that without R.P.M. the following consequences would result to the detriment of the public:

(i) the variety of goods available for sale would be substantially reduced;

(ii) the number of establishments in which the goods were sold by retail would be substantially reduced;

(iii) the prices at which the goods were sold by retail would in general and in the long run be increased; and

(iv) any necessary services actually provided in connection with or after the sale of the goods by retail would cease to be so provided or would be substantially reduced.

Three features of the confectionery market are particularly important to an understanding of the case for the registered suppliers. First, whilst there existed hundreds of different types of confectionery (called 'lines' in the case), many of which were sold only in local or regional markets, fifty leading lines accounted for 71 per cent of the total value of chocolate confectionery sales and fifteen leading lines for 21 per cent of sugar confectionery sales. Second, a high proportion (49 per cent) of total sales were of lines individually priced at 1s. (5 p) or less, and purchases for an aggregate price not exceeding 1s. (5p) formed 34.5 per cent of all expenditure. Lastly, chocolate and sugar confectionery were sold through a large number of retail outlets, ranging from confectionery shops (many of which also sold tobacco and newspapers) to supermarkets, other self-service grocers, counter-service grocers, other food retailers, variety and department stores, other non-food outlets, and non-shop outlets – e.g. cinemas. These outlets accounted for 48, 3.5, 5.5, 13, 6, 10, 2 and 12 per cent of sales respectively. An important feature of the retail distribution system was that, whilst sweetshops tended to stock a wide range of lines, supermarkets and self-service grocers usually only sold the leading lines.

The main features of the case for the registered suppliers are contained in the following summary of the evidence given by their principal witness, Mr Wadsworth, a managing director of Cadburys.

In the absence of resale price maintenance on confectionery some retailers will cut prices. Price cutting will not be confined to supermarkets, but they will start the cutting. Price cutting in these shops will be of two types: (1) regular cuts of a small number of leading lines; and (2) special cuts lasting for not more than one or two weeks on a succession of leading lines including those in (1), some of which may be deep cuts. In general, supermarkets will sell other lines at manufacturers' recommended prices particularly because a substantial part of the trade is at round prices of 3d., 6d. and 1s. (1.25, 2.5 and 5 n.p. respectively). The overall effect on the price level of confectionery sold in supermarkets will, therefore, be less than the impression created by the price cuts made.

A trader who stocks a wide variety of products is in a better position to cut prices on a particular product than is a trader who specialises in that produce, because he can expect to draw people into his shop to buy other goods.

Overall demand for confectionery is static. Total demand is not significantly price or income elastic in our affluent society. Thus, any increase in sales by any one class of distributor will be at the expense of the sales of other distributors.

The Outlets most seriously affected will be the large and medium sweet shops (particularly those near supermarkets), which offer a wide variety of confectionery and act as the 'shop window' for the industry. The trade of such sweet shops will also be adversely affected by the impression created by supermarkets' price cuts. Widespread closure of such shops would: (1) result in a fall of total consumption because of the loss of many sales which are made on impulse or are otherwise dependent upon the existence of these shops, and (2) result in a fall in variety available because these are the distributors who stock the variety and upon whom manufacturers depend for its distribution.

Cadbury, and we believe other manufacturers, will not acquiesce in the disappearance of important outlets for confectionery and will seek to increase the percentage margin realised by sweet shops, so that their businesses remain viable on a smaller turnover. We consider that our trade will be harmed less by our increasing trade margins (or other display incentives) to the extent of, say, 2 – 3 per cent of consumer prices, than by the demise of outlets which this extra margin might help to save. I believe that in this affluent society the consumer would be prepared to pay and that the effect on the total demand would be relatively small.

It may be thought that this increased margin will only encourage the super-market to cut to a greater extent and, therefore, fail in its purpose; but two points must be remembered: (1) retailer price cutting is relative, and the super-market is anxious mainly to establish the impression of a differential between its prices and those of traders in general, and (2) competition at the retailer level is imperfect and many shops will be able to realise the increased margin.

The long-term position which I envisage is, therefore, one in which: (1) a larger proportion of confectionery sales is sold through supermarkets. There will be a considerable expansion of special discounts and trade deals; I believe that in the final event the costs of these discounts are passed on to the con-sumer; (2) manufacturers' recommended prices will be higher than they would otherwise be. A narrow range of lines will be price cut, but in general confec-tionery will be sold at those higher recommended prices. On average prices will be higher than they would otherwise be; (3) there will be some reduction in the number of outlets and in the variety of confectionery available since the higher margins will not be sufficient to maintain all the present day outlets in business; (4) there will be a reduction in the sales and availability of seasonal lines.

I have considered what would be the position if manufacturers did not increase realisable margins, so that the Court may be able to see the seriousness to the industry of those consequences. However, I do not believe that manu-facturers will allow this situation to occur.*

The Resale Prices Act (of 1964) provides for exceptions to the general abolition of resale price maintenance. We do not support resale price main-tenance as a generality, and do not practice it for our grocery lines. However, we believe that confectionery is different from grocery products. I have given the reasons why I forecast that the consumer of confectionery would suffer detriment as a result of higher average consumer prices in the long run, fewer retail outlets, and a reduction in variety, all of which are 'gateways' provided for in the Act. I have had to forecast because no other method is available.

Facts are, of course, preferable to forecasts and I can only conclude by reminding the Court that in the present situation with resale price maintenance: (1) the industry is competitive and efficient; and (2) that we undermine this satisfactory situation at our peril and to the detriment of the consumer.†

---

*It was estimated that out of a total of about 250,000 retail outlets which sold confectionery, 6800 were large sweetshops, 10,500 medium and 26,400 small. If trade margins did not increase, it was predicted that by 1972 there would be a reduction of 50, 40 and 30 per cent in the number of large, medium and small sweetshops respectively, leading to an 11 per cent fall in the total sales of confectionery.

†Source: *Weekly Law Reports* (17 August 1967) vol. I, pp. 1182–4.

The Case for the Registrar

The Registrar replied to the attempts to establish 'gateways' by denying that the ending of R.P.M. in the industry would have the consequences predicted, and by arguing that, even if it did, they would not be to the detriment of the public as consumers of confectionery. He also claimed that R.P.M. led to higher prices than would otherwise exist, and argued that this detriment would outweigh any detriments which the registered suppliers might be able to establish under the 'gateway' clauses.

The Decision

The Court based its decision upon what would happen in the long term if R.P.M. were to be abolished, rather than on what could be expected to happen in the short term, when the cutting of confectionery prices would be 'news' and would therefore have a substantial publicity value to price-cutting supermarkets.

It was held that the ending of R.P.M. would not lead to a substantial diversion of trade from confectionery shops to supermarkets and self-service grocers since (*a*) the public, whose purchases of confectionery tended to be for small amounts, would not travel more than a very short distance to obtain confectionery at reduced prices, and (*b*) the extent of price-cutting would be restricted because most supermarkets and self-service grocers only stocked a narrow range of leading lines, the prices of which they would only cut for a limited period each year and then only for items in the higher and medium price ranges. Such diversion of trade as did occur would lead to the closure of no more than 10 per cent of those confectionery shops in close proximity to supermarkets and perhaps a smaller proportion of other sweetshops. The Court felt that a fall in the total sales of confectionery would be unlikely to result from the abolition of R.P.M., and stated that, if anything, it expected a small increase in consumption. As the Court believed that the closures anticipated would not have any material effect on the public – that is, would not significantly reduce the choice of lines, cause inconvenience arising out of the location of outlets, result in higher retail prices, or lead to the failure to provide necessary services connected with the sale of the goods, it refused to exempt chocolate and sugar confectionery from the general ban on R.P.M.

Exercises

(4.22) Why do supermarkets have more scope for price-cutting than large sweetshops?

(4.23) Why did Cadburys argue that the ending of R.P.M. would lead to higher sweet and chocolate prices?

(4.24) Why did the Court not accept that ending R.P.M. would cause a substantial diversion of trade from sweetshops to supermarkets?

(4.25) To which of the market structures you have studied in the theory of the firm, does the retail distribution of confectionery most closely correspond: (*a*) in the high street of a large town; (*b*) in a neighbourhood shopping precinct or suburban corner shop; and (*c*) in a small village? How does retail distribution differ in each case from the model you have selected?

CASE 13. COMPETITION POLICY IN THE EUROPEAN ECONOMIC COMMUNITY – THE INTERNATIONAL QUININE CARTEL

From the bark of the cinchona tree, two products are extracted: quinine and quinidine. Quinine is primarily used for the treatment of malaria, indeed for the treatment of some forms of the disease no substitute exists, and is also used as a tonic by the food industry. Quinidine is a drug used in the treatment of heart ailments.

Although a Dutch firm, Nedchem, was for many years the leading supplier of raw materials, it was ultimately overtaken by a German firm, Boehringer. In 1960, the converging interests of Nedchem and Boehringer led to their initiating the International Quinine Agreement. The other parties to the Agreement were a German firm, Buchler, and three French firms, Pointet – Girard, Nogentaise and Pharmacie Centrale. The Agreement involved co-ordination in the purchase of raw materials and the sale of quinine and quinidine.

In 1962 changes in the supply situation ended collaboration in the buying of raw materials. Sales co-operation continued with three major features. First, all members of the cartel charged common prices for quinine and quinidine in all countries, increasing such prices by about 50 per cent during 1964. Second, members agreed to protect their home markets against imports from other members and established export quotas for all other countries. Third, the French companies were not allowed to produce quinidine.

After 1965 the Agreement was not strictly applied because of an unexpected change in market circumstances – a surge in demand caused by the Vietnam War and a shortage of cinchona bark. During 1966 there was a spectacular increase in the price of quinine in the United States, which led to anti-trust investigations. Following the publication in 1967 of the results of these inquiries, the European Commission initiated its own investigations. The Commission concluded that the price-fixing, production-control and market-sharing aspects of the agreement violated Article 85 of the Treaty of Rome (members of the cartel controlled 80 per cent of the Community quinine market). Fines totalling 500,000 units of account were levied on the six firms, ranging from 10,000 units of account on Pharmacie Centrale to 210,000 units of account on Nedchem. The fines reflected the market position of each firm, and degree of responsibility for the infringements which the Commission concluded were committed knowingly.

Exercises

(4.26) (i) How did the International Quinine Agreement affect trade between member states of the European Community?

(ii) Suggest why the effects of the International Quinine Agreement on trade between member states of the European Community were thought to be undesirable.

Supplementary exercises

(4.27) Suggest and discuss alternative solutions to those proposed by the Monopolies Commission which might have reduced prices whilst at the same time strengthening British-based competition in the colour-film market.

(4.28) Why are there special provisions for newspaper mergers in the U.K. legislation?

(4.29) *How* and *why* does the control of restrictive practices differ from the control of monopoly and mergers in the United Kingdom?

(4.30) 'If a proposed merger is soundly based, the time needed for investigations to be completed by the Monopolies and Mergers Commission, or the European Commission, is unlikely to cause abandonment of the proposal.' Discuss.

(4.31) Contrast and compare the objectives of U.K. and European Community competition policies.

Sources and References

SIR GEOFFREY HOWE, 'Government Policy on Mergers', *Trade and Industry* (1 Nov 1973).

In addition to newspapers, and such journals as *The Economist*, reports of cases decided by the Restrictive Practices Court can be found in the *Weekly Law Reports* (see 1962, vol. I, pp. 781 – 816 for Case 10, and 1963, vol. I, pp. 1175 – 91 for Case 12), and *The Restrictive Practices Law Reports.* Monopolies and Mergers Commission reports are summarised in *Trade and Industry.*

O.E.C.D., *Guide to Legislation on Restrictive Business Practices.* Details of U.K. legislation and summaries of Monopoly Commission reports and Restrictive Practices Court cases can be found in vol. III. E.E.C. regulations and summaries of decisions by the Commission and judgements by the Court of Justice of the European Communities are in vol. VI (including Case 11). The Guide includes a detailed bibliography and is continuously updated.

Report on the Supply and Processing of Colour Film, The Monopolies Commission (London: H.M.S.O., 1966).

Restrictive Trading Agreements: Report of the Registrar 1 July 1969 to 30 June 1972, Cmnd. 5195 (London: H.M.S.O., 1972).

ROBERT SHEAF, 'Controlling Mergers (The Commission's New Proposals)' *European Community* (Sep 1973).

E. LLEWELLYN SMITH, 'The Fair Trading Act', *Trade and Industry* (9 Nov 1973).

D. SWANN, D. P. O'BRIEN, W. P. J. MAUNDER and W. S. HOWE, *Competition in British Industry: Restrictive Practices Legislation in Theory and Practice* (London: Allen and Unwin, 1974): a major study of the effects of the 1956 and 1968 Acts.

CHAPTER 5

Selective Intervention in Industry

M. S. Bradbury

Summary of Background Material

This chapter is primarily concerned with three interrelated aspects of government intervention in private industry:

(1) the promotion of changes in industrial structure other than via competition policy;

(2) the encouragement of investment by means of selective financial assistance; and

(3) the stimulation of performance by exchange of information and discussion between management, workers and government, other than via the framework of indicative planning.

When considering the evolution of such selective intervention in the United Kingdom, attention should be paid not only to the emerging legislative framework, but also to the changing motives which influence the extent and nature of selective intervention.

Selective Intervention Before 1966

Before 1966 peacetime selective intervention by the government in the private sector of U.K. industry was primarily *ad hoc*, that is legislation was mostly confined to Acts dealing with the problems of specific industries on a 'one-off' basis. The allocation of resources between industries was largely determined by market forces, and selective intervention was usually confined to cases where rapid and drastic resource re-allocation was expected to cause severe local unemployment. An example of such intervention was the cotton industry, which at the end of the 1950s was confronted with the major problems of a declining market: excess capacity, declining labour productivity and a low rate of new investment. *The Cotton Industry Act* of 1959 subsidised the removal of obsolete capacity and the installation of modern equipment and encouraged the payment of adequate redundancy compensation to displaced workers (financed via a levy on firms remaining in the industry). Further support to the industry was provided by a three-year 'voluntary limitation' quota on imports from Hong Kong, India and Pakistan.* Such intervention was usually intended to be temporary.

The Industrial Reorganisation Corporation

In January 1966 the government outlined in a White Paper proposals to establish an Industrial Reorganisation Corporation (I.R.C.). The government argued that the need to improve the balance of payments made it essential to strengthen the competitive position of British industry; that:

> In some sectors the typical company in Britain is too small to achieve long production runs; to take advantage of economies of scale; to undertake effective research and development; to support specialist departments for design and marketing; to install the most modern equipment or to attract the best qualified management. Moreover, large groups may often have been built up haphazardly or solely to achieve wide diversification and may not therefore be organised to secure full efficiency in current conditions.

Market forces alone could not, the government argued, be relied on to produce the structural changes needed, at the pace required, since:

(1)   Some of the industries most in need of rationalisation have an inbuilt tendency to stay as they are. Either there are a few large firms which are tempted to live and let live; or there are a number of small ones, none of which alone is strong enough to achieve the scale of operations needed for international competition.

(2)   Some mergers simply lead to a concentration of ownership without securing a more effective deployment of the assets of the merged companies and result in loosely knit groups of comparatively small production units ranging over a wide variety of manufacturing activities.

(3)   Whilst merchant banks and similar institutions helped to arrange mergers, they could only do so if asked and if market conditions were favourable. Thus it was possible that some opportunities to change the structure of industry were being lost, because of the lack of an institution to take the initiative in promoting mergers. The I.R.C. was intended to fill that institutional gap.

The *Industrial Reorganisation Corporation Act* of 1966 established the I.R.C., and empowered it, in the interests of industrial efficiency:

(*a*) to 'promote or assist the reorganisation of any industry; or
(*b*) if requested to do so by the Secretary of State, establish or develop, or promote or assist the establishment of, any industrial enterprise.'

*A fuller treatment of government intervention in the cotton industry during 1959 – 65 can be found in N.M.M. Dorward, 'The Cotton Industry', in *Case Studies in Economics: Economic Policy*, 1st edn (London: Macmillan, 1970) ch. 8.

The I.R.C. had no compulsory powers and was free to carry out its functions in almost any way it wished, including the granting or underwriting of loans; buying, holding and selling shares; forming new companies; and acquiring premises, plant, machinery and other equipment. In practice, the I.R.C. was able to achieve some of its objectives simply by issuing a public statement that it considered a particular takeover bid to be in the public interest. Whilst the I.R.C. was free to decide the terms on which it would lend money, it was expected to earn a commercial return *over-all* on its operations.

The I.R.C. had the right to draw up to £150 million from the Exchequer, consisting of £100 million in fixed-interest loans and £50 million of public dividend capital, that is money which did not bear a fixed rate of interest, but on which the Corporation could propose a dividend, the amount of which could be varied by the Secretary of State with the approval of the Treasury.

Criteria for I.R.C. Support

In deciding which reorganisation schemes to support, the I.R.C. (according to its Report and Accounts for 1967 – 8) took the following factors into account:

(1) structural changes which have a significant impact on the industry concerned and on the economy as a whole;

(2) industries making a significant contribution to the development of technology;

(3) strategic moves which will have repercussions throughout the industry (e.g. where one merger may make possible further mergers which were previously prevented);

(4) strong and unified management able to exploit the rationalisation possibilities created by the merger;

(5) schemes which offer good prospects of quick returns in the form of greater exports or smaller imports;

(6) the government's regional policy;

(7) the need for redundancies which follow rationalisation to be planned and carried out in consultation with the trade unions and government departments concerned.

Similar criteria applied to proposals which involved I.R.C. support for individual company investment schemes. The I.R.C. also undertook various specific government assignments, e.g. a study of the telecommunications industry and its relationships with its largest customer, the Post Office, and a report on the financial position of the Cunard Steam-Ship Company and the possible terms of the government's assistance. The I.R.C. also helped to solve a major commercial dispute.

The Industrial Expansion Act, 1968

In January 1968 the government outlined in a White Paper its reasons for wanting to increase its powers to give financial assistance towards the 'modernisation and technological advance of industry and in the expansion of its capacity'. The government did not intend to displace existing commercial sources of capital, or other more general schemes of assistance, e.g. grants payable under the *Industrial Development Act* of 1966. Instead, the government wanted to be able to help projects which it considered to be 'in the national economic interest but which, because of a divergence between national and private costs and benefits, especially in the short term, could not be expected to go ahead solely on the basis of finance from existing sources'.

The government advanced four reasons for wishing to widen its powers to support such projects:

(1) there was a need to encourage the more rapid application of advanced technology;

(2) in the absence of a general power to give such assistance, it would be necessary to pass a separate Act for each of several proposals which the government was considering (e.g. to authorise an additional loan to complete the *Queen Elizabeth II*).

(3) since the timing of assistance was often important to the success of a project, the government wanted to be able to respond quickly to any proposals it received;

(4) there was a need for a rigorous, independent and consistent system of appraisal and for effective but speedy Parliamentary examination of such projects.

The proposals were not designed to prop up declining industries, or to cause different price and output decisions than would occur in a free market. Instead, the government wanted the power of selective short-run intervention.

The *Industrial Expansion Act* of 1968, put the proposals into effect. The main provisions were as follows:

(1) In order to assist an industry or section of an industry, Ministers were authorised, subject to Treasury and House of Commons approval,

(*a*) to grant financial assistance to projects for improving their efficiency and profitability;

(*b*) to create, expand or sustain productive capacity; and

(*c*) to promote or support technical improvement.

Assistance could only be given if the project was likely to benefit the economy of the United Kingdom or any part of the United Kingdom, and if it would not be undertaken in the absence of such support. Financial assistance could take any form, including loans or grants; the guaranteeing of loans and interest payments; the underwriting of trading losses; the purchase of goods and services; the purchase of shares in companies; and the purchase of undertakings or parts of undertakings.

(2) The power to make a general scheme for an industry or part of an industry; an industry board might be created to make recommendations to the Minister concerned and to administer the scheme.

(3) Financial assistance was limited to £100 million but could be increased to £150 million.

(4) A committee (including representatives of the National Research Development Corporation and the I.R.C.) was established to advise Ministers on the merits of investment proposals and industry schemes.

The Industry Act, 1972

Following the change of government in 1970 the I.R.C. was abolished in May 1971. In March 1972 a White Paper on *Industrial and Regional Development* argued that the growth of the U.K. economy had been low compared with that achieved by other major industrial countries, and that an improved industrial base was a necessary condition if a higher rate of national economic growth was to be sustained. The government announced that to encourage improvements in the industrial base, investment incentives were to be improved on both a regional and a national basis. The policy was implemented by the *Finance Act* of 1972 and the *Industry Act* of 1972. In addition to the measures described in Chapter 3 (pp. 37 - 9), the *Industry Act* of 1972 enabled selective financial assistance to be given outside the assisted areas where this was in the national interest and could not be given in any other way. Irrespective of whether or not the firm receiving selective financial assistance was in an assisted area, the state could only acquire share or loan capital in the firm if no other appropriate way of giving financial assistance was available, and only then if the company consented. Furthermore, the Secretary of State was under an obligation to dispose of shares and stocks as soon as practicable. Where selective financial assistance to a project exceeded £5 million, Parliamentary approval was required. The Act limited selective financial assistance to a total of £150 million (with provision for this to be increased to £250 million). If the firm receiving selective financial assistance was outside an assisted area, state shareholdings could not exceed 50 per cent of the equity share capital.

The Industry Act, 1975

After the change of government in 1974, a White Paper on the *Regeneration of British Industry* outlined a new approach to selective intervention. After arguing that higher economic growth required both more investment and higher returns on investment, the White Paper continued:

> the attitude of Governments to industry, and indeed of industry to Governments, has been too remote, too much coloured by the concept that the Government's main function towards industry is that of regulation to prevent the activities of industry, or the abuse of its powers, damaging the interests of other sectors of the community. That relationship is no longer enough. Industry and the Government should also be partners in the pursuit of the objectives which spell success for industry and prosperity for this country. This requires a closer, clearer and more positive relationship between Government and industry; and the construction of that relationship requires the development of new institutions.

The government then proposed a system of Planning Agreements with major firms in key sectors of industry and a National Enterprise Board.

Amongst the items to be covered in Planning Agreements were:

Investment, with particular reference to its timing and location;
Prices policy;
Productivity;
Employment, with special reference to its regional balance;
Exports and import saving and investment directed to these ends;
Product development;
Implications of company plans for industrial relations and arrangements for
    negotiation and consultation;
Interests of consumers and the community.

It was envisaged that, following consultations between the government and companies (and between companies and their employees), the resulting Planning Agreements would run for three years (subsequently amended to whatever planning period was used by the firm concerned) and be reviewed and rolled forward annually. During the consultations the government would review requirements for selective financial assistance. Planning Agreements would not be a civil contract enforceable at law. However, the government envisaged that once an Agreement had been concluded, regional assistance under the *Industry* and *Local Employment Acts* of 1972 for the projects it covered, would, during the currency of the Agreement, continue to be available on the original terms. Although initially only a few firms would be covered by Planning Agreements, it was envisaged that ultimately all major firms, whether in private or public ownership, would be covered.

The National Enterprise Board was to have three functions:

(1) take over the ownership of state shareholdings in a number of companies;
(2) provide a new source of investment capital for industry (usually in return for a share in the ownership of recipient companies); and
(3) act as an agent for the government in the restructuring of industry.

Assistance to Scottish and Welsh industry was to be channelled through newly created Development Agencies.

The proposals for Planning Agreements and the National Enterprise Board were implemented by the *Industry Act* of 1975. The Act also included reserve powers to prevent important British manufacturing companies from passing into foreign control, provision for the publication of some Treasury macroeconomic forecasts, and reserve powers to require the disclosure of specified information about company plans to the government and to workers through their trade unions. The 1975 *Industry Act* removed the requirements in the *Industry Act* of 1972 that the state could only acquire share or loan capital in a firm requesting selective financial assistance if no other method was available, and should dispose of such shares or stocks as soon as practicable.

Illustration by Case Studies

Case 14 shows the application of both of the I.R.C.'s powers to the paper industry. Notice in this case the link between the machinery of indicative planning and the I.R.C.'s activities.

Case 15 shows the use of the I.R.C.'s powers to rationalise a fragmented industry, and to prevent a U.K. industry falling ultimately into foreign ownership.

Case 16 shows the use of the *Industrial Development Act* of 1966, the *Industrial Expansion Act* of 1968 and the *Industry Act* of 1972 to assist the development of the aluminium industry. It also illustrates the interaction between location, expansion, nationalised-industry pricing and international trade policies.

CASE 14. INTERVENTION IN THE PAPER INDUSTRY BY THE I.R.C., 1967 – 9

Why the I.R.C. Intervened in the Paper Industry

Unlike its Scandinavian and North American rivals, the British paper-manufacturing industry lacks substantial indigenous sources of low-cost wood pulp. Consequently, instead of being produced at integrated pulp and paper mills, where the economies of integration are obtainable, most British paper is made from reconstituted imported pulp or from waste paper. As a result British production costs, particularly for lower-quality papers, e.g. newsprint, have tended to be higher than those of their rivals.

For many years the industry was protected from the consequences of this cost disadvantage by substantial tariff barriers. When tariffs were reduced following U.K. membership of the European Free Trade Area, domestic producers faced a severe increase in competition in their home market. In 1968 imports reached 2.23 million tons, exactly two-and-a-half times more than in 1954, and their share of U.K. consumption rose from 24.3 to 33.6 per cent. Indeed, in 1968 half of the additional paper consumed in the United Kingdom was accounted for by imports.*

Growing concern about the consequences of rising imports led the Paper and Board Economic Development Committee to produce a confidential report on 'Structure and Productivity'. In June 1967 the British Paper and Board Makers' Association invited the I.R.C. to examine the industry's structure in the light of the E.D.C. report and suggest ways in which the industry might proceed. The report, which was not published, was completed by November 1967.

Import-Saving Projects: I.R.C. Assistance to the Reed Paper Corporation and Peter Dixon and Son

On 31 January 1968 Mr A. Currall, Assistant Under-Secretary of State at the Department of Economic Affairs, sent the following letter to Mr C. R. E. Brooke of the Industrial Reorganisation Corporation:

Dear Mr Brooke,

I refer to the proposals put by the Reed Paper Corporation at the Government's suggestion, to install facilities for de-inking waste paper which can then be used in the manufacture of newsprint.

The Secretary of State understands that the Corporation have given detailed consideration to these proposals and have satisfied themselves as to the technical feasibility of the scheme and as to the need for the Corporation's support

*'Paper Deficit to Grow', *The Times Business News* (22 Oct 1969).

if it is to be carried through. He further understands that the Corporation would be prepared to use their powers under Section 2(1)(*b*) of the Industrial Reorganisation Corporation Act to lend to the Reed Paper Group the £1$\frac{1}{2}$ million needed to finance the project.

The Government consider that the development of facilities for de-inking waste paper for use in United Kingdom manufacture of newsprint would make a valuable contribution to the economy and the Secretary of State has accordingly instructed me to convey to the Corporation his request, as required by Section 2(1)(*b*) of the Act, that the Corporation will afford the Reed Paper Group the financial assistance that the Corporation consider appropriate to enable this project to be undertaken.

In making this request, the Secretary of State understands that the Corporation are prepared to consider similar approaches from other newsprint producers.

Yours sincerely,

A. Currall*

Giving further details of this import-saving project in February 1968, the I.R.C. stated that repayments of the medium-term unsecured loan would be based on the cash flows expected to be generated by the investment. Although Reed could defer interest payments for an initial period, the I.R.C. expected to receive a commercial rate of return over the life of the loan.

In July 1968 an unsecured loan of £350,000, at an annual interest charge of 7$\frac{7}{8}$ per cent, was given to Peter Dixon and Son by the I.R.C. for a similar import-saving project.

I.R.C. Assistance Towards the Rationalisation of the Coated Paper Industry: The Donside Mill

The Donside Mill, Aberdeen, employed 600 people and specialised in the production of high-quality coated papers of the type used for mass-circulation magazines and colour supplements. The mill was a financial disaster for its owners, the Inveresk Paper Company Ltd, who spent £4.2 million rebuilding it, only to find that its 1968 operating loss of £871,104 (after depreciation) turned a small profit on the company's other activities into an over-all loss of £584,078.

The I.R.C. first approached the Reed Paper Group and the Bowater Paper Corporation independently during the autumn of 1968, and suggested that one or other of them might be interested in forming a link with the mill. However, because of the mill's poor profitability and the better returns available on competing projects, neither company was interested. Just before Christmas 1968, the I.R.C. suggested to Reed and Bowater that a joint acquisition of the mill might be worth while.

*Industrial Reorganisation Corporation, *Annual Report and Accounts* (1967 – 8) appendix 2.

In January 1969 it was announced that:

(1) The Donside Mill had been sold to Reed and Bowater by Inveresk for £2 million.

(2) An agreement had been made between Reed and Bowater providing for:

(*a*) the rationalisation of production of coated papers between Bowater, Reed and Donside (it will be the aim to fill Donside's production capacity as soon as possible);

(*b*) the preparation of a phased investment programme (to be formulated and implemented through the joint Donside company) particularly with a view to meeting the anticipated growth in demand for lightweight coated mechanical printing and publication papers for mass-circulation magazines and colour supplements expected within the period 1969 - 75;*

(*c*) a defined common marketing policy for all coated papers produced by Bowater, Reed and Donside which will be supervised by the joint Donside company.†

(3) The I.R.C. was to grant unsecured loans of £1 million each to Reed and Bowater for eight years at an over-all rate of interest of $8\frac{1}{4}$ per cent. Both companies had the right to defer interest for the first two years of the loan.

(4) The Board of Trade had agreed in principle to grant an exemption order under s. I of the *Restrictive Trade Practices Act* of 1968 (see p. 65), in respect of the production, investment and marketing agreement outlined above.

The rationalisation achieved by this move was unlikely to have occurred in the absence of I.R.C. assistance and the Board of Trade exemption order.

Gains from Rationalisation

The advantages to Inveresk of the sale are clear from the following statement:

> The trading results before you are dominated by the unhappy experience at the Donside Mill. Although the output of the mill improved progressively during the year, as did the quality of the product manufactured, heavy operating losses continued. Your Board, therefore, concluded regretfully that the Group's resources were not adequate to bring the Donside project to a profitable level in an acceptable time.‡

*Reed and Bowater were together to provide £2 million over the next two years for further capital spending and working capital.

†'Bowater Paper Corporation and Reed Paper Group: Exemption of Proposed Agreement from Registration', *Board of Trade Journal* (7 Feb 1969) p. 323. The Reed and Bowater marketing companies were to act as agents for each other's coated papers, as well as for those of the Donside Mill. Donside's output would also be sold through Inveresk.

‡Extract from Chairman's statement at the Annual General Meeting of the Inveresk Paper Company, *The Times* (31 Mar 1969).

Bowater and Reed gained from the production, marketing and investment arrangements, as each produced a complementary range of coated papers. (The agreement covered 40 per cent of all the United Kingdom's coated paper sales.)

From the I.R.C.'s point of view, the project had three advantages:

(1) it strengthened British participation in the expanding £32 million U.K. coated paper market, where rapidly growing imports accounted for about one-eighth of total sales;

(2) by delaying the construction of new facilities which might otherwise have been built by Reed and Bowater, it reduced the prospect of surplus capacity in the industry; and

(3) by protecting the employment of 600 workers in a development area, it assisted the government's regional policy.

Exercises

(5.1) What difficulties led to I.R.C. assistance to the paper industry?

(5.2) Under which of its powers under the *Industrial Reorganisation Corporation Act* of 1966, did the I.R.C. assist (*a*) import substitution schemes, and (*b*) rationalisation?

(5.3) How was I.R.C. assistance expected to strengthen the competitive position of the U.K. paper industry?

CASE 15. REORGANISATION OF THE BALL-BEARING INDUSTRY BY THE I.R.C., 1968-9

The U.K. Market for Ball-bearings

In 1968 total U.K. production of ball-bearings was valued at £70 million, of which £15 million was exported. Given imports of £11 million, total U.K. consumption was £66 million. Ball-bearings had a wide range of applications in the electrical and mechanical engineering industry. The dominant consumer, however, was the motor industry, which took about 30 per cent of production.

Of the six major manufacturers, three were foreign-controlled: Skefko (a subsidiary of S.K.F. of Sweden), British Timken (division of the Timken Roller Bearing Co. in the United States), and Fafner (subsidiary of Textron Inc. in the United States). The U.K.-controlled companies – Ransome and Marles, Hoffmann, and Pollard – shared about 35 per cent of domestic consumption. The largest single producer was Skefko with about 27 per cent of domestic consumption.

Faults in the Structure of the U.K. Ball-bearing Industry

Two major indications showed that all was not well in the U.K. ball-bearing industry.

(1) The balance of imports and exports. In 1963 the value of exports exceeded that of imports by 75 per cent, whilst in 1968 the figure had fallen to 36 per cent. Also, exports were mainly to the slow-growing Commonwealth markets, the U.K. share of European imports being only 6 per cent.

(2) Output per employee in the U.K.-owned companies averaged just over £2000 per annum, compared with a European (other than U.K.) average of about £3000 per annum.

The cause of these difficulties was the fragmentation of output between too many producers, in an industry where substantial economies of scale existed. The two largest British-owned companies were each producing between 7000 and 13,000 different types of bearings. Also, a major part of the three British-owned companies' output overlapped. Consequently much of the output of U.K.-controlled producers was made in sub-optimal production runs.

Why the I.R.C. Intervened

In May 1968 the I.R.C. decided to make a detailed investigation of the industry because:

(1) The industry's output was an important input into major export industries such as the motor industry.

(2) Compared with other advanced economies, the structure of the U.K. industry appeared to be fragmented. The Scandinavian markets were dominated

by S.K.F., who also controlled 70 per cent of Italian and French production and shared over 80 per cent of the German market with Kugelfischer F.A.G. and were strongly entrenched elsewhere.

(3) There was the possibility of a merger between Ransome and Marles and Skefko, which could have meant that there would soon be no viable British-owned company in the industry. It was feared that S.K.F., 'as with any strongly based international group, might well find it advantageous to rationalise its production facilities, locate its research and development, buy its raw materials and machine tools and direct its marketing policy in ways which would not necessarily benefit the U.K. economy'.

A Simplified Calendar of the Emergence of a Major British-owned Producer

September 1968

The I.R.C. decided to support the creation of a major British-owned company, consisting if possible of Ransome and Marles, Hoffmann, and Pollard. This decision was greatly influenced by the observation that Kugelfischer F.A.G., the independent German producer, made a substantial contribution to Germany's overseas trade surplus in bearings. (Apart from Sweden, Germany was the only country in Europe with a large surplus.) It was felt that the new British group would be similar to Kugelfischer and strong enough to compete with Skefko in the tariff-free EFTA markets. The I.R.C., with the support of the government, then asked S.K.F. not to pursue the proposed merger with Ransome and Marles.

October 1968

The I.R.C. told S.K.F. of its plans for the industry, and invited Skefko to become associated with the group in some way.

November 1968

The I.R.C. sponsored negotiations to find a basis for the merger needed to create the new company.

December 1968

Skefko were invited to join the negotiations, but discussions with them broke down almost immediately over the question of control.

January 1969

Faced with a slowing-down in the negotiations, the I.R.C. decided to create a base from which to negotiate. The I.R.C. therefore made an offer for Brown Bayley Ltd, which owned 60 per cent of the shares in Hoffmann (Brown Bayley Ltd also owned 50.1 per cent of the share capital of Brown Bayley Steels, which the I.R.C. wanted to use as the foundation of a strong private-sector special steel group based in Sheffield).

February 1969

A revised bid for Brown Bayley was successful. The I.R.C. therefore invited Pollard to discuss terms for joining the proposed company.

April 1969

After leaving the I.R.C. negotiations, Pollard had started negotiations with Skefko. In April it was announced that terms had been agreed for Skefko to take a 15.6 per cent interest in Pollard by subscribing for new shares, at a price above the then market price. The I.R.C. had then to decide whether to create a smaller group, that is Hoffmanns and Ransome and Marles, or whether to support a take-over bid for Pollard by Ransome and Marles (which it had decided to make the focal point in the new company). On 30 April such a bid was made, with the full support of the I.R.C.

May 1969

On 21 May the Pollard board recommended shareholders to accept a revised bid from Ransome and Marles.

Subsequent events

In July it was announced that the bid for the minority shareholding in Hoffmanns had been successful. The new group, called Ransome, Hoffman Pollard, then came into existence. Hence the I.R.C. had created the conditions in which a start could be made by the new company's management in raising productivity to an internationally competitive level.

Exercises

(5.4) What indicators suggested that all was not well in the British-owned sector of the U.K. ball-bearing industry? Would these indicators necessarily be relevant if used for other industries?

(5.5) How would the reorganisation strengthen the British-owned sector of the U.K. ball-bearing industry?

CASE 16. THE CREATION OF AN ALUMINIUM-SMELTING INDUSTRY IN THE UNITED KINGDOM, 1968

The Smelter Location Decision

The production of a ton of aluminium ingot required between 15,000 and 18,000 units of electricity. As shown in Table 5.1 there were wide variations in the cost of electricity from one country to another. Consequently, although electricity was not the largest component of total costs – capital charges accounted for about one-fifth of the running costs of a smelter – it was the variation of power costs which tended to determine the smelter location decision.

TABLE 5.1

Costs of electricity in different countries

Canada and the United States (hydro-electric)	under 0.2d. – 0.3d. per unit
United States (coal)	0.2d. – 0.4d. per unit
Norway (hydro-electric)	0.3d. – 0.4d. per unit
Germany (lignite)	0.6d. – 1d. per unit
Britain (bulk tariff)	0.8d. – 1d. per unit
Germany (coal)	1d. – 1.5d. per unit

SOURCE: 'Suddenly it's Smelters', *The Economist* (24 Feb 1968) p. 62.

Since electricity prices above about 0.4d. priced smelters out of the market, Britain had traditionally imported most of the ingots needed for its aluminium-fabricating industry.

However, in the mid-1960s two factors began to make smelting potentially more profitable in the United Kingdom.

(1) Nuclear power and natural gas offered the prospect of electricity at between 0.4 and 0.5d. per unit.

(2) Assistance under the *Industrial Development Act* of 1966 offered the possibility of a cut in the capital cost of such projects to their sponsors; for example, it was estimated by *The Economist* that a cash grant of 40 per cent on manufacturing plant and associated equipment reduced British production costs by 6 to 7 per cent. (Similar changes, plus the existence of import duties, were also encouraging an expansion of smelter capacity in Germany, another traditional importer of ingots.)

The Smelter Projects

After more than a year of intricate negotiations, it was announced in July 1968
that three smelters were to be built in the development areas, all of which it was
hoped would be in full production by 1971.

At Lynemouth in Northumberland, Alcan Aluminium (U.K.) Ltd was to build
a smelter with a capacity of 120,000 tons of ingots per year. The smelter was to
draw electricity from its own integrated power station, using coal supplied by the
National Coal Board from Lynemouth Colliery, under a long-term commercial
contract.

At Invergordon in North-east Scotland and Anglesey in North Wales, the
British Aluminium Company and the Rio Tinto Zinc/B.I.C.C./Kaiser Aluminium
and Chemical Corporation consortium respectively were to build smelters each
with a capacity of 100,000 tons of ingots per year. Both smelters were to be
powered by electricity supplied under unusual contracts with the electricity
generating boards.

The bulk tariff under which electricity is usually supplied to industry is based
on the costs of a range of power stations of varying ages and efficiencies. Under
the terms of the contracts, the aluminium companies made capital payments
towards the cost of two advanced gas-cooled reactor power stations, which represented the most advanced generating capacity then being installed. These payments in each case purchased a reserve of capacity capable of producing electricity
to meet the smelter's needs, as well as the associated electricity transmission
installations. The companies then paid operating charges based on the costs of
operation of that capacity. The Board of Trade announced that other companies
would be able to buy their way out of the bulk tariff if they could fulfil the same
criteria as the smelters, including the fact that it must be a substantial new demand,
or provide substantial evidence that existing operations were becoming unecono-
mical. (This announcement was made in response to demands from the steel and
electro-chemical industry for similar concessions. To date no further agreements
of this type have been announced.)

Loans of up to £30 million and £33 million, at an interest rate of 7 per cent
(equivalent to the capital payment to be made to the generating boards), were
made to British Aluminium and the R.T.Z./B.I.C.C./Kaiser consortium, under
the *Industrial Expansion Act* of 1968. British Aluminium have received a further
loan of £7 million maximum under the *Industry Act* of 1972 because of the
effects of inflation on the costs of construction. In addition, all three projects
were eligible for investment and building grants under the *Industrial Development
Act* of 1966 and subsequent legislation.

Benefits from the Smelter Projects

It was claimed that importing raw materials instead of aluminium ingots would
produce import savings of about £40 million per year. During the construction

period, about 2000 workers would be employed on each of the three sites. On completion, the Lynemouth, Invergordon and Anglesey smelters were expected to give direct employment to about 550, 600 – 50 and 720 people respectively. (In practice employment has been higher than expected – 750, 750 and 800 respectively.) Also, the long-term contract for the supply of coal to Alcan gave greater security of employment to miners at the Lynemouth Colliery. Whilst in the long-term some extra employment might be created by aluminium fabricators locating close to the smelters, this was unlikely in the immediate future because of excess capacity in the fabricating industry elsewhere in Britain.

The Norwegian Objection

At the time of the smelter negotiations, Norway was the largest aluminium ingot producer in Europe. Of its total output of about 400,000 tons per year, 300,000 was exported, of which about one-third was sold in the United Kingdom. In April 1968 Norway made a formal objection to Britain, claiming that by using regional policy and the *Industrial Expansion Act* of 1968 to subsidise the smelters, the government had breached the rules relating to competition within EFTA. Whilst rejecting the allegations of subsidy, the government made a concession to Norway by cutting the capacity of the Anglesey and Invergordon smelters from 120,000 to 100,000 tons each. It appeared likely that substantial imports of Norwegian aluminium would continue to be required as, in an expanding market, the new smelters would not have sufficient capacity to meet all U.K. demand for aluminium ingots.

Exercises

(5.6) (*a*) Why were very few aluminium smelters located in Britain before the mid-1960s?

(*b*) Why did Britain become a more attractive location for aluminium smelters after 1966?

(*c*) What benefits were expected to result from building the three smelters?

(5.7) (*a*) How did the electricity contracts for the Anglesey and Invergordon projects differ from those normal in British industry?

(*b*) What would happen to the tariffs paid by the remainder of British industry if several existing firms were offered such contracts?

(*c*) Would your answer to (*b*) be different if the industries offered the contracts were new users of electricity?

(*d*) 'The contracts were not a subsidy since the payments made to the generating boards covered the full costs of production'. Discuss.

(5.8) Discuss critically the Norwegian objection to the smelter project.

Supplementary exercises

(5.9) What were the advantages to the companies concerned of I.R.C. loans which included an option to defer interest payments for an initial period? Answer in the context of I.R.C. assistance to the paper industry.

(5.10) 'International mergers are an inevitable and desirable outcome of a free-trade area.' Discuss with reference to the ball-bearing industry.

(5.11) Why was an exemption order under the *Restrictive Trade Practices Act* of 1968 essential to the success of rationalisation in the coated paper industry?

(5.12) How do you reconcile the simultaneous existence of the Monopolies Commission and the Restrictive Trade Practices Court on the one hand, and the government encouragement of mergers on the other?

(5.13) In what respects could the loans to the R.T.Z./B.I.C.C./Kaiser consortium and to British Aluminium under the *Industrial Expansion Act* of 1968 and the *Industry Act* of 1972 be regarded as a subsidy?

(5.14) Discuss the opportunity cost of (*a*) the labour and (*b*) the capital employed in the aluminium smelter project.

Sources and References

'Aluminium Smelters', *D.E.A. Progress Report: Industrial and Regional* (Aug 1968).

'Coated Pill', *The Economist* (8 Feb 1969) p. 86.

E. DELL, *Political Responsibility and Industry* (London: Allen & Unwin, 1973) pp. 109–21.

Financial Times (31 Jan 1975).

Industrial and Regional Development, Cmnd. 4942 (London: H.M.S.O., 1972).

Industrial Expansion, Cmnd. 3509 (London: H.M.S.O., 1968).

Industrial Investment – The Production of Primary Aluminium, Cmnd. 3819 (London: H.M.S.O., 1968).

Industrial Reorganisation Corporation, Cmnd. 2889 (London: H.M.S.O., 1966).

Industrial Reorganisation Corporation, *Statement on the U.K. Ball and Roller Bearing Industry* (21 May 1969).

Industrial Reorganisation Corporation, *Report and Accounts* (1967–8 and 1968–9).

DAVID JONES, 'I.R.C. Puts up £2m. for Paper Mill Deal by Reed, Bowater', *The Times Business News* (3 Feb 1969) p. 1.

ANTHONY MORETON, '£2m. I.R.C. Aid for Paper Industry Rationalisation', *Financial Times* (3 Feb 1969) p. 30.

R. W. SHAKESPEARE, 'Episodes in the Smelter Saga', *The Times Business News* (25 July 1968).

The Regeneration of British Industry, Cmnd. 5710 (London: H.M.S.O., 1974).

E. VARLEY, 'The Enactment of the Industry Bill', *Trade and Industry* (21 Nov 1975) p. 474.

CHAPTER 6

Agriculture

M. J. Sargent

Summary of Background Material

The Common Agricultural Policy (C.A.P.) of the European Economic Community (E.E.C.) became operational in 1962 and contained certain fundamental principles:

(i) farm incomes should be derived from market returns, determined by 'support prices' set by the Community;

(ii) a fair standard of living for the agricultural community should be ensured;

(iii) the efficiency of agricultural production should be encouraged;

(iv) the market for farm products should be stabilised; and

(v) the delivery of supplies to consumers should be at reasonable prices.

The essential feature of the C.A.P. was a complete harmonisation of agricultural prices, a prerequisite to the removal of trade barriers between member countries. It followed that there must also be a common system of market organisation and protection against imports from so-called 'third countries'. Long before the Treaty of Rome (1957) the countries of 'the six', in common with most other countries, gave protection to their agricultural industries. They did this mainly because of agriculture's special characteristics of, for example, a general income inelasticity of demand for agricultural products and widely fluctuating supplies as a result of the effects of seasonal, regional and weather extremes. Furthermore, the operation of this 'common market' for agriculture depended upon the establishment of a common currency exchange. In the absence of a European currency this has been established as so called 'units of account', and their value is adjusted from time to time by the Council of Ministers. For example, at October 1974 one pound (the so-called 'green pound') was fixed at 2.0053 units of account.

Each member country has gradually brought its support measures into line, and new members are given a transitional period within which to standardise their methods of giving support and the levels of prevailing prices. Between 1 February 1973 and 1978 this will apply to the United Kingdom. Compensatory payments are made to bring this about. In the same way as lock-gates allow boats to move between higher and lower levels, so compensatory amounts may either be a levy or a payment. A high-priced continental exporter selling in the United Kingdom would receive an export refund, bringing his price down to U.K. market rates.

Conversely, a U.K. exporter selling relatively low-priced produce in the higher-priced E.E.C. market would have to raise his prices. The compensatory payment is gradually reduced during the transitional period until there is complete harmonisation of prices.

A C.A.P. was a necessary feature of the E.E.C. for three main reasons. First, agriculture occupies a key role in the economy of the Community, comprising from 3.4 to 18.3 per cent of the G.D.P. of the member states in 1972 (see Table 6.1). In 'the nine', agriculture employs between 3.3 (United Kingdom) and 24.1 (Eire) per cent of the working population. Second, the need to modernise and restructure agriculture was, and still is, a problem in the E.E.C. Over-all average farm sizes have a wide variety as shown in Table 6.1, ranging from only 7.2 hectares in Italy to 34 hectares in the United Kingdom. Approximately two-thirds of the E.E.C. farms are under 10 hectares, many being too small to provide adequate incomes to the farmers. The average age of these farmers is high, half of them in 1968 being over 57 and few of them having satisfactory training. Third, agriculture has an important role in the international trade of the E.E.C. The Community is the world's largest importer of agriculture products – and also one of the world's biggest food exporters. 'The six' bought 8000 million units of accounts' worth of foodstuffs from third countries in 1972, this being 7 per cent of their total imports. Exports of the same products by the E.E.C. amounted to 3063 million units of account, just under 3 per cent of all exports. Between 1958

TABLE 6.1
Agriculture in the E.E.C.

	Proportion of working population in agriculture (1972) per cent	*Agriculture's proportion of G.D.P. at factor cost (1972) per cent*	*Average farm size (crops and grass) (1969) hectares**
Belgium	4.1	4.3	10.4
Denmark	9.7	7.7	19.2
Eire	24.1	18.3	16.4
France	12.6	6.7	18.8
Germany (F.R.)	7.5	3.4	10.4
Italy	17.5	9.2	7.2
Luxemburg	9.8	4.4	16.8
Netherlands	6.8	5.7	10.8
United Kingdom	3.3	2.8	34.0

*1 hectare = 2.47 acres.

and 1970 agricultural imports increased by 86 per cent in value and exports doubled. Of the new members the United Kingdom is a large net importer of food (the United Kingdom is only 50 per cent self-sufficient in food) but Denmark and Eire are substantial exporters, thus retaining a degree of balance over all. With this scale of trade it is important to stabilise prices at home without disrupting world trade.

The instruments of the C.A.P. can be conveniently considered under two headings:

(i) Market price regulation; and

(ii) Structural reform measures.

It is important to realise at this stage that both instruments may well influence a single commodity, and that the actual arrangements for each are extremely complex – an obvious feature of the case studies. The C.A.P. has been called by some economists 'Mansholt's maze', after its architect.

Market Price Regulation

Official prices are set annually by the Community's Council of Ministers, on a proposal of the Commission (for examples see Table 6.2). A pre-set internal market price is aimed for, and maintained by variable levies at the common external frontier of the E.E.C. and by intervention in the internal market when

TABLE 6.2
Some examples of support prices in the E.E.C.

		1969 - 70	1970 - 1	1971 - 2	1972 - 3
		£ per ton			
Wheat (soft)	Target* price	45.00	45.00	46.33	48.20
	Intervention	41.80	41.80	42.64	44.40
Barley	Target price	40.40	40.40	42.42	44.20
	Intervention	37.50	37.50	38.96	40.60
		£ per live hundredweight			
Fat cattle	Guide price	14.40	14.40	15.24	15.88
Calves for veal	Guide price	19.37	19.37	19.83	19.95
		£ per score (dead weight)			
Fat pigs	Basic price	2.83	2.92	3.02	3.12
		p per gallon			
Milk	Target price	20.08	20.08	21.26	23.00

*For definition of terms, see Glossary at the end of chapter.

over-supply occurs. The variable levies on imports bridge the gap between world and E.E.C. prices. If prices are higher in the community, there is provision for restitution payments (refunds) when produce moves outwards. Internal market intervention arrangements are very specific for each commodity, but in general all involve the withdrawal of produce from the market when prices are considered too low.

Structural Reform Measures

As at the middle of 1976 there is no E.E.C. structural reform policy, but the need for such reforms was recognised by the Community authorities at the outset. Before the Treaty of Rome individual countries had operated schemes, and these have continued within the broader framework of the E.E.C. In 1968 a document entitled *Agriculture 1980*, usually known as the 'Mansholt Plan', was produced. This stated the need for Community action to improve the structure of agriculture, and after much discussion modernisation directives were formally adopted by the Council of Ministers in March 1972. These directives dealt with the following:

(i) modernisation aid at up to 25 per cent of cost for specifically defined and approved projects;
(ii) financial help to give up farming;
(iii) provision of information services and training facilities for those staying in agriculture and to assist those choosing work outside agriculture and those retiring from farming; and
(iv) special measures to encourage and further producer grouping, particularly to improve marketing.

The Commission has also outlined certain conditions of the proposed E.E.C. structural reform plans, for example:

(i) they be sufficiently flexible to accommodate regional differences;
(ii) farmers must accept them of their own free will without state imposition; and
(iii) the responsibility for running the schemes rests with individual governments even though the schemes have common features and objectives.

Financing the C.A.P.

Since December 1970 the expenses of operating the C.A.P. have been met from the European Agricultural Guidance and Guarantee Fund (FEOGA – from its French designation). The Fund is derived from import levies and negotiated contributions from member countries. From the beginning of 1975 all levies and duties imposed at the common external frontier have automatically accrued to the Fund. Individual countries have of course still continued acting as collecting agents.

Further financial needs will be provided by member countries according to a special contribution fixed as a proportion of the value-added tax base in each country. Not more than the equivalent of 1 per cent is payable in practice. The United Kingdom, Denmark and Eire will gradually adopt this system. Table 6.3 gives an indication of the increasing relative importance of the Fund, both between commodities and the expenditure on market support (guarantees) and social and structural reform (guidance). Market support is now nearly ten times as costly as the latter – which has been static.

TABLE 6.3

The European Guidance and Guarantee Fund (FEOGA)
(Actual or estimated expenditure in million units of account:
1967- 70 £1 = 2.40; 1973 £1 = 2.1644)

	1967 – 8	*1968 – 9*	*1969 – 70*	*1973*
Cereals	430	657	921	953
Dairy products	320	380	850	1458
Pork	41	44	50	91
Eggs	1	2	1	} 22
Poultry	3	5	5	
Beef and veal	6	14	27	16
Rice	7	10	17	11
Fats	130	207	285	363
Fruits and vegetables	18	27	32	34
Sugar	68	195	221	127
Other	12	18	20	559
TOTAL GUARANTEE PAYMENTS	1036	1559	2429	3634
TOTAL GUIDANCE PAYMENTS	285	285	285	325

SOURCE: Commission of the European Communities, *The Common Agricultural Policy* (1974).

Problems and Controversies

The crucial feature of the C.A.P. is the agreed internal market prices. Agreement has in reality not always been easy. Germany has had to accept lower price levels and France and the Netherlands have tried to avoid setting prices at too high a level. Italy, now a significant importer of grain for livestock feeding, has more recently been campaigning to avoid excessive increases in cereal prices. Apart from these nationalistic issues the real problem is one of 'balance'. If the price is set too high, incentive is given to production, and surpluses may accrue and prove costly to remove from the market. These surpluses can quickly turn to shortages if the price is then set too low. Since price is the dominant parameter of agricultural incomes, it is hardly surprising that the price levels prevailing or negotiated have often led to civil disobedience by farmers in different parts of the community.

The general monetary system and the lack of a common currency have been major sources of strain to the C.A.P., devaluations and revaluations only accentuating national differences of currency. Short-term solutions are usually found to such distortions of trade, for example by operating a temporary export-rebate/import-levy system. The C.A.P. system of protecting against third countries is controversial. Since the variable levy increases as world prices fall, thus insulating the internal markets, overseas exporting countries consider it too protective. The export restitution payments have facilitated an export trade in agricultural products strongly contested by the developing countries in particular. Lastly, the C.A.P. has not closed the disparity of incomes between farmers and non-farmers. Some farmers with very large and efficient holdings have benefited, and so the policy is seen as selective and linked to regional development problems.

U.K. Agriculture and the E.E.C.

In contrast to the C.A.P. system where farmers receive their support mainly from the market, the cost being borne mostly by the consumer through higher prices, in the United Kingdom the burden has fallen on the taxpayer. A so-called 'deficiency payment' scheme has operated, the payments representing the difference between a predetermined forward guaranteed price and the market price received by the farmer. Together with additional direct grants, these subsidies amounted to £203 million in 1973 – 4. It was this fundamental difference in method of support that proved a major stumbling block in Britain's earlier unsuccessful attempts to gain admission to the E.E.C. even though its objective was the same – massive protection for home producers. It is interesting that, at the time of writing, it is being seriously advocated by some that the E.E.C. should consider the possible use of deficiency payments. In the meantime the United Kingdom is committed to a period of transition within which these payments will be phased out and C.A.P. measures adopted; this is to be completed by 1978.

Illustration by Case Studies

The first case, wheat-market price regulation, demonstrates the main principles of the E.E.C. agricultural policy. It further illustrates how the Community copes with production surpluses of a commodity important in world trade and as a human and a farm animal feed. The market control therefore affects the cost of production of animal products and the standard of living of consumers both inside and outside the Community. The second case (sugar) illustrates again the importance of E.E.C. policy to international trade, particularly with respect to the developing countries, and reveals the very complex co-ordination required to maintain a market involving nine countries, processors, farmers and agents. In the third case, consumers' interests in E.E.C. and U.K. agricultural policies are highlighted. The causes of a period of exceptionally high prices for beef are examined in the context of world trade conditions and contrasting agricultural policies. Lastly, a case study of Italian agriculture's structural and regional problems is presented to illustrate the potential for structural reform policies in the future.

CASE 17. WHEAT-MARKET PRICE REGULATION

This case considers only so-called 'soft' wheats, not the hard or durum wheats used mainly for pastas. A target price (sometimes called 'indicative' price) is set annually and fixed at a level which it is hoped producers will achieve on the open market in the area of the Community where grain is in shortest supply – Duisburg, West Germany. It is a price after delivery to a store or merchant, and all other prices are linked to it, and hence there are differences in prices at the farm level in the E.E.C. A threshold price is calculated which is the same in all parts of the E.E.C. but is stepped seasonally to allow for the upward trend of storage costs of the home crop during the year. It is determined so that wheat landed at Rotterdam and transported to Duisburg will sell at, or a little above, the target price. Variable levies are calculated daily in Brussels to make up the differences between the lowest c.i.f.* offers on world markets and the E.E.C. threshold price. All imports from non-member countries are subject to this levy, and the protection is effective for as long as the internal price level exceeds the external. If, however, there is surplus production within the Community, then internal market operations are necessary.

An internal market intervention price is set about 8 per cent below the target price but moving upwards in steps as the cereal marketing season proceeds. The intervention price is determined at wholesale level and is also related to trade at Duisburg. From it a *derived* intervention price is set at a lower level than the basic, making allowances for transport to areas needing to buy in cereals. There are agreed buying-in centres throughout the Community committed to accepting grain offered to them at the derived intervention price. They will of course only be offered grain at this low price if a higher price is not obtainable on the open market.

Excess wheat in the Community may be exported but a subsidy or restitution is necessary because, generally, Community prices are higher than those prevailing externally. Another way of dealing with excess wheat is that of *denaturing*. The wheat crop is usually grown for human consumption and the price fixed slightly higher than for animal feed. At times of excess supply a premium is payable to encourage the use of surplus wheat as animal feed and the grain is dyed or treated with fish oil or used under licence by feed compounders. This treatment prevents the wheat being resold in the open market after it has received a premium payment, or even being offered again to the intervention agency and receiving yet another premium. It is a method of creating coarse grains without adjusting market price differentials for quality.

*C.i.f.: a contract in which the payment for the goods includes the cost of insurance and freight.

Exercises

(6.1) The prevailing world price of wheat on a particular day is £42 per tonne and the E.E.C. target price is £50 per tonne. If £5 per tonne is allowed by the Commission for transport and insurance, what would be the variable levy imposed on foreign suppliers at Antwerp?

(6.2) What would be the effect of

(i) setting threshold prices too low for soft wheat?

(ii) an exceptionally heavy crop of wheat throughout the E.E.C. followed by a period of relatively high prices on world markets?

CASE 18. REGULATION OF THE E.E.C. SUGAR MARKET

Sugar is produced from sugar-cane or from sugar-beet, the former being a tropical giant perennial grass and the latter a temperate root crop, home produced within the E.E.C. Sugar-beet is an attractive crop to European arable farmers and the Community of 'six' was more than self-sufficient in sugar production. In the United Kingdom, by contrast, as much as 60 – 70 per cent of sugar has been supplied by imports of cane sugar under preferential Commonwealth Agreements. Higher prices for U.K. producers as members of the E.E.C. could therefore lead to an expansion of beet production. But sugar is also a vital crop to some developing countries, for example Mauritius, Barbados, St Kitts and Fiji, where sugar accounts for more than two-thirds of exports. Alternative satisfactory crops to sugar are not always easy for the producers to find. Sugar is a test case for the developed world to show its real concern for the developing countries.

Each country of the Community is allotted a 'basic quantity', a quota of white sugar based on amounts marketed between 1961 – 2 and 1965 – 6. Individual countries then divide this quota between various companies and refining factories in their territory to ensure that they get supplies of sugar beet to meet the quota. A total basic quantity for the Community is determined and the FEOGA guarantees the intervention price up to 105 per cent of the anticipated consumption. If production is further in excess of the basic quantity, between 105 and 135 per cent, then the sugar factory is obliged to pay a levy back to the Fund. Production in excess of 135 per cent is not bought at the intervention price and cannot be sold in the Community but must be exported without restitution payments.

Target and intervention prices are determined for the area of greatest surplus production – Northern France; a series of prices is then derived increasing towards the highest deficit areas. In 1974 – 5 these prices were as shown in Table 6.4. Sugar-beet growers also operate under a three-tiered price system, each factory's white-sugar quota being translated into a required quantity of beet. For production up to the basic quota the farmer receives a guaranteed price on his contract, and for quantities between the basic and the maximum quota a lower guaranteed price is paid. Any beet produced in excess of the quota receives no guaranteed price.

TABLE 6.4

	u/a per metric tonne
Minimum price for beet	18.84
Price for beet between basic and maximum quotas	11.08
Target price for white sugar	265.50
Intervention price for white sugar	252.20

Threshold prices are determined for white sugar and molasses and a variable levy is payable by importers if world prices plus transport and insurance are lower than this. Certain French (African) territories are included in these arrangements, receiving the same price guarantees as European producers for a basic quantity of sugar.

Exercises

(6.3) How could the E.E.C. adjust its sugar-market regulations to allow greater access to sugar from developing countries?

(6.4) Does the regulated sugar market conflict with E.E.C. competition policy?

CASE 19. BEEF PRICES IN THE UNITED KINGDOM, DECEMBER 1972

Between January and the beginning of November 1972 beef prices in the United Kingdom increased by about 15 per cent. In the next four weeks they increased to a peak approximately 70 per cent higher than the previous January. The Prime Minister ordered an inquiry which was carried out by a three-member team in four days. It is the sequence of events which led to this inquiry that concerns us in this case study.

World demand for beef had been increasing faster than supply in previous years in response to increasing consumer incomes. For ten years, at least, positive encouragement to beef production has been given in the United Kingdom through increases in the home guaranteed prices and direct subsidies. Expansion of production by some 100,000 tons in ten years has been achieved. However, due to the world shortages and resultant high market prices, this expansion has not been as costly in deficiency payments as might be expected, and home production has varied between 75 and 85 per cent of total supplies. Since 1967, because of foot-and-mouth disease, there has been a ban on imports of beef on the bone from the Argentine, previously a significant supplier.

Our price-escalation story begins in the E.E.C. in 1969. On 16 September 1969 the Community's Ministers of Agriculture approved a scheme to discourage dairy farmers from milk production. Premiums of about £85 per cow were paid for slaughtering in an attempt to halt a mounting surplus of butter which had resulted from over-attractive prices set previously for milk. Support prices were also reduced at the same time. It is in fact from the dairy herds that most beef comes, surplus calves being fattened for beef or veal. This is because the birth of a calf occurs before the cow can produce milk so the dairy and beef enterprises are complementary to each other. The result of this policy was that supplies declined, causing a rise in beef prices, and buyers began to look overseas for supplies. This trend continued in the E.E.C. and on 5 June 1972 the E.C.C. external tariff on beef imports was abolished, attracting supplies from the United Kingdom and Eire. As the latter is an important supplier of the U.K. market this caused a further upward pressure on prices in the United Kingdom. The tariff was restored in mid-July but on 23 June the pound sterling had started to float and depreciated so that U.K. and Eire beef prices gradually became more attractive to continental buyers.

At home, producers had increased the numbers of beef heifers in calf by 72 per cent but few extra animals were ready for slaughter. Furthermore, with Christmas approaching and consumer demand showing little regard to price, further impetus was given to the upward trend in beef prices. This coincided with the imposition by the U.K. government of a general price standstill. This legislation did not apply to food markets but did to retailers' margins. Initially, retailers reacted by narrowing their margins, containing the price increases to some extent, but as it became obvious that the beef shortage would be prolonged so prices continued to rise.

The committee that reported (unpublished) to the Cabinet on beef prices just after Christmas concluded that retailers and wholesalers had not benefited excessively from the price increases but that farmers had gained most. They were very critical of the exportation of publicly financed beef, suggesting that as much as £60 million had been contributed through direct grants. They acknowledged, however, that these had increased output and were therefore beneficial to consumers. It was to the housewives that the committee directed its main advice; to transfer their purchases to other meats or cheaper cuts of beef. They rejected a call for an export ban on beef from the United Kingdom and recognised the dominant effect as being the continual outstripping of supply by world demand.

Exercises

(6.5) What measures would you advocate in case study 19 to alleviate the exceptionally high prices of beef in the short and longer term?

(6.6) What would the effect have been in December 1972 of the following:

    (i) a severe outbreak of foot-and-mouth disease?

    (ii) a shortage or surplus of lamb and pigmeat?

    (iii) the E.E.C. tariff being increased?

CASE 20. STRUCTURAL AND REGIONAL PROBLEMS IN ITALIAN AGRICULTURE

Italy has only existed as a unified state for just over a century and her colonies were lost in the Second World War. Since then, attention has,been focused on the development of the home economy. The country has been divided into fifteen 'ordinary statute' regions with five other 'special statute' regions. These regions were established belatedly, mainly due to fears that the powers of the central government in Rome would be undermined. In relation to agriculture, however, the regional problem is more than just political. Geographically, Italy can be divided into two very distinct areas. First, the Northern part, which includes the Alpine zone and the North Italian plain, and, second, the Apennine region and the Italian peninsula including Sicily. The climate and geology of these two broad regions are very different, making for inevitable differences in farming potential.

Farmers' incomes in Italy are the third lowest in the E.E.C., only Luxembourg and Eire's farmers receiving less on average. The average size of holding of 7.2 hectares is easily the lowest in the Community and the productivity of manpower is also relatively low. There are also fewer co-operatives in Italy than in other countries of the Community. As well as being small, holdings are often fragmented, and may comprise many parcels of land. The traditional agriculture that prevailed in Italy before the Second World War was based on small-scale holdings and ownership, with obsolete forms of land tenure, such as share-cropping, where farmers share the profits from their crops with landlords. In central Italy many holdings are still share-cropped and it is widely practised further south. In recent years owner-occupancy has been encouraged to combat the spread of Communism. The greater agronomic potential of land in the north compared to the south is reflected in land prices, which in 1967 were twice the southern level.

The population of Italy today is about the same as that of the United Kingdom but Italy still has one of the highest birth rates in Europe, and emigration has been a prominent feature in the past; 41 per cent of this population was engaged in agriculture in 1950, declining to 24 per cent by 1967. Although agricultural workers declined by 47,000 between 1962 and 1966, it was only by 2.7 per cent, nearly the lowest rate in 'the six'. Furthermore, it is the young who have left.

Capital will clearly have to replace labour as the basis of Italian agriculture, and without worsening the regional problems. A common national policy towards all Italian agriculture has only maintained differences. Farmers have found it easier to gain access to capital from the banks in the north. In the early 1950s land-ownership reforms were attempted through what was called the *Riforma Agraria* but it subsequently proved unsuccessful. More recently a grant organisation, *Cassa del Mezzogiorno* (the Southern Fund), has been in operation and includes schemes to finance reafforestation, soil conservation, flood control and, particularly in the uplands, the resettlement of wastelands. This measure appears to be diametrically opposed to the real need –to get people out of agriculture.

Large sums have been invested in the home economy in general by post-war governments, the evidence being particularly plain in the south. Foreign capital as well as domestic big business is encouraged to build new factories in under-developed regions, especially the south, usually with guarantees by the state. This helps to provide jobs and stabilise conditions, and of course encourages more workers to leave agriculture to seek the higher wages offered.

Italy increased expenditure on agricultural structural policies from $347.5 million in 1960 to $585.6 million by 1967, but this was actually a decline as a proportion of the total expenditure on policy from 72.2 to 63.4 per cent. During 1972 – 3 there has been much political pressure for changes in government attitudes towards agriculture and thousands of farmers have demonstrated in Rome against current policies. At the same time a related threat to move a southern provincial capital from Regio Calabrio to Catanzaro resulted in street fighting, murder and arson. It is towards a unified C.A.P. regional and structural policy that Italian farmers look with most hope. A common regional policy has so far eluded the E.E.C.

Exercises

(6.7) Identify the factors leading to regional economic imbalance in Italy.

(6.8) Which of the features referred to in (6.7) apply in the United Kingdom?

Supplementary exercises

(6.9) Why is it generally assumed that consumer prices for food will continue increasing as the United Kingdom adopts the E.E.C. agricultural policy?

(6.10) Why was agriculture a problem in the negotiations leading up to Britain entering the E.E.C.?

(6.11) Do the countries of the E.E.C. benefit from the FEOGA fund in proportion to their contribution?

(6.12) What would be the effect of (i) a devaluation of the French franc and (ii) a revaluation of the West German mark on trade in agricultural produce within the E.E.C.?

(6.13) Make a list of policy measures that might lead to an 'improvement' in farm size.

(6.14) What would be the effect of setting (i) support prices too high for milk, (ii) threshold prices too low for soft wheat, and (iii) target prices too high for sugar?

(6.15) Re-examine the principles of the C.A.P. set out on the first page of this chapter. How are the principles embodied in policy measures?

Sources and References

The following provide very inexpensive supplementary information to the case studies.

G. R. ALLEN (ed.), *British Agriculture in the Common Market* (The School of Agriculture, University of Aberdeen, 1972).

Britain and the European Communities: an Economic Assessment, Cmnd. 4289 (London: H.M.S.O., 1970).

Cereals, Pigs and Pigmeat, Milk and Milk Products, Potatoes, Eggs, Sheep and Wool and Grassland, a series of booklets published by the Agricultural Economic Development Committee of N.E.D.O. through H.M.S.O. (obtainable free of charge).

T. KEMPINSKI, *The EEC Agricultural Reform Plan and its Relevance to British Agriculture*, University of Manchester, Department of Agricultural Economics Bulletin, no. 134 (1971).

J. MARSH and C. RITSON, *Agricultural Policy and the Common Market*, European Series (Chatham House: Political and Economic Planning, 1971).

F. MULLER, *FEOGA – The Agricultural Guidance and Guarantee Fund of the EEC* (The Agricultural Adjustment Unit, University of Newcastle-Upon-Tyne, 1970).

The Common Agricultural Policy (1974) and *Regional Policy in an Integrated Europe* (1969): both published by the Commission of the European Communities (obtainable free of charge from 20 Kensington Palace Gardens, London, W8 4QQ).

'World Demand a Key Factor in Beef Prices', Report of the Prime Minister's Team of Inquiry, *Financial Times* (12 Jan 1973).

Glossary of C.A.P. Prices

Basic price – applied to pigmeat and to fruit and vegetables. Surplus produce is bought from the market once the average market price falls below the basic price.

Guidance price – applied to beef and veal and acts as a target price and as a 'trigger' for import control and support buying. A single rate is operated throughout the Community.

Intervention price – is set below the target price and is the level at which national intervention agencies are obliged to buy commodities from the market when offered them. It is from basic intervention prices that intervention prices for particular areas are derived to allow for differences in supply and demand.

Reference price – applied to fruit and vegetables and is also used to describe Community average prices (weighted) for livestock. Similar to the sluicegate price in principle.

Sluicegate price – is reckoned to represent the cost of production in non-member countries. Sluicegate prices are used for pigmeat, eggs and poultry, and a levy is payable on imports above this price and a supplementary levy is payable on imports below this price.

Target price – Community policy aims to keep market prices as close as possible to the target price. Used for cereals, sugar and milk it is seasonally adjusted, to allow for storage costs in the case of cereals, and is highest in areas which are most in deficit in grain.

Threshold price – imports arriving at the E.E.C. frontier below the threshold price are subject to a levy to raise their cost to the threshold level. They are therefore the minimum import prices for cereals, milk products and sugar.

CHAPTER 7

Nationalised Industry

M. S. Bradbury

Summary of Background Material

This chapter does not attempt to discuss all the economic issues which follow from the existence of nationalised industries. Instead, it concentrates on the pricing and investment policies of nationalised industries and the related problem of their financial obligations.

The Optimum Allocation of Resources

The conditions needed to achieve an optimum allocation of resources between one nationalised industry and the remainder of the economy are very controversial, involving detailed arguments in welfare economics beyond the level of this book. However, a considerably simplified argument does enable us to state some of the more important conclusions of this controversy.

If we assume:

(1) a given distribution of income;
(2) that the money costs actually incurred by the enterprise reflect the real cost of production to the community;
(3) that the enterprise's receipts per unit of output represent the community's valuation of its product; and
(4) that over the appropriate range of outputs price (average revenue) is constant or falling, and the cost of marginal units is rising, that is a horizontal or downward-sloping average-revenue curve and a rising marginal-cost curve;

then welfare is optimised, in the sense that it would be impossible by any reallocation of resources to make anyone better off, without making at least one person worse off, if the output produced is that at which average revenue (price) equals marginal cost. If price exceeds marginal cost, then economic welfare could be raised by shifting some resources from other parts of the economy into the nationalised industry concerned. Conversely, if price is less than marginal cost, then economic welfare could be raised by shifting some resources out of the nationalised industry concerned.

However, this deceptively simple conclusion raises difficulties, including the following.

(1) The existence of market imperfections such as monopoly, a failure of all firms to attempt profit maximisation, or divergences between private and social costs and benefits, will mean that the market prices which enterprises pay for their inputs may not reflect their real opportunity cost to the community.

(2) Where the enterprise uses factors of production which are fixed in the short run, marginal-cost pricing will not necessarily ensure that total costs are covered by revenue. For example, if marginal cost is less than average cost at equilibrium, . there will be a deficit. Conversely, if marginal cost exceeds average cost, there will be a surplus.

Economists are divided in their approach to this problem. Some argue that any surpluses or deficits should be accepted as merely the logical outcome of following the correct pricing policy. Other economists argue that surpluses or deficits which are ultimately part of the general pattern of government revenue and expenditure imply a change in the distribution of income between users of the service concerned and the rest of the community. It then becomes a matter of value judgements whether or not one considers any particular redistribution of income to be desirable.

(3) Marginal costs can be very difficult to identify in practice, particularly where there are joint costs, e.g. where part of the cost of providing a large group of different railway services is one railway station which happens to be common to all of them. In such cases, marginal cost can become somewhat arbitrary.

Given that price has been equated with marginal cost, it follows that the optimum distribution of investment will occur if the marginal project (the one just worth carrying out) in the enterprise concerned has a return which is equal to that of the marginal investment project elsewhere in the economy (assuming identical degrees of risk and no externalities).

Hence we have deduced optimum pricing and investment policies on the assumption that a given distribution of income is accepted as correct. Given that the acceptance of any one distribution of income is a value judgement, it follows that in the last resort so are the resulting pricing and investment policies. Notice, in this analysis, that the financial obligations of nationalised industries emerge as a residual consequence of pricing and investment policies and not as a starting-point which will be used to determine prices and investment.

The Financial Obligations of the Nationalised Industries

Statutory obligations

In general, the nationalising statutes required undertakings at least to break even on revenue account, taking one year with another. The undertaking was then expected to ensure that total revenues were not less than sufficient to meet all items properly chargeable to revenue, including interest, depreciation, the redemption of capital and the provision of reserves. Four aspects of these obligations are particularly important to an understanding of subsequent events.

(1) They are a minimum and not a maximum obligation.

(2) The period over which break-even is to be achieved is not specified.

(3) Surpluses and deficits on revenue account are not directly comparable with the traditional accounting concept of profits or losses. This is because some of the items which are charged to revenue account, e.g. redemption of capital and the provision of reserves, are usually regarded as an allocation of profit and not as something to be deducted when calculating profit.

(4) Following from (3), a nationalised undertaking which did break even on revenue account would in fact be making a profit in the traditional accounting sense.

*The 1961 review of the financial and economic obligations of the nationalised industries**

The government noted that for a variety of reasons, amongst which were the social obligations of the nationalised industries, such undertakings had achieved a low rate of return on capital. Consequently they had been unable to finance either the replacement of assets or expansion from their own resources. The result was a rise in borrowing; between 1954 and 1959 annual investment by the nationalised industries increased from £480 million to £810 million, whilst borrowing increased from £290 million to £570 million. The government feared that borrowing on this scale might lead to higher taxation and greater Exchequer borrowing requirements.

The government then proposed a new financial framework, including the following provisions.

(1) The obligation to break even on revenue account was to be interpreted as meaning that, as a minimum performance, undertakings were to offset deficits with surpluses within a five-year period.

(2) It was not sufficient to allow for depreciation on the basis of historical cost, that is to seek to recover the original purchase price of the asset. Instead, in a period of rising prices, undertakings should also earn sufficient to meet the difference between historical and replacement cost.

(3) An adequate contribution was to be made to general reserves, towards the cost of premature obsolescence and the financing of expansion.

Financial targets were subsequently set for each industry 'in the light of its needs and capabilities'. For example, the electricity boards in England and Wales were asked to earn a gross return of 12.4 per cent (income before interest and depreciation, expressed as a percentage of average net assets). It was estimated that the gross return represented $5\frac{3}{4}$ per cent for depreciation, $4\frac{1}{2}$ per cent interest

*The Financial and Economic Obligations of the Nationalised Industries, Cmnd. 1337 (London: H.M.S.O., Apr 1961).

and $2\frac{1}{4}$ per cent surplus. The British Railways Board, on the other hand, was asked to reduce its deficit and break even as soon as possible.

The 1967 review of the financial and economic objectives of the nationalised industries*

Two of the conclusions of the 1967 Review are particularly relevant to the purpose of this chapter.

(1) The government accepted that 'targets should reflect sound investment and pricing policies and not vice versa'.

The 1961 Review had said little about the criteria to be used in choosing individual investment projects, beyond expressing the view that in general such projects should earn a return which was at least sufficient to replace the assets and cover interest charges. In the 1967 Review the government argued that it expected nationalised industries to use the best methods of investment appraisal available. For several reasons, e.g. the ability to borrow at a rate which reflected the government's credit standing, the rate of interest which nationalised industries paid on borrowed funds did not reflect the opportunity cost of the real resources pre-empted by the investment. The government therefore established a test rate of discount of 8 per cent (raised to 10 per cent in 1969), which had to be achieved by commercial projects, appraised by discounted cash flow techniques.† The test rate of discount was intended to reflect the opportunity cost of capital, that is the return which could be achieved on a low-risk project in the private sector, after making certain adjustments. Projects with a return below the test rate of discount could be undertaken if considered desirable on wider social or economic criteria.

Where possible, pricing policy was to be based on long-run marginal costs, that is on the costs of a continuing supply, including the replacement of the asset and an appropriate return on capital. In some cases, however, pricing could be based on other criteria, e.g. an undertaking with long-lived specific assets, faced with inadequate demand for its products, could base prices on short-run marginal costs, that is aim to cover its escapable costs. Subject to certain exceptions, it was still expected that undertakings would aim to cover their accounting costs.

(2) A clearer distinction was made between commercial and social obligations, thus:

Where there are significant social or wider economic costs and benefits which ought to be taken into account in their [the nationalised industries'] investment and pricing, these will be reflected in the Government's policy for the industry: and if this means that the industry has to act against its own commer-

---

**Nationalised Industries: A Review of Economic and Financial Objectives*, Cmnd. 3437 (London: H.M.S.O., 1967).

†See *Case Studies in Economics: Principles of Economics*, ch. 9, case 25, for a description of discounted cash flow (D.C.F.) techniques of investment appraisal.

cial interests, the Government will accept responsibility. (Where necessary the Government will make a special payment to the industry or make an appropriate adjustment to its financial objective.) Except in such cases the industries should provide goods and services which consumers want and are willing to pay for at prices which reflect their own costs as accurately as possible, and keep these costs at the lowest levels consistent with providing satisfactory conditions of employment and earning a proper return on capital.*

Subsequent Events

In the late 1960s considerable efforts were made to implement the recommendations of the 1967 Review. In several nationalised industries financial arrangements distinguished more clearly than before between social and commercial obligations, and pricing policies became more sophisticated and less dependent on traditional rule-of-thumb methods. Likewise, the use of discounted cash flow methods of investment appraisal became more widespread than hitherto and most nationalised industries introduced Corporate Planning procedures.

More recently, the microeconomic aspects of the 1967 Review have tended to be overshadowed by the price and investment controls imposed to meet the needs of macroeconomic policy. However, in his March 1974 budget speech the Chancellor of the Exchequer announced that nationalised industries were to be given greater freedom to increase prices, so as to check the growing revenue support needed to offset their deteriorating financial performance.

Illustration by Case Studies

Case 21 illustrates some of the problems discussed in the 1967 Review. After showing how British Railways' social obligations were isolated and paid for separately and its capital structure changed in an attempt to solve the 'railway problem', the case describes subsequent policy.

Reference should also be made to Case 16, which illustrates the interaction between nationalised industry pricing policy and other aspects of industrial policy.

*Nationalised Industries, p. 14.

CASE 21. THE JOINT STEERING GROUP REPORT ON BRITISH RAILWAYS

This case is based on the Report of the Joint Steering Group* set up by the Minister of Transport in 1966.

The Joint Steering Group (hereafter called the Steering Group) suggested ways in which the railways' obligations, financial and general, could be redefined to enable them to operate as an efficient and viable organisation. The Steering Group took particular account of the distinction between the commercial and social functions of the railways, a problem that had bedevilled them since nationalisation in 1947, and suggested courses of action which the government could take to establish a target that would give the railways an incentive to operate efficiently. The Steering Group recommended that the railways' activities should be divided into those which should be self-supporting and commercial and those sections that could not be commercial and would be maintained in the public interest with the help of subsidy from the government; the carriage of sundries freight (freight less than three tons) presented a special problem, but this was dealt with in the context of freight transport over all. The core of the Steering Group's work consisted of detailed studies of the railways' future profit potential, estimating the likely level of subsidies from the government and then, in the light of these factors, considering the railways' capital accounts to decide how much of the Board's debt needed to be 'written off' if the railways were to break even.

TABLE 7.1
British Railways' financial performance, 1955 – 65

Year	Profit or loss (£m.)
1955	− 38.2
1956	− 57.5
1957	− 68.1
1958	− 90.1
1959	− 84
1960	− 113
1961	− 136
1962	− 159
1963	− 133.9
1964	− 120.9
1965	− 132.4

Railway Policy, Cmnd. 3439 (London: H.M.S.O., Nov 1967).

Difficulties Facing the Railways in the mid-1960s

The arguments on how far the railways' problems arose from their own failings, and how far from other causes, will not be discussed here. Suffice for us to note that in the period from 1955 to 1965 the railways ran a series of massive deficits (see Table 7.1)

Table 7.1 shows only the general background to the problem; to analyse the nature of the railways' difficulties we must examine in detail the financial results of the various traffic categories carried on the railways. The Steering Group produced a breakdown of the performance of the main traffic categories, and this is reproduced in a somewhat modified form in Table 7.2.

Table 7.2 indicates the margin of revenue over direct cost, that is costs that vary with the traffic volume and would not be incurred if the services concerned terminated. However, looking at the margin of earnings over direct expenses ignores the very high level of indirect costs which have to be met by the railways; the main indirect cost is that of track and signalling. In total these costs came to £154 million in 1966. Adding these figures to give a net total results in an out-turn of a loss of £78 million; in addition to this, interest charges of £64 million had to be met. (These figures exclude net ancillary income of £6 million.)

TABLE 7.2
Viability of traffic flows on British Railways, 1966

	Revenue (£m.)	*Allocated expenses (£m.)*	*Margin over direct cost (£m.)*
Passenger			
Principal	74	43	31
Suburban	52	43	9
Other	54	59	− 5
Parcels and mails	58	43	15
TOTAL	238	188	50
Freight			
Coal	100	68	32
Iron and steel	34	31	3
Train load	59	57	2
Sundries	24	40	− 16
TOTAL	217	196	21
Miscellaneous receipts and expenditure	9	4	5

SOURCE: *Railway Policy*, p. 63.

Establishing a financial target for the industry

Nationalised industries are set financial targets in order to provide an incentive
for their managements to act as efficiently as possible and also to set some sort
of standard to compare their performance over time. However, before a sensible
target can be established, a full review is necessary of the situation of the industry;
it would clearly be impracticable to set all nationalised industries the same target.
Because the railways were in a weak competitive position, a review should take
account of the underlying conditions and trend of demand, trends in over-all
costs and also the cost of the social obligations that the industry had to meet
which constrained their commercial freedom. The Steering Group had to forecast
the railways' future net revenue position, and examine ways of identifying those
sections of the railways' activities that could not be operated commercially and
which were likely to be socially necessary.

Forecasting the railway's future position

The Steering Group were supplied by the Railways Board with two long-term
revenue forecasts, one for 1969 and the other for 1974.

On the basis of economic assumptions which the Steering Group noted as
being somewhat optimistic, the margin of earnings over direct expenses was estimated to be £126 million in 1969 and £151 million in 1974. When indirect costs
(excluding interest) and net ancillary income were taken into account, the net
position would become a loss on operating account of about £30 million in 1969
and break even in 1974. These estimates excluded losses on freight sundries traffic,
which it was assumed would be transferred to a new National Freight Organisation. The Steering Group concluded 'unless there are major changes in policies,
the likely results in 1974 might well be up to £40 million worse than the Board
have forecast; on the other hand, at best, they would be unlikely to be more than
£10 million better.'

Identifying the unremunerative sections of railway business

The Steering Group considered the question of government assistance to meet the
cost of the following:
   (1) loss-making passenger services;
   (2) stand-by track and signalling facilities;
   (3) the carriage of sundries freight traffic; and
   (4) historical obligations, e.g. road bridges, level crossings and museums.
   Leaving aside the last as comparatively unimportant, the three main items
represented very large sums of money. Approximate estimates by the Board
indicated that the loss on the passenger business could be as much as £52 million
per annum, even after the closure of certain services which the government had
provisionally decided could be considered for closure. The loss on sundries freight

traffic was also very heavy (estimated at over £20 million per annum). The Steering Group found that the railways had no stand-by capacity as such. The Railways Board claimed that they were maintaining stand-by track and signalling capacity at a considerable cost to themselves against the eventuality of some national calamity such as a war. However, the Steering Group decided that there was a considerable amount of surplus capacity, in the commercial sense of capacity, in excess of what was economically desirable, and the total cost of maintaining this surplus was estimated at £11 million to £17 million per annum.

The impact of compensation

The Steering Group recommended that a grant ought to be payable 'wherever the Minister on broad, social and economic grounds, decides to retain a particular passenger service, the revenue reasonably attainable from which falls short of the properly attributable costs'. Allowing for some loss-making services which were unlikely to be submitted for grants (either because managerial action could eliminate losses or for commercial reasons), annual grants for unremunerative passenger services were not expected to exceed £40 million in 1969 and £35 million in 1974. The Steering Group also recommended a grant for track rationalisation, estimated at about £15 million in 1969, but reducing to zero in 1974 when track cost savings of about the same order were expected.

After allowing for the above grants, the Steering Group estimated a deficit for the Board in 1974 of between £5 million and £55 million.

The reconstruction of the Board's capital debt

Clearly a reconstruction of the Board's capital account would be necessary to reduce interest payments to a level that the Board could realistically be expected to meet from the surplus they hoped to earn over direct expenses. The main item in the Board's capital account in 1966 consisted of interest-bearing capital liabilities to the Minister of Transport of £912 million. In addition there was a net suspended debt of £390 million.

The problem for the Steering Group to decide was how to adjust the interest payments, by writing off debts, to a level that the Board could be expected to meet. As the main aim of the Steering Group was to suggest a financial framework for the Board that would ensure financial viability, this capital-reconstruction problem was clearly of the first importance. The Steering Group stated that their aim was to put the Board in a position of viability by 1971.

The reconstruction of the Board's capital debt could be matched by an equivalent writing-down of asset values in the Board's accounts. This revaluation of assets would initially benefit the Board's financial position by reducing the depreciation provisions that have to be met out of the surplus on earnings over direct cost. Although this is something of a notional benefit to the Board, it is important in the context of creating the right financial environment in which

their results are to be judged. In practice this would not be a real benefit to the
Board unless they were able to reduce the level of capital investment, which
would obviate the need to borrow to finance the investment. In the past the
government had loaned the Railways Board the necessary finance to meet a
depreciation provision in addition to any loans necessary to meet their immediate
financial needs.

The Steering Group was unable to recommend the precise form of the recapitalisation, as estimates still had to be made of the Board's financial position. However, the Steering Group did make two points regarding the order of magnitude
necessary for the recapitalisation.

(1) If all the suspended debt were written off and asset values adjusted accordingly, the depreciation allowances to be provided in the Board's accounts could
be reduced by some £15 million to £20 million. There would be no immediate
effect on the interest burden.

(2) If, say, £100 million of the 'live' capital debt to the Minister were written
off, and asset values were written down correspondingly, the interest burden
would be reduced by £6 million per annum and the depreciation provisions
would be reduced by £5 million per annum.

Conclusion

The combined effect of these various measures, the identification of loss-making
services, the giving of grants for such features as surplus track, combined with the
reconstruction of the capital accounts, would, it was hoped, establish British
Railways in a financial position such that they could meet the targets that were
set for them.

The points to note in this solution to the Railways Board's problems are the
following:

(1) The separation of commercial and non-commercial activities and the
establishment of different criteria for each of these;

(2) The attempt to estimate the earning power of the railways' assets and to
adjust the notional value of these assets to match the real value of the earnings
they would produce; and

(3) The establishment of specific grants for facilities which the government
thought were necessary in the public interest but were impossible to operate
viably – the fact that these grants were given for specific services would enable the
government to control them fairly closely and to ensure that they represented
value for money.

Postscript

In general the recommendations of the Steering Group found their way into the
Transport Act of 1968, amongst the provisions of which were the following.

(1) The railways were to be relieved of the burden of operating uneconomic passenger services, by means of government grants paid for specific services.

(2) The Board were to be paid a grant fixed in advance, and on a tapering basis for five years, to assist with the removal of surplus track and signalling capacity.

(3) The sundries freight business, which made a loss of about £20 million per annum, was to be transferred to a newly formed National Freight Corporation (N.F.C.). A tapering grant was to be paid to the N.F.C. for five years, by which time it was hoped that the division (now renamed National Carriers Ltd) would be viable.

(4) The capital debt of the Board was written down to the level at which it was reasonable to expect interest payments to be payable out of prospective revenue in the early 1970s.

It will be seen from Table 7.3 that although the new financial framework provided by the *Transport Act* of 1968 was modestly successful in 1969 and 1970, the British Railway Board's financial performance continued to deteriorate

TABLE 7.3

British Railways Board's financial performance,* 1969 - 74

	1969 (£m.)	1970 (£m.)	1971 (£m.)	1972 (£m.)	1973 (£m.)	1974 (£m.)
Total income	611.4	659.0	696.5	741.3	795.0	926.5
Expenditure (before depreciation, amortisations and interest)	511.4	562.1	618.0	665.1	734.7	959.0
	100.0	96.9	78.5	76.2	60.3	− 32.5
Provisions for depreciation and amortisation	43.8	45.2	48.3	51.3	54.6	53.4
Operating profit/loss after depreciation and amortisation but before charging interest	56.2	51.7	30.2	24.9	5.7	− 85.9
Interest and other charges	41.5	42.2	45.6	51.1	57.3	71.9
Balance	14.7	9.5	− 15.4	− 26.2	− 51.6	− 157.8

*Includes all activities, e.g. hotels, ferries; the better performance of the non-railway activities improved the over-all results.

SOURCE: British Railways Board, *Annual Report and Accounts 1973 and 1974.*

(particularly after 1973). Furthermore, the above results were arrived at after allowing for government grants towards unremunerative passenger services, which rose from £61.2 million in 1969, to £68.2 in 1972, and then accelerated from £91.4 million in 1973 to £154.3 million in 1974. By 1974 the Board were experiencing cash-flow difficulties and a special additional grant of £215 million was paid.

Although some of the deterioration in the Board's financial performance could be attributed to the depressed state of the economy, price controls and industrial disputes (both on the railways and at major customers), the effectiveness of the Joint Steering Group's solution to the 'railway problem' was clearly in doubt. Following the policy review initiated in 1972, the Board's preferred solution was 'to seek support for the infrastructure of the whole railway, over which the Board in most cases would run passenger and freight services on a commercial and competitive basis'.* However, the government rejected this approach in favour of a totally supported passenger railway with commercial freight services superimposed on the passenger system.

The change of government policy was implemented by the *Railway Act* of 1974, the key features of which were the following:

(1) the reduction of the Board's debts from £439 million to £250 million (repayments of debt were also delayed for five years);

(2) the support of up to £1500 million was expected to last five years to compensate the Railways Board for the net cost of operating the whole or any part of their railway passenger system. (This general support for the passenger system marked the end of grants for specific passenger services, a major feature of the *Transport Act* of 1968);

(3) the provision of grants towards the cost of facilities for loading or unloading railborne freight where these were considered to be in the environmental interest of any locality; and

(4) the provision of assistance towards meeting the Board's historic pension-fund obligations.

Further changes in railway policy are likely to emerge from the transport policy review now under way, a stage in which is the publication of *Transport Policy: A Consultation Document* (London: H.M.S.O., Apr 1976).

Exercises

(7.1) (*a*) What social obligations did the railways have to meet out of revenue before the passing of the *Transport Act* of 1968?

(*b*) How were these social obligations paid for under the *Transport Act* of 1968?

*British Railways Board, *Annual Report and Accounts 1974*, p. 4.

(7.2) (*a*) Why did the Steering Group suggest that the British Railways Board's capital structure be changed?

(*b*) What was the economic reasoning behind the adjustment of B.R.B.'s capital structure under the *Transport Act* of 1968?

(7.3) How do you explain the existence of large indirect costs on the railway system?

Supplementary exercises

(7.4) Comment on the outcome of the 1968 *Transport Act's* solution to the railway problem. Compare and contrast the solutions to the railway problem proposed by the Joint Steering Group of 1966 with those of the 1976 *Consultation Document*.

(7.5) How does a nationalised industry's surplus or deficit on revenue account differ from the traditional accounting concepts of profits and losses?

(7.6) (*a*) What is the difference between historical cost and replacement cost depreciation?

(*b*) What would happen in the long run if an industry covered historical cost depreciation, but failed to earn the difference between this and replacement cost depreciation?

(*c*) Is depreciation a relevant cost when the demand for the services of specific and long-lived assets is declining?

(7.7) 'Self-financing is an irrelevant objective for nationalised industries; if a project offers an adequate return, the finance should be found for it; if a project has an inadequate return, it should not be carried out merely because the finance is available.' Discuss.

Sources and References

W. J. BAUMOL, *Economic Theory and Operation Analysis*, 2nd edn (Englewood Cliffs, N.J.: Prentice-Hall, 1965) ch. 16.

K. LEE, 'The Nationalised Industries: Pricing and Investment Policy in Theory and Practice', *Economics* (Spring 1968).

Part 3

Government Revenue and Expenditure and the
Management of the Economy

Introduction

C.T. Sandford

Macroeconomic Policy

Part 2 of this volume emphasised the more specifically microeconomic policies; Part 3 emphasises macroeconomic policy, attempts by the government to control or influence the broad aggregates of the economy – the level of employment and the level of prices, the balance of payments and the rate of economic growth. The distinction between microeconomics and macroeconomics is one of convenience, which is never absolute. In the first two chapters of Part 3, in which we look at government expenditure and taxation, we examine issues with a distinctly micro significance – the cost of Concorde, the costs and benefits of the Severn Bridge and the firm of J. Sainsbury Ltd 'going public'. None the less, these cases illustrate broad issues raised by public expenditure and taxation: the first two relate to the methods and problems of con·rolling government expenditure; whilst the change in the firm of Sainsbury exemplifies the way in which taxation may affect the organisation of the business enterprise.

The Great Divide

In the post-war history of macroeconomic policy there is a great divide that can be dated at around 1970. Before then there had been a fairly consistent pattern; the intellectual framework of policies seemed reasonably secure and the policies themselves fairly predictable in their results. Since 1970 the intellectual framework of policies has been insecure: economists have disagreed about the appropriateness of particular measures; the measures themselves have been much less predictable in their results; and the failure of governments to manage the economy satisfactorily has become increasingly apparent.

1945 – 70

From the Second World War to 1970, governments attempted to regulate the economy mainly by fiscal policy, to a less extent by monetary policy. Whilst the level of employment achieved was satisfactorily high, the policy came under increasing criticism for a failure to control inflation (which averaged about 4 per cent per annum) and for the failure of the United Kingdom to achieve a rate of economic growth comparable to that of most advanced industrial countries. Both those failures were intimately linked with an unsatisfactory performance in international trade. The pattern of economic activity in the United Kingdom became characterised as 'stop – go' – a three- or four-year cycle in which, for a year or two, activity, wages and prices rose; a balance-of-payments deficit followed; deflationary measures were then adopted to check the price rise and correct the balance of payments; then a year or so later, when unemployment had risen and the deficit in the balance of payments had been reduced or eliminated (and, the cynic would add, when a General Election was in the offing), there was a switch to the 'go' stage, and the whole cycle started again.

This alternation of expansion and contraction reduced Britain's rate of economic growth; investment plans were disrupted and the comparatively low rate of investment lowered the rate of increase in productivity. With strong trade-union pressures for higher wages, the low productivity in turn led to larger price increases in Britain than in most industrial countries. Further, in the expansionary phases of the 'stop – go' cycle wages rose well ahead of prices, whilst in the 'stop' phase wage increases were, at best, contained, never reduced. These various factors thus generated a marked upward trend of prices. Given a policy of fixed exchange rates, balance-of-payments deficits became endemic.

Prices and incomes policies and indicative planning were both tried in this period as attempts to break out of the 'stop – go' cycle. Indicative planning was conceived as a method of increasing the rate of economic growth in which firms would be encouraged to take a rather longer look ahead in their investment plans and to 'stick to trend'. A prices and incomes policy was seen as an attempt to restrain prices, wages and other incomes so as to check cost inflation without increasing unemployment and sacrificing growth.

1970 – 5

Since 1970 the record on demand management has deteriorated. Unemployment has twice risen above a million and (at the time of writing in 1976) is still rising; and the experience of inflation since 1970 makes the earlier period seem like a success story. For the first time since the war rising rates of inflation have been accompanied by growing unemployment. Inflation has begun to feed on itself as the expectation of its continuance has been written into the terms of economic bargains, thus generating further inflation. The attempt to enforce a prices and incomes policy has had traumatic consequences for the Conservative Party and perhaps for the country. A floating exchange rate has replaced a fixed rate, perhaps preventing a point of crisis, but removing an effective check on the rate of inflation and resulting in a downward slide in the pound. Equally traumatic events in world markets, a prolonged rise in raw-material prices, capped by huge increases in petroleum prices, have provided the international setting to Britain's difficulties. At the same time there has been disagreement amongst economists on the main cause of Britain's inflation – monopolistic trade unions or an irresponsible increase in the money supply.

Interrelationships

In Chapters 10 – 12 we attempt to span both periods of post-war demand management. Whilst the case study on fiscal and monetary policies relates to the period just before 1970, the background material reviews events to 1975. Conversely, the cases on prices and incomes policy concern 1972 – 4, but they are set in the context of earlier attempts at such policies, and a postscript outlines the subsequent policies of the Labour government to the end of 1975. If Chapter 12 on indicative planning is necessarily concerned with the attempts of the 1960s, yet some of the features of indicative planning survived in the public expenditure surveys, and there are other signs of a possible movement in the direction of such planning.

Finally, it remains to stress the interrelationships between all the chapters in this part of the book. The links have already been made clear between Chapters 10 – 12 – fiscal and monetary policy, prices and incomes policy and indicative planning, but there are important interrelationships between these chapters and those on taxation and government expenditure. Thus the over-optimistic growth expectations of the National Plan (Chapter 12) encouraged government spending (Chapter 8) and fostered expectations of higher wages (Chapter 11); whilst the disincentive effects of high marginal rates of taxation (Chapter 9) may partly account for the limitations of fiscal policy in curbing inflation (Chapter 10). Once again is demonstrated the truth of the adage: 'in economics everything depends on everything else.'

CHAPTER 8

Growth and Control of Government Expenditure

C.T. Sandford

Summary of Background Material

Theories of Public Expenditure

Various attempts have been made by economists to develop general theories of government expenditure; Pigou and Dalton, earlier this century, offered a theory of 'maximum social welfare', according to which government expenditure should be pushed to the point at which the disutility from the marginal pound raised in taxation was just equal to the utility derived from the expenditure of the marginal pound by the government, whilst the allocation of funds to the various government services should be such that the utility from the expenditure of the marginal pound on all services was the same. In this situation no adjustment of expenditure as between the private and public sectors of the economy or as between one government service and another could increase social welfare. This theory has an attractive conceptual simplicity and elegance, but suffers from overwhelming practical defects: it equates the incommensurable, treats 'the government' as one simple unitary being, and is a normative theory (concerned with what ought to be) rather than a positive theory (concerned with what is).

More recent economists (Downs, Buchanan and Tullock) have sought to develop a theory of expenditure based on the concepts that the members of a government seek to maximise the life of that government and tax and spend accordingly, whilst voters seek to maximise their real income. This is an attempt at a positive theory to which some general historical credence can be given, but it is an over-simplification limited by uncertainty and by ignorance of the effects of different measures to achieve the objects of maximisation.

A more helpful, if limited, theory is the hypothesis of Peacock and Wiseman, who are less concerned to provide a general theory of expenditure than to offer a working explanation of the time pattern of the growth of expenditure. They see public expenditure rising as a result of social disturbances (most notably wars) and then settling after the disturbance at a higher level than before. Their explanation is that in normal times governments are reluctant to incur the unpopularity of raising taxation; increases in government expenditure will tend to be limited to increases in revenue from given tax rates as incomes rise. A social emergency, however, both leads people to a new acceptance level of taxation and reveals and partly creates the need for higher government expenditure. Thus a major war is the justification for a huge increase in expenditure and taxation; after the war, expenditure remains above its pre-war level because people have come to accept higher tax levels and also because the war has revealed social needs (e.g. for an improved health service because of the poor physical condition of army recruits or evacuated children) and created new expenditure commitments (e.g. on debt interest and war pensions). This theory fits the pattern of government expenditure in the United Kingdom well for the first half of the twentieth century, but is less applicable to the expenditure growth of the 1960s and early 1970s.

Measuring Government Expenditure

Measuring government expenditure raises a number of practical and conceptual problems. There is an element of arbitrariness about what is included in government expenditure. For example, when the U.K. government in 1968 wished to raise family allowances to the poorer members of the community, it was convenient to do so by paying it to all families and then taking back the whole of the increase from those where the parents paid income tax; this had the effect of putting up government expenditure much more than if the same result had been achieved by directly paying the increased allowances only to the poor. Moreover, meaningful figures for the growth of expenditure must make allowances for changes in prices, population and national output (or income). One of the most convenient ways of showing changes in public expenditure is to express it as a proportion of national output. This has the advantage that it incorporates some automatic adjustment for price changes when comparison is being made over a period of years (though the adjustment is imperfect because the prices of the goods and services the government buys do not change in precisely the same proportion as the average of all goods and services). It also gives an indication of what is happening to the size of the public sector of the economy relatively to the private sector. But the measure is not devoid of difficulties.

Control of Expenditure

The term 'control' has a number of different meanings. When we talk of it we really need to ask two questions: control by whom and for what purposes?

There are two answers to the first question: control is exercised by the government itself – which primarily means the Treasury, with the Chancellor of the Exchequer at its head – and, second, by Parliament and the committees of Parliament acting, according to democratic theory, on behalf of the people.

There are at least four different purposes of control that can be distinguished.

(1) To secure the 'right' over-all balance of the economy between the private and the public sectors – the determination of how large in total public spending should be.

(2) To secure the 'right' allocation of resources as between alternative directions of expenditure within the total of public spending. This entails an efficient allocation of resources between one service and another (e.g. health and education) and within a service (e.g. whether a hospital should be built at town *A* or town *B* or town *C*).

(3) To ensure that there is no waste in carrying out particular policies in the sense that any agreed policy is carried out with the least expenditure.

(4) To prevent fraud and unauthorised expenditure.

What methods are used to try to achieve these objectives? To start with there are certain constitutional practices which have grown up over several centuries particularly concerned to clarify responsibility and prevent fraud and unauthorised expenditure. Thus all receipts must flow into and all payments be made from one single Exchequer account and only the government can authorise expenditure; an ordinary M.P. is debarred from increasing an estimate.

Further, a particular procedure has developed, often referred to as 'the circle of control', which starts with the initiation of estimates by the spending departments and ends with the auditing of the accounts and the confirmation that the money has been spent in the way authorised. The main stages are set out in Figure 8.1.

These practices and procedures all developed when the philosophy of public expenditure was very different from today: when the government was expected to provide for defence, internal order, a minimum of poor relief, and not much else; their emphasis was very much on the fourth of the functions of control which we listed. Since 1960 major changes have taken place in the control system aimed at the other three objectives and mainly springing from the 1961 Report of the Plowden Committee on *Control of Public Expenditure.**

The Plowden Committee, concerned at the somewhat piecemeal way in which many public expenditure decisions had hitherto been taken, strongly recommended that 'Regular surveys should be made of public expenditure as a whole, over a period of years ahead, and in relation to prospective resources; decisions involving substantial future expenditure should be taken in the light of these surveys'. Their other recommendations included 'improvements in the tools for measuring and handling public expenditure problems . . . and more widespread use of quantitative methods'.

Following Plowden the Public Expenditure Survey Committee (P.E.S.C.) was set up to implement the Committee's first recommendation, and the period since Plowden has seen government departments increasing their use of, and experimenting with, various management and control techniques, notably cost – benefit analysis, planning, programming, budgeting systems (P.P.B.S.) and programme analysis and review (P.A.R.).

*Cmnd. 1432

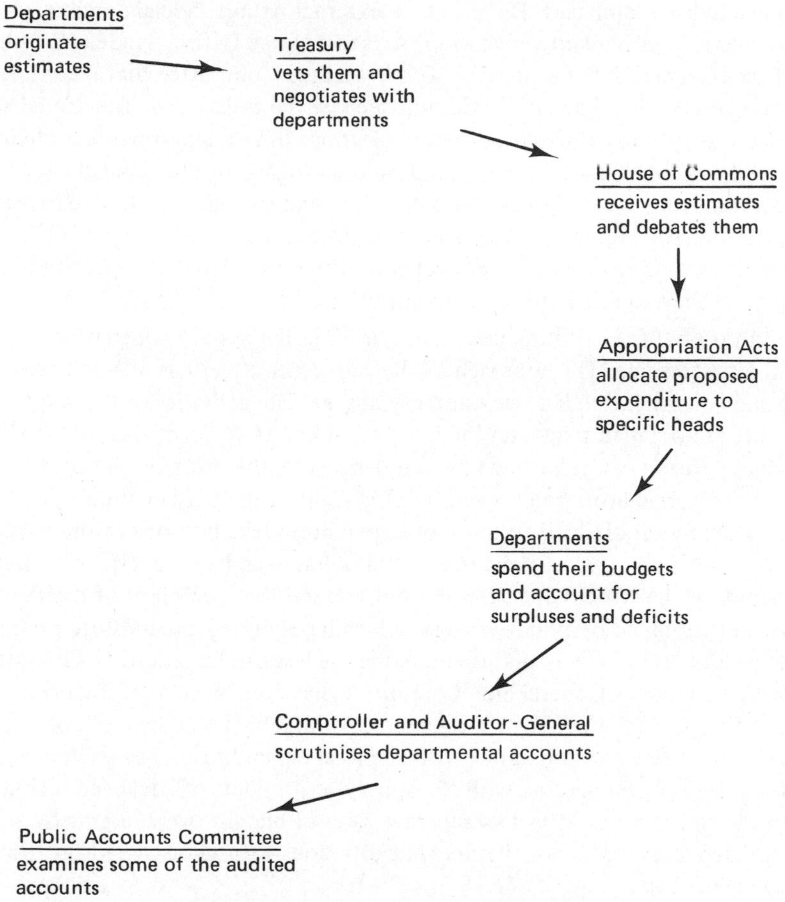

Departments
originate
estimates   ⟶   Treasury
vets them and
negotiates with
departments

House of Commons
receives estimates
and debates them

Appropriation Acts
allocate proposed
expenditure to
specific heads

Departments
spend their budgets
and account for
surpluses and deficits

Comptroller and Auditor-General
scrutinises departmental accounts

Public Accounts Committee
examines some of the audited
accounts

FIG. 8.1 *The 'circle of control'*

The development of control methods used by the executive has been followed by new opportunities for Parliamentary control. The first of a series of annual White Papers on public expenditure, outlining a five-year programme based on the work of P.E.S.C., was published in November 1969 and a debate on the White Paper takes place in the House of Commons each year. Also an Expenditure Committee was set up in 1970, replacing an earlier Estimates Committee. Whereas the Estimates Committee had very limited time in which to comment on a selection of the estimates before they were approved by the House of Commons, the Expenditure Committee is not under as tight a time constraint in looking at the five-year expenditure programmes. It has divided into a series of functional Sub-Committees: Defence and External Affairs, Social Services and Employment, Environment, Education, Arts and Home Office, Trade and Industry, as well as a General Sub-Committee. The Procedure Committee that recommended the setting up of the Expenditure Committee saw the tasks of the functional sub-committee as to study the expenditure projections of the departments in their field, to report on changes of policy and on the progress of the departments towards clarifying their objectives and priorities and to enquire into departmental administration, including the effectiveness of management. The General Sub-Committee was to scrutinise the projections of the annual White Papers and to co-ordinate the enquiries of the sub-committees.

For a variety of reasons the new methods of Parliamentary control have proved disappointing. The approach of the sub-committees has differed very much and co-ordination has been notably absent. The activities of the Expenditure Committee have failed to attract the interest, either of M.P.s or the public, which the subject warrants; nor have the annual debates on the White Paper proved, as some of their originators had hoped, 'the highlight of the Parliamentary year'. M.P.s have found it difficult to think of expenditure save in terms of the needs of their own constituencies, and the over-all view has been lacking. The technical complexity of the White Papers has not helped; and the credibility of the figures has been undermined by policy changes which have altered expenditure programmes almost as soon as they were published. None the less the Expenditure Committee, especially through its General Sub-Committee, has done some useful work.

A further particular problem connected with the third objective of control – to ensure that policies are carried out with the least expenditure – has also come to the fore since 1960 in connection with the supply of products of advanced technology by outside contractors. After two separate cases of blatant overcharging by suppliers (Ferranti and Bristol Siddeley Engines) negotiations with industry led, in 1968, to an agreement that:

(1) the government should in future have the right to equality of information with the contractor on non-competitive contracts, that is it should have right of access to the company's books; and

(2) an independent review board should be set up to which contracts could be referred where profits of more than $27\frac{1}{2}$ per cent or losses more than 15 per cent had been made.

Illustration by Case Studies

The case studies aim to demonstrate the difficulties of measuring public expenditure, to highlight the significant increase in public expenditure during the 1960s and early 1970s and to look at some of the methods of control. Case 22 describes and analyses the growth of public expenditure, 1964 – 74. Case 23 looks at one of the techniques used in the attempt to secure an efficient allocation of resources within the public sector – a particular cost–benefit analysis. The remaining two cases show the work of the two main committees of the House of Commons concerned with expenditure control – the Expenditure Committee and the Public Accounts Committee. We have chosen as the Expenditure Committee case the General Sub-Committee's analysis of the credibility of the figures in one of the public expenditure White Papers. In the case on the Public Accounts Committee we see some of the problems of securing efficiency in public expenditure on contracts for products of advanced technology and the particular problems that may arise when international agreements are also involved.

CASE 22. CHANGES IN THE SIZE AND CONTENT OF GOVERNMENT EXPENDITURE, 1964 – 74

The purpose of this case is to indicate some of the problems of measuring public expenditure; to describe the very substantial increase in public expenditure, 1964 – 74; to break down the totals into some of the significant categories; and briefly to suggest some of the reasons for the increase.

Measuring Public Expenditure

If, as a convenient summary of the size of the public sector, we measure public expenditure as a percentage of national output, we face two general problems: what should we include in public spending and what measure of national output should we use?

There are at least three measures of over-all public spending which are meaningful.

(1) The combined total of central and local government spending (including the national insurance fund) and the capital expenditure of public corporations. This gives the biggest total of the three and can be taken as some approximate measure of the total spending influence of the government in the economy.

(2) The combined total of central and local government spending (that is as (1), but omitting the nationalised industries altogether on the ground that they are more or less autonomous bodies).

(3) The combined total of central and local government spending *minus* net lending by central and local government. The justification for omitting this item is that it consists mainly of lending to private and nationalised industries where the government can be regarded as acting simply as an intermediary in the provision of capital.

The first of these measures corresponds to what is called in the *National Income Blue Book*, the 'Public Sector'; the second corresponds to the *Blue Book* figures for 'Combined Public Authorities' and the third is 'Combined Public Authorities' less the item 'Financial Assets'.

Each of these measures is valid in its own right and the choice should depend largely on the purpose in hand.

The measure of national output which it is customary to use as the denominator is Gross National Product (G.N.P.). Net National Product (N.N.P.), which is the same as National Income, might be preferable in theory, but because the figures of capital consumption (or depreciation) which represent the difference between G.N.P. and N.N.P. are very unreliable, a more consistent series for comparing a number of years is likely to be attained by using G.N.P.

TABLE 8.1

Public expenditure as a percentage of G.N.P. at factor cost

Measure	1964	1965	1966	1967	1968	1969	1970	1971	1972	1973	1974
1 Central and local government and public corporations*	43	44.7	45.7	49.6	50.6	49.6	49.9	49.4	49.6	50.0	56.2
2. Central and local government†	40.6	42.2	43.4	47.4	48.7	47.8	47.6	47.4	48.1	47.4	52.5
3. Central and local government† *less* expenditure on financial assets	38.0	39.2	40.3	43.7	45.5	45.4	45.2	44.2	45.3	44.9	49.3

*Excluding current expenditure on goods and services on operating accounts of public corporations and other public enterprises.

†Excluding financial transfers between central and local government.

SOURCE: *National Income and Expenditure, 1964–74* (London: H.M.S.O., 1975) tables 1, 52 and 57.

The factor cost measure of G.N.P. is better than the market price measure because market prices are affected by subsidies and outlay taxes, and changes in these could distort the picture.

Table 8.1 shows the total of public expenditure, using each of these three measures, for the period 1964 – 74. Whichever measure is taken, public expenditure as a percentage of G.N.P. is shown between 29 and 31 per cent higher in 1974 than in 1964; but the figures range from the rise of 43 to 56 per cent by the first measure to that of 38 to 49 per cent by the third.

Analysis of the Public Expenditure Growth

A growth in total public spending of this order is without precedent for any comparable peacetime period. Before the 1960s the Peacock and Wiseman 'social-disturbance' hypothesis seemed to fit very well the pattern of expenditure growth; but the period 1964 – 74 contained no war to act as the catalyst to a big public expenditure rise.

The period shows a clear pattern: a fairly steady growth to 1968, followed by a period of stability, and then a huge leap upwards in 1974.

We can understand the increase better if we break it down into some of its component parts. We wish, in this case, to concentrate on central and local government and not the nationalised industries, so in the following tables, with one exception, we shall use the second of our measures, central *plus* local government spending (including 'Financial Assets'). The exception is Table 8.4, where it is convenient to use measure (1), the figures of the Public Sector as set out in the *National Income Blue Book*. When taking the total of central and local expenditure together, we have to omit cash transfers between them to avoid double-counting; the biggest of these items is grants from central government to local authorities. These count as spending by local government but must not also count as central government spending.

Table 8.2 distinguishes current and capital expenditure; Table 8.3 separates government spending on goods and services from transfer expenditure; Table 8.4 looks at what has happened over the period to the largest functional categories of expenditure; and Tables 8.5 and 8.6 separate central and local government spending.

The distinction between current and capital expenditure is important because, broadly speaking, it distinguishes expenditure on goods and services currently used up from that on items with a long life which will be providing services to the community for many years to come Thus, whereas the biggest item in current expenditure is the wages and salaries of public employees, the main items of capital expenditure are new buildings – hospitals, schools and government offices – and roads. It can be seen from Table 8.2 that the expenditure growth to 1968 was characterised by a substantial rise in capital spending, which increased at more than twice the rate of current spending between 1964 and 1968, whereas in 1974

TABLE 8.2

Combined central and local government spending as a percentage of G.N.P. at factor cost
(distinguishing current and capital expenditure)*

Combined central and local government	1964	1965	1966	1967	1968	1969	1970	1971	1972	1973	1974
Current expenditure	32.7	33.9	34.6	36.9	37.8	37.6	37.7	37.3	38.6	37.8	42.0
Capital expenditure	7.9	8.3	8.7	10.6	10.9	10.3	9.9	10.1	9.5	9.6	10.5
TOTAL	40.6	42.2	43.3	47.4	48.7	47.9	47.6	47.4	48.1	47.4	52.5

*Columns do not always exactly add up because of rounding.

SOURCE: *National Income and Expenditure 1964–74*, tables 1 and 52

TABLE 8.3

Combined central and local government spending as a percentage of G.N.P. at factor cost
(distinguishing expenditure on goods and services and transfers)*

Combined central and local government	1964	1965	1966	1967	1968	1969	1970	1971	1972	1973	1974
Goods and services	23.3	23.8	24.7	26.2	26.3	26.0	26.4	26.3	26.6	26.3	28.2
Transfers	17.3	18.4	18.7	21.2	22.4	21.8	21.2	21.1	21.5	21.1	24.3
TOTAL	40.6	42.2	43.3	47.4	48.7	47.9	47.6	47.4	48.1	47.4	52.5

*Columns do not always exactly add up because of rounding.

SOURCE. *National Income and Expenditure, 1964–74*, tables 1 and 52.

the increase in capital spending was a little less, proportionately, than the increase in current spending.

The distinction between spending on goods and services (sometimes known as 'exhaustive' expenditure) and transfers is particularly important. Transfer payments are cash payments to people or institutions against which there is no corresponding economic output currently provided; the government takes money from some people (in the form of taxes and possibly loans) and transfers it as cash payments to others. Social-security benefits, retirement pensions, subsidies and grants and interest on the national debt are all transfer payments. The payment of salaries to civil servants or teachers or doctors are not transfer payments in this sense, even though the government raises the money by taxation, because in return for the payments they receive they are currently rendering services to the community which count as part of current output. The distinction has a twofold importance. First, broadly speaking, it distinguishes that part of spending which gives a government direct control over goods and services from that which does not. Take the figures for 1974; the total of government spending in that year amounted to 52.5 per cent of G.N.P. It would be incorrect to say (as is often stated) that, in 1974, the government pre-empted over half the national output for its own purposes. It would be correct to use such an expression for government expenditure on goods and services; but with most transfer expenditures the recipient determines what the money shall be spent on, not the government. (This is not true of all transfers; some, such as investment grants and at least a part of education grants, are only given on the guarantee that the money will be spent in a certain way.)

The second way in which this distinction is important is for fiscal policy (see Chapter 10). A given total of government expenditure on goods and services will be more effective in raising aggregate demand than the same total of expenditure which takes the form of transfer payments, some of which might be saved by the recipients.

Table 8.3 shows that in both periods of growth, 1964 – 8 and 1974, transfer payments rose at a faster rate than expenditure on goods and services.

Table 8.4 contains all the headings of public expenditure which, in 1974, exceeded £2000 million and compares the totals in money terms and as a percentage of G.N.P. The last column, in which money expenditure in 1974 is expressed as a percentage of money expenditure in 1964, enables us to compare easily the growth rates of the various items with each other, with the total of public spending and with the growth of G.N.P. Thus it shows, for example, that all the items have increased faster than G.N.P. except defence spending, which has risen (in money terms) much less than public spending as a whole and has declined significantly as a proportion of G.N.P.

Tables 8.5 and 8.6 distinguish central from local government spending. Table 8.6 uses the data from Table 8.5 for the calculation of an index number to show the respective growth rates. It reveals very clearly the particularly rapid growth of local government spending. Whereas (as a proportion of G.N.P.)

TABLE 8.4

Increase in major items of public expenditure,* 1964–74

	1964		1974		Money expenditure 1974 as percentage of money expenditure 1964
	£m.	Percentage of G.N.P.	£m.	Percentage of G.N.P.	
Military defence	1990	6.71	4421	5.71	212
Industry and trade†	905	3.05	3731	5.04	412
Housing	814	2.75	3942	5.33	484
Education	1417	4.78	4864	6.58	343
National Health Service	1130	3.81	3819	5.16	338
Social-security benefits	2099	7.08	6845	9.25	326
Debt interest	1257	4.24	3326	4.50	265
Total public expenditure	12759	43.03	41606	56.24	302
G.N.P. at factor cost	29648	100	73977	100	250

*Includes capital expenditure of public corporations.

†The item labelled 'other industry and trade' in the *National Income Blue Book* includes capital formation of central and local government and public corporations, subsidies, grants to the private sector and net lending.

SOURCE: *National Income and Expenditure 1964–74*, table 58.

central government spending has risen by 25 per cent between 1964 and 1974, local government spending has increased by 39 per cent; the combined total of central and local spending has risen by 29 per cent.

TABLE 8.5
Central and local government spending, 1964 – 74*

	Percentage of G.N.P.		
Years	*Central*	*Local*	*Combined*
1964	28.3	12.3	40.6
1965	29.3	13.0	42.2
1966	29.9	13.4	43.3
1967	33.0	14.4	47.4
1968	34.1	14.6	48.7
1969	33.0	14.8	47.8
1970	32.4	15.2	47.6
1971	32.5	14.9	47.4
1972	32.8	15.3	48.1
1973	31.3	16.2	47.4
1974	35.4	17.1	52.5

*The figures exclude grants and loans from central to local government and interest on loans paid by local to central government.

SOURCE: *National Income and Expenditure, 1964 – 74*, tables 1 and 52.

Table 8.6 brings out most clearly the enormous leap upwards in public expenditure in 1974. Distinguishing central government from local government spending also reveals that between 1968 and 1973 there was a noticeable fall in central government spending (as a percentage of G.N.P.) which is largely masked by the more or less continuous rise in local government expenditure.

Why Has Government Spending Risen So Fast?

In a relatively short case study we cannot attempt to offer anything like a full explanation of the rise of government expenditure, 1964 – 74. It must be recognised, also, that there is much that is problematical and controversial about the causes of the increase and that political and philosophical as well as economic influences all played a part. Clearly there were often special reasons for the increase in particular components of public spending (such as the demographic influences on expenditure on education, mentioned in Case 2 in this book). The

TABLE 8.6
*Central and local government spending as a percentage of G.N.P. at factor
cost, 1964 – 74 (expressed as an index number)*

Years	Central government	Local government	Combined
1964	100	100	100
1965	103.4	105.3	104.0
1966	105.8	108.8	106.7
1967	116.7	117.0	116.8
1968	120.4	118.4	119.8
1969	116.8	120.1	117.8
1970	114.6	123.2	117.2
1971	115.0	120.5	116.7
1972	116.0	123.9	118.4
1973	110.5	131.1	116.7
1974	125.1	138.6	129.2

following suggestions, which link up closely with the statistics we have examined,
attempt to outline some of the most important general factors at work.

(1)   *Basing public expenditure plans on over-optimistic growth rates*

Following the first recommendation of the Plowden Report, governments, as we
have seen, prepared public expenditure programmes over five-year periods in the
light of 'prospective resources', a phrase interpreted to mean the expected growth
of G.N.P. It follows from the nature of our measure of public expenditure as a
percentage of G.N.P. that the outcome is susceptible to changes in its denominator
as well as changes in the numerator. In other words, public expenditure measured
in this way might increase, not because public spending in real terms had risen
abnormally, but because the growth of G.N.P. was abnormally low. In the two
periods in which public expenditure rose very rapidly, 1965 – 8 and 1974, the rate
of growth of G.N.P. fell far short of expectations. Thus in the period 1965 – 8,
which was associated with the National Plan (see Case 33) public expenditure was
planned to rise at $4\frac{1}{4}$ per cent per annum in the context of an expected growth
rate of G.N.P. of 3.8 per cent; the actual growth rate was $2\frac{1}{2}$ per cent. Similarly,
in 1974, public expenditure shot up partly because the G.N.P. growth rate was an
unanticipated abnormal low of 0.3 per cent. In short, there have been unintended
increases in the size of the public sector when actual G.N.P. growth has been
much less than expected growth because the expenditure plans have been based on
the expected growth rate and because rigidities in public spending have made a
sharp cut back very difficult to apply.

(2) *The changing source of local finance*

We have seen that one marked characteristic of the growth in public spending
from 1964 to 1974 has been the much larger growth of local than of central
government expenditure. This phenomenon has coincided with a significant
change in the source of local finance. In 1958 local authorities obtained fractionally
more of their revenue from local rates than from central government grants. By
1964 the ratio of rates to grants was 49 : 51; by 1968 it was 45 : 55; by 1974 it was
38 : 62. At the risk of over-simplifying a very complex matter it can be said that
most of the increase in local spending from 1964 to 1974 has been paid for by
grants – by the taxpayer rather than the ratepayer. Local spending which benefits
local residents must always seem a good bargain if the cost is wholly or largely
met by the whole body of national taxpayers. There can be little doubt that
local authorities' attitudes to spending would have been very different if they had
been obliged to find most of the increased revenue from local taxes.

(3) *The 1974 inflation*

Much of the huge upsurge in public spending in 1974 is closely associated with the
treatment (or non-treatment) of galloping inflation. Thus large sums have been
paid out by central government to subsidise food and rents and to keep down the
prices charged by nationalised industries; payments on pensions of public employees (which were made 'inflation-proof' by the *Pensions (Increase) Act* of 1971)
and state retirement pensions (guaranteed an annual review) have soared; a huge
public-sector deficit has meant more payments on debt interest; and subsidies
have been made to private firms to bale them out of economic difficulties. All
these items, and a growing bill on unemployment benefits, have put up current
expenditures of transfer payments. At the same time, big wage and salary awards
to central and local government employees, partly to make up for some earlier
falling behind, go a long way to account for the increase in government current
expenditure on goods and services.

Exercises

(8.1) 'Central and local government expenditure, taken together, was £23
million in 1790; in 1974 it was £38,830 million. Therefore government expenditure has increased 1688 fold.' Comment on this statement

(8.2) The four items of expenditure – housing, education, the National Health
Service and social-security benefits – might be regarded as expenditure on 'human
resources'. Compare the growth in the combined expenditure on these items with
that of public spending as a whole in the period 1964 – 74.

(8.3) Plot the data of Table 8.6 in the form of a graph. Comment briefly on
the main points of significance that the graph reveals.

(8.4) In 1966 the government introduced a new method of encouraging investment in manufacturing industry: investment grants, which were a cash subsidy, replaced investment allowances (a tax relief). Apart from any difference in the aggregate financial benefit received by industry, what, if anything, would be the effect of the change in method on the statistics of government expenditure?

(8.5) 'Unintended increases in government spending resulted from the operation of the very system set up to control it.' Explain this paradox.

CASE 23.   THE COSTS AND BENEFITS OF THE SEVERN BRIDGE

Cost – benefit appraisals are a method of seeking to improve the efficiency of decision-making in the public sector. A private producer makes a comparison of costs and benefits when he compares his costs of production with his receipts (which indicate the minimum values his customers put on the benefits they receive). A cost – benefit study differs from the assessment of the private producer because it seeks to incorporate social (as well as private) costs and benefits, and to make an appraisal where no prices (or only nominal prices) are being charged.

Cost – benefit studies are concerned with the second function of control set out in the 'Summary of Background Material' – the efficient allocation of resources within the public sector. Their application has been primarily in relation to alternative expenditures within a service rather than between services, and they have been applied most in transport; the most notable have probably been the studies of the M1, the Victoria Line and the Third London Airport.

The Severn Bridge study was not, however, undertaken to decide whether or not the bridge should be built; it did not precede the decision to construct the bridge. The cost – benefit study was part of a wider assessment of the economic consequences of the bridge,* undertaken after its construction. It was hoped that the cost – benefit study would have relevance to investment decisions elsewhere (such as Humberside and Deeside), and the study illustrates clearly the methods employed and the difficulties of cost – benefit studies.

The Severn Road Bridge was opened in 1966. Previously there had been a very tedious and time-consuming car-ferry service, which terminated at the opening of the bridge; and a rail link through the Severn Tunnel, which continued in existence. The bridge reduced the journey by road between the eastern and western sides of the estuary by up to 50 miles.

Method

Some very limited data on the situation before the bridge opened was available from a traffic survey on roads likely to be affected by the bridge. After the opening of the bridge a further traffic survey was undertaken on the same roads. In addition to data obtained in the process of toll collection, a series of traffic surveys were conducted on the bridge itself, and other data were collected by industrial surveys in the surrounding regions. By these means much information was collected on bridge-users which made it possible to calculate, with a fair degree of accuracy, the number and type of vehicles crossing the bridge, the origins, purpose and

---

*E. J. Cleary and R. E. Thomas, *The Economic Consequences of the Severn Bridge and its Associated Motorways* (Bath University Press, 1973). The project was jointly sponsored by the South West Economic Planning Council and the Welsh Economic Council.

destination of the trips made, the number of passengers and the type of commodity carried.

Three stages can be distinguished in a cost – benefit analysis:

(1) the enumeration of the costs and benefits to be included;
(2) the value to be placed on those costs and benefits; and
(3) the basis of comparison of costs and benefits.

(1) *Enumerating costs and benefits*

The costs of the Severn Bridge consisted of the capital costs of construction, together with a part of the adjacent motorway costs providing the necessary approach roads, and the maintenance charges throughout the life of the bridge.

The benefits taken into account covered both benefits to diverted traffic (trips which would have been made anyway had no improvements been made) and to generated traffic (the increase in trips following the improvement). The benefits consist of reduced journey times resulting in both a mileage saving (petrol, wear and tear on the car) and a time saving.

Certain other costs and benefits were considered for inclusion. There was saving of motorist's time on many other routes (e.g. through Gloucester and Chepstow) because of reduced congestion resulting from the diversion of traffic to the bridge; on the other hand, there was an increase in congestion on roads leading to the bridge. There was also a reduction in accidents for diverted journeys, but additional accidents resulting from generated traffic. In the event, estimates for these items were not included: the data were inadequate; even if an extended field survey were undertaken, the results would be likely to need much qualification; and quantitatively the costs and benefits appeared likely to be relatively unimportant.

(2) *Valuing costs and benefits*

The distance saved was arrived at by using a series of traffic zones, and the miles saved were multiplied by an operating cost per mile to obtain a monetary value. Savings for light vehicles throughout the life of the bridge were based on forecasts of car-ownership, based in turn on population forecasts in each of the zones. With heavy vehicles the forecasting was subject to a wider margin of error, being affected by government policy on factors, such as permitted maximum lorry sizes, that could only be guessed at. Evidence collected in the three years after the opening made it clear that firms adjusted only slowly to the opening of the bridge; to allow for the uncertainties in the adjustment process alternative assumptions were made about the length of time heavy vehicles took to adjust to the bridge before the traffic settled at a steady growth rate.

Mean periods of time saved were obtained by timing vehicles on the main roads affected. In valuing the time saved a distinction was made between work time and the remainder. Work time for commercial drivers was valued at a higher rate than that for other work travellers, in accordance with estimates produced by the Road Research Laboratory and based on current earnings. Non-working time was given a lower value at rates recommended by the (then) Ministry of Transport, of around 30 per cent of the commercial drivers' wage rates. A further calculation was made at a still lower rate (of about 20 per cent of the commercial drivers' wage rates).

(3) *Comparing costs and benefits*

To compare costs and benefits they must all be converted to the same basis. In the Severn Bridge study, the year 1966 was used as the basis for comparison. Some of the construction costs of the bridge were incurred before 1966, so interest had to be added to these costs at a compound rate in order to obtain their 1966 value. Costs incurred after 1966 and benefits resulting after 1966 need to be discounted to obtain their 1966 value (a process of compound interest in reverse) to take

TABLE 8.7

Estimated costs and benefits of Severn Road Bridge
(discounted to 1966 values at a discount rate of 10 per cent)

	Value of saving in		
Estimated gross benefits	*Miles*	*Time*	*Total*
	(£m.)	*(£m.)*	*(£m.)*
Light vehicles			
Firm's business	19.7	15.3	35.1
Holidays	5.5	4.2	9.7
Visiting	10.1	7.9	18.0
All other and multiple	10.5	8.0	18.5
Total	45.8	35.5	81.3
Heavy vehicles			
Lower traffic forecast	47.6	10.7	58.3
Total	93.4	46.3	139.6
ESTIMATED COSTS			
Capital costs			20.9
Maintenance			0.6
Total			21.5
ESTIMATED NET BENEFIT			118.1

SOURCE: *The Economic Consequences of the Severn Bridge and its Associated Motorways*, table 8.6.

account of the fact that, quite apart from any question of inflation, £100 next year
is not as valuable as £100 this year. Three different discount rates were used in
the study: 5, 8 and 10 per cent.

Table 8.7 summarises the outcome of the calculation at the 10 per cent discount
rate, and using the lower heavy vehicle traffic forecast. The calculations show a
huge net benefit, with total benefits emerging as between six and seven times the
cost. If the upper traffic forecast had been used, the net benefit would have been
£5.8 million higher.

Various alternative calculations all give a very large net benefit. The lowest net
benefit recorded in the study (which is based on the lower heavy traffic forecast,
the lower values for non-working time and a calculation of the value of the
distance saved by light vehicles on the basis of running costs only) comes out at
£99.8 million.

Problems of Cost – Benefit Analysis Illustrated by the Study

Besides some difficulties peculiar to this cost -benefit appraisal (e.g. that the full
benefits of the bridge would not be realised until the completion of the motorway
network with which the bridge was linked), the study reveals a number of problems,
both practical and conceptual, which are common to all or most cost -benefit
studies.

(1) Which costs and which benefits to include?

In theory a cost - benefit study is supposed to take into account all relevant costs
and benefits. In practice this is impossible and there is an element of arbitrariness
in what is omitted. In the Severn Bridge study the authors recognised the existence
of effects on users of other roads and on the number of road accidents, but did
not include them in their calculations. But (like most cost - benefit studies of road
transport) they did not explicitly recognise the effect on other transport users.
Thus, for example, the road link across the Severn may well have reduced rail
traffic through the Severn Tunnel and led to a deterioration in the rail service, to
the detriment of those who continued to use it. On a still broader plane, whilst
other aspects of the full study by Cleary and Thomas dealt with the effects of the
bridge and the associated motorways on the prosperity of South Wales and the
West of England, no attempt was made to include an assessment of these broader
aspects in the cost -benefit appraisal. This is not to criticise the authors, for the
difficulties of doing so would be enormous. But such omissions indicate one of
the limitations of cost -benefit studies.

(2) Inadequate data

Cost - benefit studies invariably suffer from inadequacy of the data available. In
this particular study reliable data was collected for the period immediately
after the opening of the bridge, but very little quantitative data existed for

the previous period. When cost – benefit studies are being used as a basis for decision-making, the situation is usually reversed; data can be collected for the situation before the decision to invest, but what will happen after the investment is hypothetical – although useful guidelines can be obtained from looking at other similar investments in this and other countries.

(3)   *Forecasting problems*

The problem of inadequate data links up with the difficulties of reliable forecasting. In order to calculate the full costs and benefits, an assumption has to be made about the length of life of the asset. In this case it was assumed that the bridge would last until 2050, that is eighty-four years from its opening – quite a short life by most comparable standards. On the other hand, because of the discount factor, any benefits accruing in the second half of the next century would have such little value that to assume a longer life would make little difference to the results.

Another difficult item to forecast is future growth in light traffic – depending on such general considerations as the growth of real incomes and population, affecting car-ownership and the increase in leisure. Whilst past trends in car-ownership have been fairly consistent, the intrusion of OPEC, causing the huge rise in petrol prices, will obviously upset any calculations based on these trends.

The growth of commercial traffic is likely to depend heavily on economic growth. In the period in which traffic crossing the bridge was studied, national growth rates were lower than they had been, on average, since the war. Therefore, the authors of the study suggested that their figures were likely to be an underestimate of the growth in commercial traffic. In 1975, growth prospects look less favourable and there is less reason for believing that the growth in traffic has been underestimated.

(4)   *Valuation problems*

A variety of problems of valuation are always raised by cost – benefit studies. Outstanding among these is the problem of valuing time. In valuing work time the question has been raised whether small individual amounts of time saved can be put to use; are twelve savings of five minutes each as valuable as one saving of one hour? More difficult still is the problem of valuing non-work time. Clearly, leisure time saved has some value to the individual, but it could lie anywhere between nothing and the individual's wage rate. Much ingenuity has been exercised in trying to value non-work time saved, but no wholly satisfactory answer has been reached. In this particular study, even if non- work time had been valued at zero, the investment would still have been amply justified; but in some other transport studies the saving in non-work time has formed a major part of the benefit, and whether or not the investment was actuarially justifiable depended on which of a number of possible values was put on non-work time.

Exercises

(8.6) What considerations would be properly taken into account by a government department assessing whether or not to build a particular bridge which would not be taken into account by a private entrepreneur, with the right to levy a toll, who faced the same decisions?

(8.7) Discuss the significance of the valuation of time in a cost – benefit transport study.

(8.8) 'There is an irreducible element of subjectivity in a cost – benefit analysis.' Discuss this assertion in the light of the Severn Bridge study.

CASE 24.   ASSESSMENT OF PUBLIC SPENDING PROGRAMMES, 1974/5 – 1978/9

This case study summarises the main comments of the Report (of March 1975) of the General Sub-Committee of the House of Commons Expenditure Committee on the White Paper, *Public Expenditure to 1978/79*. It illustrates both the work of the General Sub-Committee, which, in recent Reports, has begun to take on something of the role of a General Economic Policy Committee, and the system of public expenditure projections, and it gives some indications why the public expenditure survey system has recently fallen somewhat into disrepute.

The General Sub-Committee took evidence from Treasury witnesses on three occasions and had the benefit of the services of Mr T. S. Ward of the Department of Applied Economics, University of Cambridge, as Specialist Adviser.

The Main Criticisms

The Committee made a series of cogent criticisms and comments on the White Paper, including the following.

(1) *Incompatibility of balance-of-payments target and projected growth rate*

The White paper on public expenditure contained medium-term projections of the demands on resources on the basis of three growth rates, of which the so-called 'central case' postulated a $3\frac{1}{2}$ per cent average rate of growth per annum in domestic output, 1974–9.* At the same time the White Paper stated that the government's aim was to close the non-oil deficit on the balance of payments as soon as possible and to go on to achieve an over-all balance. The Committee expressed extreme doubt about the compatibility of the balance-of-payments target and the growth rate. The Committee's Specialist Adviser calculated that, at this growth rate, to achieve the balance-of-payments target, the volume of exports would need to increase by an average of 10 per cent per annum. Previous experience suggested that such a rate was most unlikely to be achieved. The Committee accepted that it would be feasible to eliminate the balance-of-payments deficit at a lower growth rate – which would generate less imports, and hence would not require as high a rate of export expansion – but they concluded' 'We cannot see how the Treasury's balance of payments target and the White Paper's assumed $3\frac{1}{2}$ per cent rise in output can be attained simultaneously.'

(2) *The strange relationship between public expenditure and growth*

The Committee pointed out the peculiar relationship implied by the White Paper between the rate of growth of gross domestic product (G.D.P.) and that of public

*The 'central case' of the White Paper postulated 3 per cent growth 1973–9; this corresponds to $3\frac{1}{2}$ per cent for the period 1974–9.

expenditure. The economic situation in 1974 and 1975 was such that little growth would occur in these years; a $3\frac{1}{2}$ per cent average growth rate in G.D.P. over the five-year period of the survey therefore implied a growth rate of over 4 per cent per annum for the later years. But the public expenditure profile in the White Paper was the exact reverse of this. The Committee recognised the possibility that this inverse relationship between public spending and G.D.P. might be regarded as counter-cyclical – but this was certainly not clear from the Treasury's evidence. The Committee recommended that in future years the White Paper should state the expected path of output growth (not just the average growth over the period).

(3)   *The nearer the year the higher the estimate*

Following up this second point the Committee drew attention to the fact that the White Paper's pattern of big increases in expenditure in the near future followed by small increases later was the same pattern as in the previous three White Papers. The forecasts in all three for what were originally 'later' years were subsequently revised upwards. The Committee continued: 'We suspect that this pattern has the primary purpose of reducing the average rate of increase in forecast expenditure over each survey period. Were this to become a perpetual feature of the Public Expenditure White Papers, the Treasury would create a credibility gap which would largely nullify their usefulness and cast doubt upon the whole P.E.S.C. system.'

(4)   *The costs of variations in spending plans*

The Committee reiterated their concern, mentioned in an earlier Report (*Public Expenditure, Inflation and the Balance of Payments,* 1974), at the potentially large costs of disruption caused by many switches in direction in the expenditure plans for one year. They recorded their opinion that these costs were 'not fully taken into account, quantified and weighed against the benefits of the proposed action when changes were made for short-term demand management reasons'. The Committee therefore recommended the Treasury to undertake a research study into the effect and cost of changes in forecasts of capital expenditure, even if it had to be restricted to a limited field.

Exercises

(8.9) In what ways did the House of Commons Expenditure Committee (through the Report prepared by its General Sub-Committee) query the credibility of the projections contained in the White Paper, *Public Expenditure to 1978/79*?

CASE 25.   THE COST OF CONCORDE

Introduction

This case study is based on the Sixth and Seventh Reports from the Committee of
Public Accounts, session 1972 - 3, *Development and Production of the Concorde
Aircraft.* The two reports were published together because the Seventh Report
simply up-dates the figures of the Sixth.

The purpose of the case study is (1) to show how the Public Accounts Committee (P.A.C.) Works; (2) to give some idea of the difficulties of public expenditure control of the cost of products of advanced technology; (3) to show the
particular difficulties which arise where the product is subject to international
agreements.

The Committee examined witnesses from the Ministry of Defence and the
Department of Trade and Industry on four occasions in April 1973; it was able to
draw on the Reports of early P.A.C.s which had looked at the expenditure on
Concorde and the Reports of an Estimates Committee in 1963 and of an Expenditure Committee, 1971 - 2; the P.A.C. also had the benefit of specialist advice
from the Comptroller and Auditor-General and his staff.

The Reports

In its Reports the Committee reviews the history of the Concorde project; examines
the Anglo - French agreement; analyses the escalation in estimated costs; scrutinises
in detail the arrangements for control of contractors' costs; looks at the production,
sales and pricing arrangements; and then records its conclusions.

The background to the project

Concorde had its origin in a committee set up by the Ministry of Supply in 1956
to examine the technical feasibility of a supersonic aircraft. In 1959 the committee reported that the time had come for industry to begin serious design work
on a transatlantic aircraft carrying a payload of about 150 passengers at about
twice the speed of sound. The manufacturers were asked to consider collaboration
with foreign industries. A project submitted by the British Aircraft Corporation
came nearest to the committee's specifications (there were slightly fewer
passengers), and discussions between the French and British governments, and the
firms concerned eventually led to an Anglo - French agreement in November
1962. This agreement provided that the principle of collaboration should be
equal responsibility for the project as a whole, with equal sharing of the work,
the expenditure incurred by the two governments and the proceeds of sale.

Escalation of costs

When the Concorde Agreement was signed in 1962, the cost of development, including jigging and tooling for production, was estimated at £150 – 170 million (excluding expenditure at government research departments). Tables 8.8 and 8.9 indicate the successive increases in estimates and costs and summarise the causes of the escalation.

TABLE 8.8

Date of estimate	Total estimate (£m.)	U.K. share (£m.)	U.K. expenditure (£m.)
Nov 1962	150– 70	75 – 85	
July 1964	275	140	
June 1966	450	250	45
May 1969	730	340	170 to 31 Mar 1969
May 1972	970	480	330 to 31 Mar 1972
June 1973	1065	525	380 to 30 Apr 1973

SOURCE: *Development and Production of Concorde Aircraft,* Seventh Report of P.A.C. (July 1973) table A, appendix 2.

TABLE 8.9

Changes in estimates from Table 8.8	Cause of escalation				
	Changes in economic conditions* (£m.)	Programme slippage (£m.)	Revision of estimates (£m.)	Additional development tasks (£m.)	Other adjustments (£m.)
Nov 1962 to July 1964 (£m. 170–275)	18	–	47	40	–
July 1964 to June 1966 (£m. 275–450)	34	–	38	103	–
June 1966 to May 1969 (£m. 450–730)	107	–	58	115	–
May 1969 to May 1972 (£m. 730–970)	83	26	22	70	39
May 1972 to June 1973 (£m. 970–1065)	65	20	10	–	–
INCREASE IN ESTIMATES	307	46	175	328	39
TOTAL					895m.

*Covers changes in the levels of wages and prices of materials and in exchange rates.

SOURCE: *Development and Production of the Concorde Aircraft,* Seventh Report of P.A.C. (July 1973) table B, appendix 20

The 'additional development tasks' included major modifications to wings, fuselage and engines if the plane was to achieve the desired performance and to meet new requirements of the airlines and of civil-aviation authorities responsible for airworthiness certification. Major design modifications, in their turn, resulted in programme slippage.

Even if all increase due to economic conditions were eliminated, the June 1973 estimates would still be well over four times the original estimates. As the Committee puts it: 'The history of rising costs makes it clear that neither the contractors nor the responsible departments have been able to assess with any accuracy the magnitude of the technical problems or the expenditure involved.' As the Department argued, once a project like Concorde was started, if the engineers of both countries agreed that massive changes were essential to meet the specification, either the modifications had to be introduced or the project discontinued. In these circumstances the Department could only consider whether the estimated cost, and any later increase in costs, were reasonable, and control then became a matter of ensuring that only approved work was paid for.

Conclusions

From its detailed consideration of the costing arrangements the Committee concluded that there were 'weaknesses in the administrative and control arrangements'. For example, there was a long delay in introducing costing schemes which gave an incentive to the contractor to economise; that when introduced, these schemes offered only mild incentives; and the Committee endorsed the Ministry's view that in principle it would have been better had the company's money been at risk as well as the government's. None the less, the Committee appreciated that the officials administering the project 'attempted to exercise some control in intractable circumstances'.

> Officials have worked within two constraints: the first was the decision of the British and French governments to launch an advanced technology project of an exceptionally speculative kind: the second was the decision to proceed with the project in one stage only, that is to completion, instead of breaking such a speculative enterprise into a number of phases at which the option to withdraw would have been open to each government. Given these constraints, we do not believe that it was in the hands of officials to make major savings in this project.

On the Anglo-French agreement, the Committee expressed concern about the decision to divide the work equally (irrespective of which contractors in which country might be able to do the work most efficiently), and about the lack of arrangements for rectifying imbalances in spending between the two countries. The Committee then further explored the second of the constraints referred to in the previous paragraph. They concluded:

We question whether in future, and in the light of the Concorde experience, governments should be as willing to deprive themselves of all unilateral discretion as to their continued involvement in projects the costs of which might rapidly escalate far above target. Perhaps some reconciliation can be found between the conflicting demands of genuine national commitment to international collaboration in advanced technology on the one hand, and the need to retain some national discretion about the extent of involvement in particular projects on the other, by defining stages at which an option can be exercised unilaterally if certain criteria of cost or performance are not met.

The 'General Conclusions' of the Report contained one further comment of interest. The Committee complained of 'excisions from the evidence on grounds of confidentiality' and warned 'Commercial confidentiality must not be made an excuse for the concealment of facts material to the determination of the public interest.'

Exercises

(8.10) What proportion of the addition to the original estimate of Concorde's costs was due directly to major modifications of design?

(8.11) in what ways did the terms of the agreement between the British and French governments make more difficult the attempt to secure an efficient use of resources in relation to the Concorde project?

Supplementary exercises

(8.12) Using the latest *National Income Blue Book*, extend Table 8.1 to bring it up to date.

(8.13) 'Private opulence and public squalor.' With what justification can this dictum of Professor J. K. Galbraith be applied to Britain in the mid-1970s?

(8.14) Compare and contrast the work of the House of Commons Public Accounts Committee and the General Sub-Committee of the Expenditure Committee.

Sources and References

Control of Public Expenditure, Plowden Report, Cmnd. 1432 (London: H.M.S.O., 1961).

National Income and Expenditure Blue Books (London: H.M.S.O., annually).

A. J. PEACOCK and J. WISEMAN, *The Growth of Public Expenditure in the United Kingdom* (London: Allen & Unwin, 1961).

M. PESTON, 'On the Nature and Extent of the Public Sector', *Three Banks Review* (Sep 1965).

G. H. PETERS, *Cost - Benefit Analysis and Public Expenditure,* Eaton Paper 8, 3rd edn (London: Institute of Economic Affairs, 1973).

Public Expenditure White Papers (London: H.M.S.O., annually).

Report of the Committee of Enquiry into Certain Contracts made with Bristol-Siddeley Engines Ltd. (London: H.M.S.O., Feb 1968).

Reports of the Inquiry into the Pricing of Ministry of Aviation Contracts: First Report, Cmnd. 2428 (London: H.M.S.O., July 1964); *Second Report,* Cmnd. 2581 (London: H.M.S.O., Feb 1965).

C. T. SANDFORD and A. ROBINSON, 'Public Spending', *The Banker* (Nov 1975).

CHAPTER 9

Taxation

C.T. Sandford

Summary of Background Material

In general taxes are levied to cut down demand for goods and services by the
private sector of the economy (households, private firms) so that resources are
available for the government's purposes without creating inflation.

A tax, however, is rarely 'neutral' in its effects. Its imposition has consequences
additional to the release of resources for government purposes; economists seek
to unravel these consequences in 'incidence' analysis.

These modifying effects of taxation include the 'distortion' of consumers'
choice, alterations in the organisation and methods of production, variations in
the total supply of the factors of production and changes in the distribution of
income and of capital (or wealth).

Sometimes these 'distortions' are an incidental and unintentional effect of the
general purpose of taxation. At other times a government may choose a particular
form of tax to promote particular changes – indeed, often because the government
considers that there are other 'distortions' in the economy which it wishes to
counteract; e.g. it is often argued that heavy taxation of tobacco and alcoholic
drinks can be justified on the grounds that the consumption of each involves
social costs (e.g. health and driving hazards) not included in the private costs of
production.

Income Tax and Demand for Leisure

One of the most important and controversial of the issues of tax incidence concerns
the so-called 'disincentive effects' of income taxation, more specifically the effect
of income tax on willingness to undertake paid work. Consideration of the problem
in terms of the demand for leisure is convenient, for we can then use concepts
familiar in demand theory. A man's time is considered to be divided into two
parts, work and leisure; hence an increased demand for leisure necessarily reduces
willingness to work.

An increase in income tax reduces net personal income; a taxpayer, feeling
worse off, can afford less of most things, including leisure; he therefore tends to
reduce his consumption of leisure, that is, he does more work. This is the income
effect.

However, at the same time there is a substitution effect. The cost of leisure has fallen; less income is forgone by taking an extra hour of leisure (that is doing an hour's less work). On this count the taxpayer will tend to consume more leisure, that is do less work. Thus these two effects work in opposite directions,* and economic theory does not tell us which is the stronger.

However, theory can take us a little further. The income effect works through the change in the terms on which income can be acquired at the margin. The larger the substitution effect relatively to the income effect, the larger the disincentive (or the less the incentive) effects of tax. Progressive taxes (where the rate of tax rises more than proportionately to income) are characterised by marginal rates which are high compared with average rates. Thus an income-receiver paying a progressive income tax is likely to reduce work more (or increase it less) than if he had paid the same sum under a proportional income tax.

From our theory, however, we still do not know whether more or less work will result from a progressive income tax; this issue can only be resolved by empirical study.

Taxation and Welfare Payments

Taxation affects the distribution of income either as an incidental effect of government policy or by deliberate intent. Welfare benefits not only affect income distribution, but, like taxation, may influence the supply of labour. Thus, where welfare benefits are subject to an income means test, if a man increases his income by extra work, he may lose welfare payments; the effect is then the same as if he had suffered a tax on the extra income. The loss of cash (or cash-equivalent) benefits resulting from an extra £1 per week of income has been called by Professor Prest an 'implicit' marginal tax rate. †

A person who increases his income may be subject to both explicit and implicit marginal taxation. Indeed, it is possible for the combined explicit and implicit tax rates to exceed the increase in income, that is to amount to over 100 per cent of marginal income. In these circumstances, at that range of income, if the individual realises what is happening, he can hardly fail to be deterred from work effort. The income and substitution effects both operate in the same direction – to reduce the amount of work done; not only will the substitution effect encourage him to replace work by leisure, but cutting his work effort actually adds to his income.

---

*Students familiar with general demand theory will know that a fall in the price of a commodity leads to a positive substitution effect and usually a positive and invariably a small income effect. Hence, save in the most exceptional circumstances, a fall in a commodity price leads to an increase in purchases. A fall in the price of leisure, however, whilst it has a positive substitution effect, also has a negative, and possibly large, income effect.

† A. R. Prest, *Social Benefits and Tax Rates* (London: Institute of Economic Affairs, 1970).

Taxation and the E.E.C.

With Britain a member of the E.E.C. the structure and rates of tax have to take account of harmonisation policy. The rationale behind the E.E.C. is the promotion of economic efficiency, and the emphasis in harmonisation policy has been on the removal of tax barriers which would hamper or distort the movement of goods or factors of production. The main taxes which it is intended should be harmonised are therefore taxes on goods and services (general sales taxes and excise duties) and corporation tax (which affects the movement of capital). But other considerations also affect harmonisation. The Community budget requires a tax with the same base throughout the Community. Also, if economic and monetary union ever becomes a reality and rates of exchange between Community members become effectively fixed, then it will be important to ensure that members have the flexibility to be able to adjust some tax rates as a means of controlling balance-of-payments disequilibria with other members.

Tax harmonisation involves three stages: agreement on a common form; a common base; and common rates, to the extent that this is held to be necessary.

So far progress has been very slow. Most progress has been made with the general sales tax, and V.A.T. has been adopted by all Community members, but the second and third stages of harmonisation of V.A.T. are very much in the melting pot; and harmonisation of excise duties and corporation tax is much further behind.

Illustration by Case Studies

Case 26 briefly illustrates the effect of taxation on industrial structure. Case 27 outlines two connected research studies of the effect of income tax on work effort. This is followed by Case 28 which demonstrates the 'poverty trap', the way in which taxation with unco-ordinated means-tested benefits can lead to implicit and explicit marginal tax rates which together may reduce incentives to work, undermine the welfare intention and combine to keep a man in poverty. Finally, in Case 29, we examine the progress of harmonisation of V.A.T. in the E.E.C. up to 1975.

CASE 26   TAXATION AND BUSINESS STRUCTURE: FIRMS 'GO PUBLIC' TO MINIMISE THE EFFECTS OF DEATH DUTY ON THE BUSINESS

The shareholders' only reason for parting with a portion of their interest in the business is to create a marketable security thus enabling them to make provision for possible future taxation and death duties without creating financial embarrassment to the business.

The above notice appeared as part of the 'Offer for Sale' of shares in the famous whisky company, Teacher's Distillers, which was converting from a private to a public company. Although the Offer for Sale was published in *The Times* as long ago as 10 January 1949, the example remains no less relevant today and is a good one because of the explicit statement of the tax reason for going public.

Another famous private company which has gone public much more recently, partly because of death duties, is J. Sainsbury, the grocery and supermarket chain, which in 1972 had 192 branches. A report in *The Times Business News*, 20 October 1972, based on a statement issued by the company, said that a public flotation was under consideration for the latter part of 1973. The report stated: 'Death duty considerations rank high among the reasons for contemplating a public offer.'

The problem for the private company is that, although death duties are levied on personal wealth and not on companies as such, where a major shareholder in a private company dies, his executors may only be able to meet death-duty liabilities by selling a large block of shares. The market for shares in a private company is narrow. Where existing shareholders are unable to buy up the shares, new shareholders must be found. Especially if the majority of the shares are held by members of the same family, outsiders will be reluctant to buy; as minority shareholders they would be at the mercy of the family on vital matters like dividend policy and directors' remuneration. Thus, especially under conditions of forced sale, if an outside buyer can be found, the price realised for the shares might be low. This would not only be hard on the heirs of the deceased shareholder, it might also prejudice the terms on which the firm could raise new capital in the future. One method of meeting the situation is to invite a takeover. Another method, where the firm is large and profitable enough, as in the examples quoted, is to convert to a public company, thus dispersing the shareholding and widening the market and so reducing the likelihoood that the death of a large shareholder will adversely affect the business.

The conversion to public-company form of Teacher's Distillers and of J. Sainsbury took place when the death duty was estate duty. The change from estate duty to capital transfer tax in 1974 – 5 has accentuated the problem of death duty for the private firm. Estate duty (but not any capital gains tax) could be avoided if the shareholder gave his shares away and survived the gift by a prescribed number of years (which was seven at the time estate duty was abolished). Capital transfer tax blocks this loophole by taxing gifts and also providing that taxable gifts should be added together and taken into account in determining the rate of tax on future gifts and on the estate left at death.*

Exercises

(9.1) (i) Explain how it is that death duty, which is levied on personal wealth, may have adverse effects on a private company.

(ii) How may these effects be reduced by a private company converting to a public company?

---

*In fact, to ease the problems which capital transfer tax causes the private business, the *Finance Act* of 1976 provided for a 30 per cent reduction, for tax purposes, in the value of business assets transferred.

CASE 27. THE EFFECTS OF TAXATION
ON THE SUPPLY OF LABOUR

Our study under this heading consists of two related surveys of the effects of income tax on the work effort of two groups of highly paid professional men. The first survey was carried out by Professor G. F. Break in 1956, published in the *British Tax Review* (June 1957); the second was a 'replication' of Break's survey some twelve years later by D. F. Fields and W. T. Stanbury, published in *Public Finance* (1970). We shall look at the first in some detail, but as the second was identical in methodology, we shall concentrate on the main difference in the findings.

Professor Break's Survey of 1956

Characteristics of the survey

The method revolved around interviews with respondents who consisted of self-employed accountants and solicitors. They were relatively free to vary their work effort. Nearly two-thirds were subject to surtax.* They were knowledgeable about tax rates. The sample was divided into two parts: (1) London; (2) small and medium-size towns and cities in predominantly rural and agricultural areas. Selection was by random means from the lists of the Law Society and the Institute of Chartered Accountants. Of the 327 names obtained, 306 were actually interviewed.

Interview procedure

Stage I.   The respondent was invited to discuss his decisions to take on or refuse work for the firm, and his outside earning opportunities. Respondents over 45 were asked about retirement plans. The influence of taxation on the respondent's incentives to work entered the discussion only if he introduced it.

Stage II.   Those who had not mentioned taxation on their own initiative were invited to consider its effects on the amount of work they did.

Stage III.   The respondent was asked to indicate his pre-tax professional income and pre-tax total income by marking the appropriate bracket on a prepared card. Only eight of the 306 refused to disclose income.

Unadjusted tax incentive and disincentive ratios

Table 9.1 summarises the responses.

*Surtax was a separate tax, additional to income tax, on high incomes. In 1973 income tax and surtax were combined into one unified personal income tax.

TABLE 9.1

Type of tax effect	Proportion	Percentage
(1) Day-to-day tax disincentive	54/306	18
(2) Day-to-day tax incentive	18/306	6
(3) Incentive influence at retirement (postponement)	78/150	52
(4) Disincentive influence at retirement (earlier)	Nil	Nil
(5) Total tax incentive	92/306	31
(6) Some kind of tax influence	128/306	42

Adjusted tax incentive and disincentive ratios

When doubtful cases were removed (those who were vague about effects of taxation, or where the influence cited referred to some hypothetical circumstance in the future, such as a still distant retirement), the definite tax influences were as follows.

(1) Total disincentives: 40/306 or 13 per cent;
(2) Total incentives: 31/306 or 10 per cent; and
(3) Total influenced by taxation: 71/306 or 23 per cent.

Types of tax disincentive: refusal of work offered; reduced incentive to seek new clients; shifting of work load within the firm to other partners or additional staff hired for the purpose.

Types of tax incentive: postponement of retirement (where taxation was the main reason cited and the respondents were already very close to retirement age or had already postponed it); increased work on a day-to-day basis.

If standards of admissible evidence were raised still higher and those respondents excluded (*a*) those who had reacted to taxation only on one or two special occasions, and (*b*) those for whom taxation was simply one amongst several motivating factors, the gross tax effect fell below 15 per cent, of whom just over half were incentive cases.

These figures do not enable us to say anything about how much the supply of labour was increased or decreased or the value of the services gained or lost.

Professor Break's main conclusion

Some people do indeed react to high income-tax rates by working less hard than they otherwise would, but others behave in exactly the opposite way, being more or less forced by taxation to work harder. These opposing groups are not only small but of approximately the same size, being separated in this study by only a few percentage points, and significantly (depending on the interpretation given to the evidence) the incentive group is frequently the larger of the two.

Subsidiary conclusions

(1) There was some indication that tax disincentives were less frequent amongst London respondents. Possibly the pressures or pleasures of urban life tend to offset the incentive-inhibiting effects of high tax rates. (In terms of economic theory, for some people leisure and income might be complementary goods; more leisure without more income might not seem very worth while.)

(2) Respondents who paid tax at a marginal rate of 70 per cent or more were considerably more subject to tax disincentives than those facing lower rates.

Fields and Stanbury's Survey of 1970

The sample was chosen in the same way as Break's and consisted of practising chartered accountants and solicitors. There was a response from 285 of a final sample size of 319. Break's questionnaire was used and there was a similar breakdown of the responses.

Of the unadjusted responses, 46 per cent of the sample claimed to experience some sort of tax influence: incentive 22 per cent, disincentive 24 per cent.

When the responses were adjusted to remove doubtful cases, the result was 11 per cent incentive and 19 per cent disincentive. This is a significant difference in the proportion experiencing disincentive effects compared with Break's survey (10 per cent and 13 per cent respectively).

The Fields and Stanbury survey also found (reinforcing Break's conclusions) that:

(1) The proportion of respondents experiencing disincentives increased as income increased; and

(2) The proportion experiencing disincentives in the counties was significantly higher than in London.

Exercises

(9.2) Briefly list the main types of incentive and disincentive effect as revealed by Professor Break's study.

(9.3) What was the importance of voluntary changes in the age of retirement as a response to high rates of income tax?

(9.4) Indicate the limitations of the two studies as general evidence of the effect of income tax on the supply of labour.

CASE 28. THE 'POVERTY TRAP'

It was estimated in the late 1960s that over 1500 different methods of means testing were being used by different local authorities and central government departments.* Most such means tests only applied when there was a special need, e.g. a home help or school-uniform allowance, but many low-wage households with children might in normal circumstances be eligible for four or five means-tested benefits: family income supplement (F.I.S.), rent rebate, rates rebate, free school meals and school milk. At the same time the wage earner would be paying national insurance contributions and might be liable to income tax on marginal earnings. If he gained additional wages the extra might be largely or wholly taken in combined tax and lost benefit.

The data for the following example are drawn from a letter to *The Times* (19 Aug 1975) from Mr Ralph Howell, M.P.

Household:	Man with wife and 3 children
Earnings:	£30 per week
Rent:	£C per week
Rates:	£2 per week

If the man's weekly wage rose by £5 to £35, the effect would be a weekly reduction in his income of 88p; a combined explicit and implicit marginal tax rate of *118* per cent. The details are as shown in Table 9.2.
The evil results can be summarised as follows:

(1) the poor are placed in a situation in which it is almost impossible for them to pull themselves out of poverty by their own efforts (hence the phrase 'poverty trap');

(2) where, as in the example, a household is actually made worse off by a wage increase, there is a failure to alleviate poverty; the household is left with less net income than some government departments considered was needed.

(3) there is a powerful disincentive to work effort;

(4) any incomes policy designed to benefit the low paid (like a £6 per week flat rate increase) is undermined; and

(5) in general, the lack of co-ordination of tax thresholds with means-tested benefits means heavy administrative costs incurred in collecting tax from people and then handing it back to them as means-tested benefits.

In practice some of these effects are modified by ignorance, failure to take up benefits and time lags. Thus the disincentive effect is less than might be thought because wage earners may not realise what is happening, especially as, whilst the extra tax is deducted immediately wages increase, the loss of benefits only takes

*M. Reddin, *Social Services for All* (Fabian Society, 1968).

TABLE 9.2

Extra earnings of £5		
Increase in tax	(£)	
Income tax	1.75	
National insurance contributions	0.27	
	2.02	Explicit marginal tax rate: *40.4* per cent
Loss of benefits		
F.I.S.	1.80	
Rent rebate	0.67	
Rate rebate	0.22	
School meals	0.75	
Free milk	0.42	
	3.86	Implicit marginal tax rate *77.2* per cent
Total reductions	5.88	Combined marginal tax rate *117.6* per cent

place some months later. The failure to claim all benefits due also reduces the disincentive effect – but only at the cost of accentuating poverty.

How has this situation arisen? As David Piachaud writes:

The road which has led to this situation has been paved with good intentions. Each new means-tested scheme was introduced if not to benefit the poorest households, at least to shelter them from some new charge, or from an increase in an established charge. But the burden of these charges, from which the poorest have been exempt, has dragged many more down to poverty. Each means-test appears to have been evolved by the particular central or local government department with scant regard to other means-tests. In this field co-ordinated action has been sadly lacking.*

His final comment applies equally to the relationship between the income levels at which benefits apply and tax thresholds; the problem is accentuated in the United Kingdom by the high marginal rate at which income tax begins (35 per cent in 1975 – 6) and the failure of the tax threshold to rise in line with rapid inflation.

Ideas for a negative income tax or tax-credit scheme have derived much of their recent impetus from the recognised need for co-ordination and simplification in the relationships between taxation and the various means-tested benefits.

*'Poverty and Taxation'; in *Taxation Policy*, ed. B. Crick and W. A. Robson (Harmondsworth: Penguin, 1973) ch. 5.

Exercises

(9.5) What is meant by an 'implicit marginal tax rate'?

(9.6) Explain how it can come about that a man may obtain an increase in wage only to find himself actually worse off.

(9.7) Explain the term 'poverty trap'. How has the poverty trap come about?

CASE 29.   PROGRESS ON GENERAL SALES TAX HARMONISATION WITHIN THE E.E.C. TO 1975

The objectives of this case study are to indicate the slow pace of fiscal harmonisation within the E.E.C., the difficulties of harmonisation and the continuing
process of rethinking both purposes and methods. No attempt is made to assess
the merits or drawbacks of V.A.T. as a sales tax or to analyse its economic
effects except in so far as these issues are incidental to a consideration of the
progress of tax harmonisation.

The Treaty of Rome (25 March 1957), the foundation of the E.E.C., had laid
down, in Article 99, that 'The Commission shall consider in what way the law of
the various Member-States concerning turnover taxes, excise duties and other
forms of indirect taxes can be harmonised in the interest of the Common Market.'
The Commission's method in seeking to implement this article has been to appoint
study groups (sometimes of outside experts, sometimes of internal officials), whose
reports are then discussed in the Commission and in the member states. Then
follows a Proposal for a Directive, a Draft Directive and finally a Directive passed
by the Council of Ministers with the force of law in member states.

Why V.A.T.?

The first tax to be seriously considered for harmonisation was the general sales tax.
The Neumark Report* envisaged ultimate acceptance by all E.E.C. countries of
value-added taxes which would cover all stages of production and distribution,
and which would be identical or nearly identical in all respects – structure, tax
rates and exemptions. The Report recognised that the all-round harmonisation
could only be achieved gradually, but recommended the adoption of value-added
tax by all countries as a first step, with the retail stage left out if necessary, and
with rates as similar as possible.

Why should a general sales tax come first in the programme for fiscal harmonisation, and why should it take the form of value-added tax? The answer to the
first question was that general sales taxes were most akin to tariffs which member
states were in process of getting rid of between themselves. Big differences in
sales taxes could counteract the progress from reducing internal tariffs – for
example, people could cross national boundaries to buy where taxes were lower.
The answer to the second question is that, apart from any general economic
merits that V.A.T. might have, which would apply in any country adopting it, the
tax was particularly attractive to the strongest of the E.E.C. countries; France
already had a V.A.T. – but one which stopped short at the wholesale stage – so few

*The E.E.C. Report on Tax Harmonisation: Report of the Fiscal and Financial
Committee*, Chairman, Professor Fritz Neumark, English translation (Amsterdam,
1963).

administrative changes were necessary for her if V.A.T. became the E.E.C. sales tax. Germany had a 'cascade' or 'gross' turnover tax by which tax was levied on sales of output at all stages of production but without (as in V.A.T.) a deduction of tax paid on input; this cascade tax was recognised as inefficient, creating a distortion in favour of vertical integration* and the Germans were keen to get rid of it; a change to V.A.T. remedied the defect of the cascade tax and could be made with administrative ease as the mechanisms for collecting tax multi-stage were already there. There may have been another factor influencing the E.E.C. countries in their choice of V.A.T.: as a general sales tax it is comparatively evasion-proof. Apart from the retail stage there is both a check on evasion and a self-regulating mechanism, one producer's output tax is another producer's input tax; whilst the former might like to evade by paying less than his due, to do so would be against the interest of the latter, who can offset input tax against his own output tax. At the retail stage, when goods are bought by the final consumer who cannot reclaim, there is no such check; but at least, as compared with a retail sales tax yielding the same revenue, a V.A.T. is less liable to evasion at the retail stage because only a proportion of the total revenue is collected at that stage.

The Adoption of V.A.T.

Two Directives, issued in April 1967, required member countries to accept V.A.T. in place of existing general sales taxes by 1 January 1970, but without any requirement at this stage to adopt uniform rates.

By the due date two countries, Belgium and Italy had failed to comply. Belgium did not wish to introduce the tax at a time of rapidly rising prices and was given an extension to 1 January 1971. Italy caused the most difficulty; for a variety of reasons, including opposition within the country to a whole new tax package of which V.A.T. was a part, the Italian implementation of the Directive was delayed until 1973.

The other countries which subsequently joined the E.E.C. – Denmark, Ireland and the United Kingdom – had all adopted V.A.T., partly in anticipation of membership. Denmark had introduced V.A.T. in 1967 as part of a major tax restructuring; Ireland introduced V.A.T. in 1972; and V.A.T. in the United Kingdom came into force in April 1973, three months after she had joined the Community.

Limited Progress and Changing Objectives

Apart from this universal implementation amongst its enlarged membership of V.A.T. as the common sales tax, little further visible progress has been made

---

*Vertical integration is the combination of firms at different stages in production (e.g. the merger of a spinning firm with a weaving firm) in contrast to horizontal integration, which is the combination of firms at the same stage of production (e.g. the merger of two spinning firms).

towards the objectives set out in the Neumark Report. Table 9.3 indicates the wide differences which continue to exist in rates of V.A.T. Currently, discussion is taking place in the Community on Proposals of the Commission which seek to establish a uniform base, i.e. to ensure that the tax covers the same range of goods and services in each country.

TABLE 9.3
Rates of V.A.T. in the E.E.C. *

Country	Reduced rate (per cent)	Intermediate rate (per cent)	Standard rate (per cent)	Luxury rate (per cent)
Belgium	6	14	18	25
Denmark	–	–	15	–
France	7	17.6	20	33.33
Germany	5.5	–	11	–
Ireland	6.75	–	19.50	36.75†
Italy	6	–	15	18
Luxembourg	5	–	10	–
Netherlands	4	–	16	–
United Kingdom	Zero	–	8	12.5

* U.K. rates as 1975 – 6 budget: other countries as 1974.

†Chargeable once only at importation or point of delivery: otherwise 6.75.

Some of the difficulties of obtaining agreement on harmonisation are indicated by the attitude of the British Government. Thus paragraph 94 of *Membership of the European Community: Report on Renegotiation*‡ states: 'No existing Community rules set the rates of V.A.T. The Government can prevent the adoption of any proposal which would run counter to their stipulation that there should be no harmonisation of V.A.T. which would require the taxation of necessities'; and again, paragraph 95: 'The Government had made it clear that any agreement on harmonisation of the tax base must include a provision for zero rating.'

There is also taking place a more or less continuous process of rethinking about the objectives of harmonisation. The initial emphasis was almost entirely commercial, and the Neumark Committee envisaged uniform V.A.T. rates. Then, recognising the differing dependence of the various states on indirect taxes and the different traditions about taxing 'necessities', the Commission began to think

‡Cmnd. 6003 (March 1975).

in terms of an acceptable band of rates around both a standard rate and a reduced rate, as a more practical target, which would achieve, near enough, the commercial objectives. Now a zero rate has to be accommodated in the thinking.

Further, the objectives for V.A.T. have widened with time. The intention is that the Community Budget shall be derived from its 'own resources' rather than from contributions of member states in accordance with some formula, and that the Community Budget will include sums corresponding to V.A.T. up to 1 per cent. For this purpose a uniform tax base is essential so that each member's contribution shall be fair. This does not, however, prevent some goods being zero rated – which goods would count as part of the tax base.

Finally, moves towards Economic and Monetary Union (E.M.U.) raise a further problem. The object of E.M.U. is, if not a single Community currency, at least fixed exchange rates between members. If that were to be achieved, then any balance-of-payments disequilibrium between a member and the rest of the Community could not be rectified by a movement of the exchange rate. It would therefore seem desirable to allow member states to change their rates of V.A.T. to give them a flexibility for purposes of economic management.

Thus the need for practical political compromise in bringing together countries with different fiscal objectives, traditions and administrative practices, and the continuing evolution of the Community affecting the purposes of harmonisation, mean that the progress of tax harmonisation up to date has been slow and will remain so.

Exercises

(9.8) Why did the E.E.C. begin its tax-harmonisation programme with a general sales tax?

(9.9) Why were France and Germany keen to adopt V.A.T. as the general sales tax of the Community?

(9.10) Is it (a) feasible and (b) desirable that all E.E.C. members hould have the same rates of V.A.T.?

Supplementary exercises

(9.11) What is meant by the income and substitution effects of an increase in income taxation? Compare and contrast the working of those effects in the following situations:

(i) a high-income earner paying income tax at the maximum marginal rate (83 per cent in 1975 – 6); and

(ii) a low-income receiver whose combined explicit and implicit marginal rate of income tax is 110 per cent.

(9.12) What light does the experience of tax harmonisation throw on the view that, in remaining in the European Community, Britain is abandoning its sovereignty for government by Brussels bureaucrats?

Sources and References

In addition to the publications referred to in the text, the following provide useful supplementary information to the case studies:

D. DOSSER, 'Tax Harmonisation in the European Community', *Three Banks Review* (June 1973).

C. T. SANDFORD, *Economics of Public Finance*, 2nd edn (Oxford; Pergamon, 1977) chs 6, 7, 13.

CHAPTER 10

Fiscal and Monetary Policy

C.T. Sandford

Summary of Background Material

The case study to which this background material relates focuses on the years 1967–9; the study examines the fiscal and monetary measures used to manage the economy in the context of the devaluation of sterling, November 1967. The period lends itself to case-study treatment because it shows the close interplay of national and international developments and policies and because the incident of devaluation gives the study a unity. The period can be taken as an occasion – perhaps the last occasion – on which the kinds of fiscal and monetary methods used during most of the post-war period achieved an appreciable measure of success – even though the success was not complete and the methods were currently subject to considerable criticism both on matters of detail and on fundamentals.

Since 1970 there has been a veritable ferment of change in the fields of policy and ideas: a new policy of competition and credit control in the banking world; floating instead of fixed exchange rates; a breakdown in the relationship between unemployment and inflation – which hitherto had appeared to be stable; and the growth of 'monetarism', which, already emerging in 1969, has since gathered many new adherents amongst economists and politicians; all this against a background of inflation and unemployment worse than at any time since the Second World War.

The post-1970 developments are not so much a background to the case study as a sequel. To some extent, but by no means wholly, they are an outcome of criticisms expressed in 1969 and of modes of thinking already evident then. But, in any case, the recent changes are far too important to be ignored in any survey of monetary and fiscal policy. The best way of incorporating them has seemed to be to present the background material in two parts. First, there is a review of post-war monetary and fiscal policy up to 1967–9 (much as it appeared in the first edition of this book), so that the policy measures of that period can be seen in the context in which they were taken, including the criticisms made of them at the time. Then there is a second section, by way of a postscript, which briefly reviews the main developments since 1970.

The 1944 Employment White Paper to 1970

In 1944 the coalition government, with the approval of all political parties, published a White Paper on *Employment Policy* in which government in the United Kingdom accepted the responsibility for maintaining a 'high and stable level of employment'.

The government was able to take on this responsibility because of increased understanding of the causes of unemployment – an understanding resulting from the work of economists in the 1930s and in particular of J. M. Keynes. Keynes stressed that the general level of employment depended on the level of aggregate demand (that is total expenditure) for goods and services. Employers would employ workers if they expected that there would be a demand for the products which the workers helped to make. Thus the demand for labour was a derived demand depending on the demand for goods and services.

Aggregate demand for goods and services (E) can be divided into demand for private consumption goods and services (C), demand for private investment (I), government demand (G) – which in turn can be divided into consumption and investment demand – and net exports (X), * that is exports of goods and services minus imports. All these demands create domestic employment. Thus

$$E \text{ (aggregate demand)} = C + I + G + X.$$

In the first part of this section we shall largely ignore the complications of international trade. With that simplification it could be said that the task of government was seen as being the maintenance of aggregate demand at full-employment level.† If aggregate demand fell below that necessary for full employment, then the government should increase effective demand. On the other hand, when resources were fully employed, if aggregate demand was in excess of aggregate supply, the government should curtail demand to avoid inflationary pressures on prices.

The two main groups of policy measures by which governments sought to secure full employment without inflation were fiscal and monetary.

Fiscal policy

Fiscal policy consists of altering the level of aggregate demand by variations in taxation and government expenditure. The government sets a certain target figure of employment (say, 98 per cent of those seeking work at the current wage level)

---

*Strictly speaking gross exports of goods and services create aggregate demand and domestic employment regardless of the level of imports. But imports reduce domestic demand and employment and it is therefore convenient to use the short-hand of net exports as adding to aggregate demand. X may of course be negative.

†Full employment does not mean 100 per cent employment of those seeking work; in any dynamic economy there will always be some people unemployed as a result of, for example, changing technology and changing tastes. Full employment represents a practicable target which allows for some unemployment.

and estimates for a short period ahead, say one year, the likely level of the main components of aggregate demand. If the forecast suggests that demand would be insufficient to maintain employment at the target level, then the government can add to effective demand in one or more of the following ways:

(1) increase C by reducing taxation on income and/or consumers' outlay, thus raising private disposable incomes;

(2) increase I by, say, bigger tax allowances on investment;

(3) increase G by expenditure on public investment ('public works') or on current services such as the health service or cash transfer payments such as family allowances.*

If the government budgetary forecast suggests that inflation threatens, then these measures are applied in reverse, e.g. taxes increased to curtail consumption. Such tax increases must not of course be matched by increased government expenditure. The object is that the government should receive more than it spends. Conversely, when unemployment threatens, the government should budget to spend more than it receives. A budget surplus is used to combat inflation, a deficit to combat unemployment.

The various fiscal measures open to a government vary in their efficiency as instruments for managing the economy. Important criteria are the following:

(1) The total effect on demand of any given measure, e.g. £x million of public investment will give a bigger multiplier effect than £x million of tax reduction, some of which is saved by the immediate beneficiaries.

(2) The speed of introduction and application, e.g. changes in outlay taxes can be applied more speedily than income-tax changes (where new code numbers have to be calculated), and both these measures are speedier in raising employment than increases in public investment. A particular flexibility was given to outlay taxes by the 'regulator' provisions, which, since the early 1960s, have permitted Chancellors to vary customs and excise duties by up to 10 per cent of existing rates in any one financial year without prior approval of Parliament.

(3) The extent to which a measure can be directed to a particular area, where unemployment may start and from which it may spread; e.g. investment, public or private, may be more readily directed to a particular area than changes in major taxes.

In deciding which measures to adopt, the government cannot ignore their effect on its other objectives, such as social policy and economic growth; to check inflation by raising taxes on goods of widespread consumption might increase inequalities in real-income distribution but be more favourable to economic growth than curtailing investment.

In the period up to 1970 most reliance was placed on fiscal (rather than

* Cash transfers raise private disposable incomes, and their effects can most conveniently be considered under our first heading of increasing C.

monetary) policy. During the period the fact that unemployment rarely rose
above $2\frac{1}{2}$ per cent, and was generally less than 2 per cent, suggests a considerable
measure of success in maintaining full employment; but policy was less effective
in checking inflation, retail prices rising at about 4 per cent per annum on
average over the period. Partly because of this failure to curb inflation, but also
for other reasons, notably the slower rate of economic growth of the United
Kingdom compared with most other industrial countries, the 1960s saw
increasing dissatisfaction with budgetary policy.

Limitations and criticisms of fiscal policy. These can be categorised as follows.

(1) An annual review of the economy was felt to be both too infrequent and
also insufficiently long term; too infrequent for 'fine-tuning' of the economy;
too short term for a broader perspective. Hence the later years of this period
saw more frequent tax and expenditure changes in a succession of mini-budgets,
combined with the introduction of longer-term projections in the form of
indicative plans (see Chapter 12). Neither of these changes noticeably improved
the management of the economy.

(2) In employment policy the emphasis shifted from the need to avoid
general unemployment to the need to raise employment in particular regions of
the economy at a time when employment was full or 'over-full' in other regions.
Most of the instruments of fiscal policy do not readily lend themselves to this
selective treatment, although regional variation in investment grants and Regional
Employment Premiums were introduced.

(3) Most of the criticism of fiscal policy stemmed from its inadequacy to
control inflation. Three main arguments, which overlap somewhat, were advanced.

(*a*) Cutting demand by fiscal measures is a blunt instrument in so far as inflation
is cost-generated. Cuts in demand may only be able to check cost inflation if
pressed to the point at which they cause an unacceptable level of unemployment.
Hence the attempts to formulate a prices and incomes policy.

(*b*) Increases in taxation are partly ineffective against inflation because people
react against the attempt to cut their consumption by reducing saving.

(*c*) A general argument advanced by Mr Colin Clark,* which in part comprehends
the other two, is that, for a variety of reasons, higher taxes will not, *in the long
run*, check inflation. High taxes reduce the supply of the factors of production to
the economy as a whole and hence the rate of economic growth; they generate cost
inflation by stimulating wage earners and executives to seek a level of remuneration
which offsets the tax; and high taxes, especially high profits taxes, make employers
less resistant to wage and salary demands and generally careless about increases in
other costs (e.g. expense accounts).

(*d*) Allied to these arguments on the limitations of fiscal policy as a means of
controlling inflation is the view, given increasing prominence, that fiscal policy

*C. Clark, *Taxmanship,* Hobart Paper 26 (London: Institute of Economic
Affairs, 1964).

needs to be supported by monetary policy, including control over the money supply, if its effect is not to be offset.

At this point let us examine this second means of controlling unemployment and inflation.

Monetary policy

Monetary policy has always tended to be surrounded with an aura of mystery and has often been a subject of controversy, as at present.

The traditional methods.   The classic weapons of monetary management have been Bank Rate and open-market operations.

Bank Rate was the minimum rate at which the Bank of England would rediscount (purchase) first-class bills of exchange or Treasury bills, or lend to the discount houses on the security of such bills. It was important because other interest rates, notably the deposit and advances rate of commercial banks, were linked to it by convention, so that a change in Bank Rate was associated with changes in the level of short-term interest rates and also of long-term rates, to the extent that the changes in short-term rates were considered likely to be of long duration. Changes in Bank Rate also had a psychological effect, as a symbol of government intention.

Open-market operations consist of the sale or purchase by the Bank of England of government bills or bonds. These transactions have the effect of varying the size of bankers' deposits with the Bank of England and therefore the cash – deposits ratio and are the traditional means by which the Bank controls the supply of money (that is notes, coins and bank deposits transferable by cheque). The effect of a policy to increase the supply of money (by the Bank purchasing securities, that is exchanging securities for money) is also to lower interest rates, since the purchases tend to raise the price of securities (and hence reduce their yield).

A policy of low interest rates and plentiful credit ('cheap' money) encourages borrowing and spending and hence is appropriate against a slump; high interest rates and tight credit ('dear' money) discourage spending, particularly investment expenditure, and can check inflation.

Other methods.   During this period the traditional methods of control were modified and new methods introduced. From 1951 Bank Rate changes were frequent, but open-market operations were not used in their traditional way; instead emphasis has shifted from the 'cash ratio' to the 'liquidity ratio'. After the revival of monetary policy in 1951, the banks were given to understand by the Bank of England that they were expected to maintain their liquid assets at a minimum percentage of deposits, originally 30 per cent, reduced to 28 per cent in October 1963.

This change in emphasis was accompanied by new methods of control: loan requests, special deposits and the regulation of hire-purchase terms.

(1) *Loan requests.* Requests were a made to banks in two forms: (*a*) to look sympathetically on applicants for loans for some purposes (e.g. to finance exports, 'productive' investment in manufacturing industry and agriculture) and pro-with disfavour on other applicants (e.g. for purchases of consumer goods or property development apart from house-building); (*b*) to limit their total advances.

These requests had almost the force of law, for the *Bank of England Act of 1946* conferred on the Bank the right to embody the recommendations in legally binding directives if they were not heeded. This power has never been invoked, but in June 1969 a new sanction was applied: the rate of interest paid by the Bank of England on special deposits was halved until the banks reduced their advances below the specified ceiling. During the 1960s the policy of 'loan requests' was extended to non-bank financial intermediaries, e.g. hire-purchase companies and building societies.

(2) *Special deposits.* In July 1958 the Bank was empowered to call for 'special deposits' from the clearing banks and the Scottish banks; interest would be paid on them, but they would not count as liquid assets for the purpose of calculating the liquidity ratio. Thus the effect of a call for special deposits (the first of which was made in April 1960) was to transfer part of the banks' assets from the 'liquid' to the 'non-liquid' category.

(3) *Hire-purchase regulations.* It is convenient to include government-imposed limits on consumer loan terms as part of monetary policy. Since the Second World War the government have made frequent changes in minimum down-payments and maximum repayment periods as a method of cutting consumers' demand for durable goods; e.g. to check inflationary pressures down-payments ratios are increased and maximum repayments periods reduced.

Limitations of monetary policy. The *traditional methods* - reducing interest rates, increasing the quantity of money by Bank Rate and open-market operations - may be insufficient to avoid a slump or promote recovery. Businessmen, pessimistic about the future demand for their products, may not be willing to invest even though cheap credit is readily available. Moreover, there is a limit (well above zero) below which the rate of interest cannot be pushed.

The limitations of the traditional weapons of monetary policy to check inflation are of a different kind.

(1) There is some doubt whether small increases in interest rates and credit restriction by the banks will reduce investment,* especially when banks are not

*This issue is considered in detail in *Case Studies in Economics: Principles of Economics*, ch. 9.

the only sources of credit available to borrowers; and still more doubt whether a rise in interest rates will increase saving, that is reduce consumption.

(2) A policy of really dear money is likely to conflict with government housing policy and significantly raise the cost of National Debt interest.

(3) Several disadvantages follow because the main impact of the traditional measures is on investment rather than consumption: they check inflation at the expense of long-term economic growth; although flexible in the sense that they can be speedily introduced, they take considerable time to exert full effect, for investment projects can rarely be stopped part-way through; and because they are slow-acting, there is a possibility that their effects will continue after the need has ended, with the danger that high interest rates to check inflation might precipitate a depression.

The new measures. Changes in hire-purchase regulations have the merit of a very strong immediate impact on demand for consumer durables. The other side of this coin is that they have a markedly disrupting effect on the growth of the industries concerned (most notably motor vehicles). They also tend to be inequitable between rich and poor consumers: the rich are less dependent on loans and can more easily find alternative sources of finance.

Loan requests and special deposits also carry disadvantages. Loan requests are unfair to the banks as against other financial intermediaries. (Even though recent requests have also been addressed to other financial institutions, they are not liable to the same sanctions as the banks.) Loan requests are inequitable as between banks, e.g. the imposition of a ceiling which is a proportion of advances at a base date is unfair to those banks whose advances were a particularly low proportion of deposits at the base date; and they restrict competition between banks. Requests to banks to discriminate between applicants for loans on grounds other than creditworthiness rest on doubtful assumptions: how can one arbitrarily distinguish between 'productive' and 'non-productive' business loans? 'Is a lathe or a new plant necessarily more productive than an office building or a business take-over?'*

The special deposits were intended to restrict advances by putting pressure on the banks' liquid assets. But the statistical evidence suggests that they are of doubtful effectiveness because the banks could finance them by selling government securities rather than by restricting advances.

The authorities seem to have placed reliance on these discriminatory measures because they have given priority in debt management to maintaining a stable market for government securities and to keeping down the cost of government borrowing. Hire-purchase regulations, loan requests and special deposits are all ways in which the authorities can hope to restrict credit without much increase in interest rates. To reduce the supply of money by selling bills and bonds (open-market operations), it was argued, would unsettle the market for government securities and raise interest

*John H. Karaken, 'Monetary Policy', in *Britain's Economic Prospects*, ed. Richard E. Caves (Washington: Brookings Institution, 1968).

rates; in particular sharp, short-term movements in the prices of government securities, due to official action, would undermine confidence in the market and the government's credit.

This aspect of government policy came increasingly under fire. In fact the money supply had been growing more rapidly than national output. Professor Milton Friedman of the University of Chicago was the high priest of a movement to reinstate the supply of money as the major means of controlling prices and activity in the United States. His views found many echoes amongst observers of the British scene.* Significantly, Chancellor Jenkins, in his Letter of Intent to the International Monetary Fund in June 1969, promised to try to limit domestic credit expansion (D.C.E.) to £400 million (or $2\frac{1}{2}$ per cent) for the year ending March 1970 (compared with an expansion of £1225 million in the previous twelve months), plus an additional amount equal to any surplus on the balance of payments.

International considerations

So far we have examined fiscal and monetary policy with little regard to considerations of international payments. These must now be taken into account.

Given fixed exchange rates (which applied throughout the period we are now considering), if Britain has a degree of inflation greater than that of her foreign trade competitors, this will generate a deficit on her balance of payments. High incomes at home suck in imports which are relatively cheap; exports, relatively high-priced, are difficult to sell; the easy home market pre-empts some goods which might have been exported. The rigidity associated with over-full employment inhibits the development of export growth industries. Budgetary and monetary measures to cut demand may need to be taken less because of the domestic ill-effects of inflation than because of a payments deficit and a loss of internationally liquid assets. But at least in those circumstances the needs of the balance of payments and the domestic economy are in line. (In fact the balance-of-payments deficit has mitigated the domestic inflation: in our equation $E = C + I + G + X$, X has become negative.)

But suppose unemployment occurred abroad, say in the United States. American incomes and prices would fall. Britain would tend to import more from America because of lower American prices. British exports to America would fall because, with lower incomes, Americans could afford less and the lower prices of American home-produced goods would undercut British goods. Also American goods would underprice British goods in third markets. The decline in British exports and displacement of British home-produced goods would create unemployment in the British economy (initially a fall mainly in X, followed

*See, for example, Karaken, ibid; E. Victor Morgan, *Monetary Policy for Stable Growth* (London: Institute of Economic Affairs, 196′ ; N. J. Gibson, *Financial Intermediaries and Monetary Policy* (London: Institute of Economic Affairs, 1967); W. E. Norton, 'Debt Management and Monetary Policy in the United Kingdom', *Economic Journal*, LXXIX, 315 (Sep 1969).

by reductions in *C* and *I*). But Britain would also have a balance-of-payments deficit. Increasing demand at home to counter the unemployment would accentuate the payments deficit. The needs of the domestic economy and the balance of payments would conflict.

A similar conflict would arise if sterling were overvalued. Then, if the exchange rate were to be maintained, demand might have to be cut back to the point at which there was substantial unemployment and loss of output in order to avoid a payments deficit.

One of the instruments of monetary policy in this period, Bank Rate, might specifically be used to strengthen the balance of payments. If Britain had a payments deficit, Bank Rate might be raised to encourage the short-term foreign lending to Britain to stem the outflow of reserves whilst measures taken to rectify the balance of payments were given time to work. Sometimes Bank Rate changes for payments purposes might be appropriate to the needs of the domestic economy, such as when a payments deficit was associated with continuing inflation. But at other times a Bank Rate change might conflict with the needs of the domestic economy. This might occur when there was a lag in the effect of a domestic inflation on the balance of payments and Bank Rate was raised to protect the reserves after the downturn in the domestic economy; or where Bank Rate was employed to check a speculative outflow of funds which arose, say, because of the expectation of a change in the value of another currency, regardless of the state of the British balance of payments; or, as mentioned above, where Bank Rate was used to protect an overvalued currency.

Interrelationships

In practice fiscal and monetary policies were rarely employed separately, but a 'package' of measures was proposed including both. Similarly, although it was convenient for expository purposes to present them separately, the influence of fiscal and monetary policies on the domestic economy and on international payments intermingle and interact. In the period we are considering the government was most often forced to policy action by the emergence of balance-of-payments deficits, and many economists considered that this 'balance-of-payments constraint' was a major factor in generating 'stop-go' cycles and preventing steady economic growth in the British economy.

Developments, 1970-5

The most significant developments for fiscal and monetary policy since 1969 can be summarised as follows.

(1) The year 1970 was notable for a clear reversal of previous experience on unemployment and inflation. The comforting assumption that an increase in unemployment could be traded off against a reduction in inflation, all within

acceptable margins, was overthrown; rates of inflation and unemployment were both increasing at the same time.

(2) In May 1971 the Bank of England issued a consultative document, *Competition and Credit Control,* as a basis for discussion with banks and finance houses on new methods intended to combine effective credit control with greater scope for competition and innovation. The new arrangements came into effect in September. They comprised three main features.

(*a*) For purposes of credit control all banks were to be treated by the authorities in a uniform way, in contrast to the long-standing concentration upon the clearing banks. Identical reserve requirements were imposed upon all banks, which were, in general terms, required to hold a minimum of $12\frac{1}{2}$ per cent of eligible liabilities in the form of short-term government debt, or other assets which the authorities were prepared to turn into cash. This minimum reserve assets ratio was to provide the authorities with 'a known firm base for the operation of monetary policy'. In addition calls for special deposits might also be made, again on the banking system as a whole.

(*b*) Direct quantitative control of bank lending ('ceilings') was to cease. Thus future control was to be by means of 'monetary aggregates' such as interest rates and the money supply.

(*c*) Impediments to competition in the banking system were removed. Thus the clearing banks abandoned their collective agreement on interest rates which applied primarily to the rates allowed on deposits and, in a looser form,to those charged on advances. Henceforward each bank fixed its own 'base rate' for lending. The link between Bank Rate and the deposit and lending rates of the banks was severed.

(3) In line with the principles of the new monetary policy, in July 1971 the Chancellor had removed all existing restrictions on hire-purchase, credit-sale and rental agreements.

(4) On the foreign exchanges an increased flexibility was introduced into the exchange rate after the suspension of the convertibility of the dollar in August 1971. In his 1972 budget the Chancellor stressed that a lesson of recent years was that it was neither necessary nor desirable to distort domestic economies to maintain unrealistic exchange rates. In June 1972 the sterling exchange rate was completely freed. Allowing sterling to 'float' removed one of the constraints to growth; it also removed a check on inflation, for with a fixed rate inflationary pressures generated a balance-of-payments deficit which obliged the government to take action.

(5) In October 1972 the Bank of England announced that the regular weekly Bank Rate announcement was to be discontinued and that the Bank's minimum lending rate to the money market would be the average rate of discount for Treasury bills established at the most recent tender plus half a per cent, rounded to the nearest quarter per cent above (e.g. at the time of the announcement the

Treasury bill rate was 6.69 per cent; the minimum lending rate therefore became $7\frac{1}{4}$ per cent).

(6) The balance of payments moved from a small surplus (in 1972) into a heavy deficit in 1973, in part because of rising import prices, accentuated at the end of 1973 and during 1974 by enormous and wholly unprecedented rises in the price of oil engineered by OPEC (Organisation of Petroleum Exporting Countries).

(7) The rise in import prices, accentuated by a depreciating sterling, added to domestic price rises to give double-figure rates of inflation unprecedented since the war which, between mid-1974 and mid-1975, reached over 25 per cent (see Chapter 11).

(8) The period has been marked by controversy amongst economists on the prime cause of the domestic inflation. At one extreme has been the 'institutional wage-push' view, which sees the rate of inflation as primarily a product of monopoly trade-union pressure, which can be exerted with little fear of loss of jobs when governments are committed to demand-management policies to maintain full employment. At the other extreme are the 'monetarists,' who see the growth of the money supply as the crucial factor, operating on the price level with a substantial lag of about $2\frac{1}{2}$ years. If governments spend more than they are prepared to take in taxes, and at the same time are not prepared to see interest rates rise to levels which would dissuade the public from consuming and encourage them to lend to the government in sufficiently large quantities to cover its borrowing requirement, then the shortfall will be met by increases in the money supply with a subsequent effect on prices.

Between the two extremes other economists take an intermediate position, accepting something from both sides. The dispute continues. What is undeniable, however, is the increasing support which the monetarist case has attracted over the period. This is reflected, amongst other ways, in the regular publication of two indicators of the money stock M_1 (cash plus current account balances) and M_3 (M_1 plus mainly deposit accounts); and in the frequent references by politicians and in the press to the money supply.

Illustration by Case Studies

Fiscal and monetary policy are both illustrated by the same case study: an analysis of the management of the British economy from the devaluation of November 1967 to the budget of April 1969. In one sense this is atypical: devaluations of sterling have occurred during this century about every 20 - 30 years; and, as long as the United Kingdom has a floating exchange rate, a devaluation in the sense of a move from one fixed exchange rate to another lower fixed exchange rate is impossible. But in another sense the period is ideal for a case study. Devaluation provides the study with a focus and unity: the interactions between the domestic economy and the problems of international payments are clearly demonstrated; and the period illustrates nearly all the features of fiscal and monetary policy in the form they were used at that time.

It should be stressed that we are examining this period from the point of view of fiscal and monetary policy; we are not concerned here with analysing in detail why devaluation was necessary or precisely how it might be expected to work.*

*Analysis of this aspect of devaluation is contained in *Case Studies in Economics: Principles of Economics*, ch. 14.

CASE 30.   FISCAL AND MONETARY POLICY IN THE UNITED KINGDOM FROM THE DEVALUATION OF NOVEMBER 1967 TO THE BUDGET OF APRIL 1969

Demand Management and Devaluation

Sterling was devalued by 14.3 per cent, from $2.80 to $2.40 = £1, on 18 November 1967, after several years of payments deficits, which, because they persisted even after strong deflationary measures to curtail demand, had demonstrated fairly clearly that the currency was overvalued.

The purpose of a devaluation is of course to earn more foreign currency and to spend less – to turn a payments deficit into a surplus by making exports cheaper in terms of foreign currencies (and more profitable to exporters) and imports dearer in terms of sterling. To turn a payments deficit on current account into a surplus requires an increase in visible and invisible exports (or a decrease in imports); after a devaluation a bigger change in real terms is necessary to achieve any particular improvement on the balance of payments, as *more* exports are needed at the lower exchange value to earn any given amount of foreign currencies. In other words, a devaluation is a deliberate worsening of a country's terms of trade in order to improve its balance of payments.

What does this mean in terms of the components of aggregate demand, $C + I + G + X$? X (net exports: exports of goods *and* services minus imports of goods and services) has to be changed from a large negative to a large positive sum. In real terms a massive movement of resources into exports is required; some resources which were previously unused or under-used may move into exports, and exports can grow from increased output resulting from higher productivity; but this is a relatively slow development, and increased output is also likely to mean increased imports.

At the time of the sterling devaluation there were unused resources in the economy (unemployment, seasonally adjusted, stood in November 1967 at the relatively high rate of 2.3 per cent compared with 1.8 per cent a year earlier and 1.3 per cent a year before that). But this was too small a margin to provide all the increase in X required. Thus monetary and fiscal policies to support devaluation were needed to cut one or more of C, I and G. (In January 1968, in a House of Commons debate, the Chancellor gave a conveniently round estimate of the required increase in X: 'We need to put about £1000 million in the balance of payments to get the turnround we need and to meet the additional calls imposed by the loss in the terms of trade.')

The situation can be expressed in monetary terms: devaluation generated strong inflationary pressures; the pressure on demand arising from the expected sub-stantial increase in X combined with pressures of cost inflation, particularly stimulated by the higher import prices following devaluation. Fiscal and monetary measures were needed to check the inflationary pressures; if a cut was not made in $C + I + G$, then inflation would develop which, amongst other things, would prevent the necessary improvement in the balance of payments both in the short and the longer run.

The Fiscal and Monetary Measures: November 1967 to March 1968

The sterling devaluation was not the application of a carefully prepared act of policy nor even of a detailed contingency plan; it was forced on a reluctant government by what *The Economist* described as 'the inexorable pressure of facts'. This lack of preparedness meant that the measures necessary to make devaluation work, instead of being introduced as one very large and impressive package at the time of devaluation, were introduced piecemeal in three main stages.

(1) *Measures announced with devaluation*

(*a*) *Monetary.*   *Bank Rate*, which had been increased from $5\frac{1}{2}$ to 6 per cent in October and from 6 to $6\frac{1}{2}$ per cent early in November, was raised to 8 per cent. (This was the highest rate for over half a century; its intention was probably more to attract short-term foreign capital, to strengthen the reserves whilst devaluation was given time to work, than to cut domestic demand.)

Loan requests were addressed to all financial institutions to limit their private-sector lending. The banks were not to allow their private-sector lending to rise at all, except that certain medium-term lending for exports and shipbuilding was excluded from the restrictions. Below the imposed 'ceiling', priority was to be given to loans to finance investment in 'export industries' and in agriculture, if a saving of imports could thereby be achieved, and on loans to finance house-buying; loans for imports of manufactured goods were to be regarded with particular disfavour.

Hire-purchase regulations on the sale of cars in the home market were tightened: minimum down-payments were raised from 25 to $33\frac{1}{3}$ per cent and the maximum repayment period reduced from 36 to 27 months. This was not only to reduce demand in general; cars were believed to have a high price elasticity in overseas markets, and the curtailment of home demand would stimulate the more rapid increase in car exports that devaluation made possible.*

(*b*) *Fiscal.*   No fiscal measures were *applied* immediately, but some were announced to take effect later. Cuts in government expenditure were foreshadowed, especially in defence; as from 1 April 1968 the Selective Employment Tax (S.E.T.) premium was to be withdrawn except to manufacturers in development areas, and the export

---

*Note, however, the possibility that if the home market is so reduced that total output (combined home and export) falls, the motor-vehicle industry, in which there are big economies of scale, may be forced to produce at higher average cost – which would not help exports.

rebate was to be withdrawn; the rate of Corporation Tax was to be raised from 40 to $42\frac{1}{2}$ per cent in the next budget to apply to company profits in 1967 – 8.

(c) *Miscellaneous.* Along with these measures went an undertaking to cut capital expenditure by nationalised industries and references to a strengthening of the voluntary prices and incomes policy and a strict watch on dividends.

(2) *Fiscal measures, January 1968*

A series of further measures, mainly concerned with government expenditure, were announced by the Prime Minister on 16 January 1968. The planned expenditure of central government and local authorities was to be cut, with the effect of reducing the rate of increase of public expenditure, in real terms, for 1968 – 9 from 6.9 to 4.8 per cent and for 1969 – 70 to less than a further 1 per cent. The biggest 'saving' for 1968 – 9 (of £80 million at 1967 prices) arose from postponing the proposed acceleration of the payment of investment grants (leaving the time lag between investment expenditure and repayment at twelve months). Other savings were in reductions of projected expenditure for 1968 – 9 on roads, education (including the postponement of the rise in the school-leaving age), health and welfare, housing, environmental services and home defence. Substantial savings were proposed on the defence budget, including the reduction of overseas commitments, but none of these would be effective in the year 1968 – 9. In addition, National Health and Insurance contributions of employers and employees were to be raised, and National Health charges for prescriptions and other fees, including charges for dental treatment, were increased.

(3) *The budget, March 1968*

The immediate background to the budget was that, at home, little having been done since devaluation to cut consumption (*C*), the first months of 1968 saw a spending spree (which boosted imports) in anticipation of increased taxes.

In the foreign exchange markets, the end of February saw the beginning of a speculative increase in the demand for gold, mainly in exchange for dollars, and some weakening of sterling. Arising from this speculation, the main central banks agreed on a 'two-tier' system for gold, by which gold for international currency reserves, the price of which would remain fixed, was separated from a 'free' market.

The Chancellor introduced his budget on 19 March, several weeks earlier than usual. Major tax changes were proposed, estimated to yield an additional £775 million in 1968 – 9 and £923 million in a full year. The main proposals were:

(*a*) increases on all rates of purchase tax, with a new top rate of 50 per cent;
(*b*) customs and excise duties raised on tobacco, wines and spirits;
(*c*) duties raised on hydrocarbon oils, including petrol up by 4d. a gallon;
(*d*) increases in betting duties and gaming licences;

(*e*) rates of S.E.T. increased by 50 per cent (except for part-time employees) from 2 September;

(*f*) vehicle-licence duties raised on private cars from £17.10s. to £25 per annum and on heavy vehicles by 50 per cent;

(*g*) a special charge on investment income over £3000 to be levied for one year only; and

(*h*) the promised rise in corporation tax from 40 to $42\frac{1}{2}$ per cent.

Only minor changes were made in income tax; family allowances were to be raised from October 1968, but P.A.Y.E. coding was adjusted so that the benefit was restricted to poorer families.

There were three outstanding features of the budget from the viewpoint of fiscal policy. First, the size of the tax increases (and the consequent budget surplus), bigger than ever before in peace-time. Second, the extent to which the increases were on expenditure: here was a courageous attempt to cut back personal consumption sharply. Third, the particular emphasis on the motor-car industry, affected by the November hire-purchase measures and now by increases in purchase tax, petrol duties and licence fees – clearly because of its export potential.

More stable foreign exchange markets after agreement on the two-tier gold system and favourable foreign reaction to the budget led to a *Bank Rate* reduction by $\frac{1}{2}$ per cent on 21 March. *Bank Rate* was again reduced by $\frac{1}{2}$ per cent to 7 per cent in September.

The Measures of November 1968

Developments in the domestic economy and in the foreign exchange markets combined to bring about another package of fiscal and monetary measures in November.

Improvements in the British balance of payments were coming more slowly than expected; although exports were increasing well, imports remained obstinately high. Personal spending had fallen after the March budget, but was picking up again in the later part of the year.

In the exchange markets there was a currency crisis in November in expectation of a devaluation of the franc and a revaluation of the mark, and sterling came under heavy pressure.

(1) Early in November new *hire-purchase controls* were introduced on a wide range of goods. Cars, as usual, bore the brunt; minimum deposits were raised to 40 per cent (from $33\frac{1}{3}$) and the maximum repayment period reduced to two years (from 27 months). Minimum deposits on many other consumer durables were raised to $33\frac{1}{3}$ per cent (and on furniture to 20 per cent), with reductions in repayment periods.

(2) After the currency crises, (*a*) the 'regulator' was used to raise duties on

beer, wines, spirits, petrol, tobacco and purchase taxes by 10 per cent; (*b*) a new *import deposits scheme* was introduced for a year, by which importers of all but certain goods such as basic foods and raw materials were required to place 50 per cent of the value of imports with the customs before the goods would be released, the deposit to be refunded after 180 days; and (*c*) monetary policy was further tightened by stiffer *loan requests* to the banks.

The Squeeze on the Banks

The requests to the banks in November 1967 to allow no increase in lending except for seasonal reasons had been followed by another request in May 1968, which required a further curtailment of 'non-priority' borrowing. The November measures were more severe still; excluding fixed-rate lending for exports and shipbuilding, but not other credit for exports, clearing-bank lending was to be reduced further to 98 per cent of its November 1967 level by March 1969. This general contraction of about 2 per cent in money terms implied a much larger contraction in real terms, or in advances expressed as a percentage of G.N.P.

The banks experienced considerable difficulty in reducing loans in line with this target; at the end of January 1969 the authorities urged renewed efforts by the banks to achieve speedy results. When the February figures of advances si.owed increases in bank lending, *Bank Rate* was raised to 8 per cent, partly to support this policy of credit restraint and to make it easier for the banks to reduce loans. By the March deadline, advances remained above the ceiling. The banks were given more time; but in June the sanction of halving the interest on special deposits was introduced until they complied.

The Budget, April 1969

It is not our purpose to examine the 1969 fiscal measures in detail; the budget of 1969 is the convenient terminal point for examining the fiscal and monetary policies of the previous eighteen months. The general background was of a large balance-of-payments deficit in 1968 but an improving trend in exports and some levelling-off in imports. The Chancellor felt it necessary to take a further £272 million out of the economy in 1969 - 70, about £340 million in a full year. The main changes relevant to our purpose were an increase in S.E.T., Corporation Tax and petrol duty; the broadening of purchase tax to include goods such as pet foods, potato crisps and tableware, previously exempt; and various additional betting and gambling duties. The regulator surcharge of November was incorporated in the rates of customs and excise duties and purchase tax. A different approach to the need to reduce consumption (*C*) was the announcement of proposals for a contractual savings scheme, S.A.Y.E. (Save as You Earn), with favourable interest rates for regular savings left untouched for seven years. And a further measure was the provision by which interest on loans could not longer be offset against income tax except for house purchase and business purposes.

The Effectiveness of Fiscal and Monetary Policy

It is not possible to distinguish with certainty the relative effects of fiscal and monetary policies; the following attempt is therefore tentative and limited.

Fiscal policy

The prime purpose of fiscal policy over the period surveyed was to cut consumption. The budget of 1968 was intended to cut private consumption by 1.9 per cent; in the event it rose by 1.2 per cent. This gives some idea of both the strength and weakness of fiscal policy.

On the one hand, this was a smaller increase than in periods of comparable growth. As the Chancellor expressed it in his 1969 budget speech: 'Judged by any standard other than the exceedingly stringent one which I applied last year, a growth of only 1 per cent in personal living standards, combined with a growth of 4 per cent in G.D.P., is a considerable and unusual achievement.'

The reasons that the cut was not more effective were mainly two: the tax increase was to some extent cushioned by a reduction in savings, that is there was a slight drop in the ratio of savings to disposable incomes; also there was a higher growth of earnings in relation to prices than expected. The average rise in weekly earnings in the year to April 1969 was 8.8 per cent, although prices rose only 5.5 per cent. These facts give support to the views set out earlier on the limitations of budgetary policy; they throw even more doubt on the efficacy of incomes policy.

Monetary policy

As with fiscal policy, the methods employed registered mixed success.

There can be little doubt of the immediate effect of hire-purchase restrictions in postponing demand. For example, after the November 1968 measures there was a marked fall in new-car registrations in the first quarter of 1969.

But other aspects of monetary policy were less successful. The loan requests were not fully adhered to. During 1968 there was a considerable expansion of credit. The money supply rose by £986 million, or $6\frac{1}{2}$ per cent, between end-December 1967 and end-December 1968. This was distinctly smaller than the 10 per cent increase in 1967, but nevertheless was a large rise for a period of substantial balance-of-payments deficit.

The following year saw a further tightening of the money supply, associated with the Chancellor's undertaking to the International Monetary Fund to restrict domestic credit expansion in June 1969.

The Balance of Payments

The prime purpose of fiscal and monetary policy in this period had been to make devaluation work. The ultimate test, therefore, must be what happened to the balance of payments (although of course the balance of payments is affected by other changes in world trade). Devaluation acted slowly. In the year of devaluation, 1967, the balance-of-payments deficit on current account was £322 million.; in the following year it was scarcely lower at £306 million.; 1969 saw a surplus of £437 million followed by a surplus of nearly £700 million in 1970 and over £1000 million in 1971.

Exercises

(10.1) What is the 'regulator'?

(10.2) 'Consols' (Consolidated Stock) are an irredeemable government security with a fixed interest rate of $2\frac{1}{2}$ per cent. If the market long-term rate of interest on gilt-edged securities rises to $7\frac{1}{2}$ per cent, which of the following will be the market price of Consols:

(*a*) £100; (*b*) £133$\frac{1}{2}$; (*c*) £33$\frac{1}{3}$; (*d*) £300; (*e*) zero?

(10.3) Consider briefly the relative merits in combating unemployment of (*a*) a tax reduction of £500 million, and (*b*) government investment of £500 million.

(10.4) What were the outstanding features of the 1968 budget?

(10.5) What are the disadvantages of trying to control inflation by restricting the supply of money and raising interest rates?

(10.6) Indicate briefly the merits and disadvantages of changes in hire-purchase regulations as an instrument to control the level of demand.

(10.7) What do you understand by 'discriminatory' monetary policy? What are its advantages and disadvantages?

(10.8) Why were so many fiscal and monetary measures introduced to curtail demand for motor-cars in the British home market after devaluation?

(10.9) Why is inflation in a country often associated with a balance-of-payments deficit? Must it necessarily be so?

(10.10) Examine the argument that to attempt to cure inflation by increasing taxation on a community already taxed heavily is likely to be self-defeating. How far does British experience in 1968-9 bear out this view?

(10.11) In what ways does a devaluation of a country's currency generate inflationary pressures?

(10.12) 'In Britain today the objectives which determine how much taxation should be raised relate to the pressure of demand on domestic resources and the balance of payments, not the crude relationship between the yield of taxation and government outlay' (Cmnd. 3310). Explain and comment.

Supplementary exercises

(10.13) Draw a graph of the changes in the yield on government irredeemable securities (e.g. Consols) from the beginning of 1965 to October 1972. Mark on the graph the level of Bank Rate throughout the period.

(10.14) Assess how far Chancellor of the Exchequer Roy Jenkins was successful in his management of the U.K. economy.

Sources and References

Budget details can be referred to in *Hansard* (19 Mar 1968 and 15 Apr 1969);
  The Times, Guardian or *Financial Times* of the days following the Budget;
  or *The Economist* (23 Mar 1968 and 19 Apr 1969).
RICHARD E. CAVES AND ASSOCIATES , *Britain's Economic Prospects*
  (Washington, 1968) chs i and ii.
'Competition and Credit Control' - Articles reprinted from the *Bank of England
  Quarterly Bulletin,* vol. 11 (1971).
Convenient sources of regular financial banking and trade statistics are the
  Monthly Summary of Business Conditions in the United Kingdom, published
  by the National and Commercial Banking Group Ltd; and the *Midland Bank
  Review,* which, besides regular quarterly assessments of 'Business and Finance',
  includes an 'Annual Monetary Survey' in the May issue.
Devaluation details can be found in *The Economist* (25 Nov 1967) or the *Midland
  Bank Review* (Feb 1968).
N. J. GIBSON, *Financial Intermediaries and Monetary Policy,* Hobart Paper 39
  (London: Institute of Economic Affairs, 1967).
SIR JOHN HICKS, 'What is Wrong with Monetarism?', *Lloyds Bank Review*
  (Oct 1975).
SIR JOHN HICKS *et al., Crisis' 75*? Occasional Paper Special No. 43 (London:
  Institute of Economic Affairs, 1975).
ANNA JACOBSON SCHWARTZ, 'Why Money Matters?', *Lloyds Bank Review* (Oct
  1969).
MICHAEL PARKIN, 'Where is Britain's Inflation Going?', *Lloyds Bank Review*
  (July 1975).
Public Expenditure in 1968 - 69 and 1969 - 70, Cmnd. 3515 (London: H.M.S.O.,
  Jan 1968).
The Annual *Financial Statement and Budget Report* for each of the years 1968 - 9
  to 1975 - 6 (London: H.M.S.O.).
E. VICTOR MORGAN, *Monetary Policy for Stable Growth,* Hobart Paper 27 (London:
  Institute of Economic Affairs, 1964).

CHAPTER 11

Prices and Incomes Policy

Catherine Winnett

Summary of Background Material

Ever since the Second World War, governments have made periodic attempts to
check the upward trends in prices and incomes, often through moral suasion, but
occasionally with the backing of statutory powers. As an historical fact, incomes
policies were generally introduced to counteract severe disequilibria in the balance
of payments resulting from inflation; and incomes policies were increasingly
preferred to monetary and fiscal methods since governments hoped their use
would avoid the sharp deflation and unemployment which accompanied demand-
restraint policies. Politicians of the post-war period were committed to the maintenance of full employment (having learned their lesson from the 1930s). The
major purpose of incomes policy has thus been to try to solve the problem: how
to avoid inflation at full employment.

There were three attempts to implement incomes policies between 1945 and
1964; under the post-war Labour government, from February 1948 to mid-1950;
and twice under Conservative governments, in 1956 and 1961–2. Of these, the
first is judged to have been the most successful in restraining wages and prices,
largely because it was the only policy to have won the support of the trade
unions. All three were voluntary policies. The use of incomes policy as a more
permanent and integrated tool of economic management dates from the return
of a Labour government in the autumn of 1964. Faced with a serious balance-
of-payments crisis and an inflationary economy, the government sought agreement
with business and labour leaders on the need for an incomes policy; criteria to
guide wage and price decisions were published, and a National Board for Prices
and Incomes was established in 1965 to which selected price increases, wage
claims and settlements were referred for investigation and approval. The criteria
or general guidelines, suggested in an early White Paper, indicated a 'norm' for
increases in wages, equal to the underlying growth in productivity, around 3 to $3\frac{1}{2}$
per cent per annum. Exceptional pay increases would be granted to low-paid
workers and to employees in undermanned industries which functioned in the
'national interest'. The objectives of the Labour government were to:

(1) ensure that British industry was dynamic and that its prices were competitive;
(2) raise productivity and efficiency so that real national output could increase;

(3) keep increases in wages, salaries and other forms of income in line with this increase; and

(4) keep the general level of prices stable.

All in all, it was hoped that a policy of steady and sustained growth in output could be pursued – expansion without inflation and subsequent balance-of-payments crises. Hence the aim was to break the 'stop – go' cycle, characteristic of the British economy since the war. It was hoped that the economy would follow a steady upward trend in its growth rate, and an incomes policy was introduced to help secure this. The concept of aligning the rates of growth of incomes and production, over all, was attractive but serious problems were bound to arise in ensuring equitable treatment as between fast- and slow-growing sectors, such discrepancies in sectoral growth rates often not being attributable wholly to factors within the control of capital and labour in the particular sector.

Arrangements for wage – price control were adopted initially on a voluntary basis, but proved ineffective. The upward movement of prices and incomes continued throughout 1965 and the first half of 1966, and by June 1966 the indices of both retail prices and weekly wage rates were over 7 per cent above the levels of December 1964. Continuing balance-of-payments deficits, and the consequent instability of sterling, made stronger measures imperative. In July 1966 the government announced a standstill on money incomes and prices to the end of the year, followed by a period of severe restraint during the first six months of 1967, when only minor exceptions to the freeze on wages and prices would be allowed. For the first time statutory powers were passed to enforce the policy if necessary. After the summer of 1967 wage increases were to be granted only if they could be justified by a list of criteria which emphasised direct contributions to increased productivity and the relative income position of low-paid workers. In the budget of March 1968 a ceiling of $3\frac{1}{2}$ per cent was placed on all other annual income increases. Throughout the standstill virtually no increase was recorded in basic weekly wage rates, and over the subsequent six months the rate of increase was low (about 2 per cent from July 1966 to June 1967) as compared with experience up to mid-1966. Although the index of retail prices continued to rise during the standstill at a rate only slightly below that of 1965, this was in part due to the introduction of Selective Employment Tax in September 1966. After the summer of 1967, with the emphasis on voluntary rather than statutory co-operation, the policy was rather less effective. Pressure on prices increased with the devaluation of sterling in November 1967 and various tax increases which were the outcome of the budget of March 1968. Together these accounted for a 10 per cent increase in the retail price index between June 1967 and June 1969. Earnings rose by 16 per cent in the same two-year period. Subsequent wage claims and settlements were well in excess of the recommended figure.

These inflationary trends in prices and incomes continued into the 1970s. By the close of 1970, the retail price index was almost 8 per cent higher than a year before, and weekly wage rates over 13.5 per cent higher. Throughout 1971 these increases became slightly less pronounced, probably as a result of the initiative taken by the C.B.I. in the summer of 1971 in inviting member companies not to increase prices, or to limit unavoidable increases to 5 per cent over the coming twelve months. However, by mid-1972 prices and wages were rising more rapidly than ever before, and some government intervention seemed inescapable. Prices and incomes policies under the Conservative government, 1970-4, form the content of the case studies below.

Before turning to consider in detail the post-1970 incomes policies, let us highlight the following particular feature of earlier policies which has on-going implications. It has already been noted that the incomes policy of the 1964-70 Labour government attempted to peg movements in wages to movements in productivity, with the explicit intention of providing economic incentives to management and unions to rationalise working practices and manpower use. However, whilst the policy was intended to make British industry more competitive and faster growing, it did disrupt existing differentials in pay, most seriously between the private and public sectors. The private sector gained most from productivity agreements; these were predominantly negotiated in plants where earnings were already relatively high, amongst the strongly organised groups of manual workers in private manufacturing industry. As workers in slower-growing industries within the private sector attempted to defend their existing differentials, so incomes policy was steadily eroded in the private sector in the late 1960s. In the public sector, by contrast, where the government's regulative powers were clearly greater, the policy was far more rigorously applied, the resulting discriminatory effects of the policy being to create inequities between workers in the two sectors. By the early 1970s resentment had accumulated in many public-sector industries, most notably in the mining industry, which forms the content of Case 32. Thus it is clear that incomes policies have encountered severe problems when trying to reconcile considerations of efficiency and equity; and this conflict of objectives has, in the past, most directly impinged on the public sector. In assessing the incomes policy of the 1970-4 Conservative government, the pre-1970 experience indicates that, whilst incomes policies, particularly statutory ones, may achieve some *short-run* success in restraining increases in money wages and prices, these very successes tend to generate sectoral inequalities and produce 'special cases', thereby sowing the seeds of future resentment.

Apart from these specific problems which have arisen over the implementation of incomes policies, more fundamental criticisms have questioned the very conception and theoretical basis of incomes policy. Many economists now believe that there is little or no value in a prices and incomes policy, as an on-going component of a policy designed to reduce the long-run rate of inflation; at most it may ease problems of short-run adjustment to lower rates of inflation, through effects on expectations. Underlying this view is the belief that only changes in the rate of growth of the money supply can have a persistent effect on the rate of inflation.

In spite of its weaknesses, incomes policy remains a major part of the economic strategy of British governments; and the following case studies are concerned to examine some of the complexities of implementing such policies.

Illustration by Case Studies

The following case studies consider in detail the prices and incomes policies of the 1970-4 Conservative government. Case 31 discussed Phases I, II, and III of that policy and associated Pay Board reports - the reports on anomalies and relativities issued whilst the Conservative government was in office. The case study thus focuses on the over-all incomes policy of the Conservative government. A detailed outline of the incomes policy is presented, and two problems are drawn out and given particular emphasis. First, the increasing role of international factors (in the form of rapidly rising world commodity prices) in both accelerating and sustaining domestic inflation. Throughout the duration of the Conservative incomes policy the openness of the British economy made it particularly vulnerable to international influence. Second, attention is drawn to guidelines that can be enacted in a way that is both effective and equitable, especially in relation to pay. This point is considered above and is taken up in more detail in Case 32, in which the Pay Board's final report on the relative pay of mineworkers is discussed. This last report followed the miner's dispute and, indeed, was published after the change of government which the dispute indirectly brought about. It is thus an outstanding example of the problems of devising policies which are equitable as well as effective, or at least which can secure the co-operation of the trade unions. As the background material has suggested, this is probably the major problem in implementing such policies.

CASE 31.   INCOMES POLICY, 1972 – 4: THE MAIN PHASES

Phase I

The first stage of the Conservative government's 'Programme for Controlling Inflation' was the outcome of a long series of meetings with the C.B.I. and the T.U.C. The following objectives were agreed:

(1) faster growth in national output and real incomes;
(2) an improvement in the relative position of the low paid;
(3) moderation in the rate of cost and price inflation.

On the eve of Phase I the official view was that the economy was growing at an annual rate of around 5 per cent; a number of indicators confirmed that a strong expansion was under way. However, the government remained pessimistic about the rate of inflation. Throughout 1972 a definite acceleration in the rates of increase in prices and wage rates occurred; the figures for October 1972 showed retail prices as being nearly 8 per cent higher than a year previously, and wage rates 16.5 per cent higher. It was clearly essential to reverse the upward thrust of pay and prices.

Since the government, C.B.I. and T.U.C. failed to co-operate in a voluntary policy, it became necessary for the government to introduce statutory measures. The Prime Minister announced to the House of Commons, on 6 November 1972, that there would be an immediate standstill on increases in prices, pay, rents and dividends. On 30 November, when the Bill became law, a ninety-day standstill was introduced, which was extendible by a further sixty days. The 'freeze' lasted until 1 April 1973.

Prices

The prices of goods supplied to the home market were to be subject to the stand-still, wholesalers and retailers being permitted to raise prices only if their costs increased, in order to maintain profit margins. The government did recognise that certain prices, particularly those for fresh food such as vegetables, meat and fish, and fruit, and for imported raw materials, were subject to fluctuations in the world market, and since they would not subsidise imported commodities, these remained outside the scope of Phase I.

Pay

There were to be no increases in wage and salary rates for the duration of Phase I. The only settlements which could be implemented were those reached before 6 November, where the operative date of the increase occurred no later than 6 November. Those employees in industries whose pay is determined by Wages

Councils were to be granted increases in pay during the standstill, provided the proposal had been made on or before 6 November, and if they had not had an increase in pay for at least twelve months before the standstill. These Wage Council awards did in fact account for most of the increase in earnings during the 'freeze'. Phase I also attempted to combat wage drift, and all improvements in the terms and conditions of employment, e.g. hours and holidays, were forbidden.

Rents and dividends were also controlled.

The official retail price index for March 1973 was 173.4 (January 1962 = 100) as compared with 169.3 in November 1972, an increase over four months at an annual rate of 7.3 per cent, but for items excluding food the rise was less steep. Excluding food, the annual rate of increase was only 3.2 per cent; for food

TABLE 11.1
General index of retail prices (monthly averages)

		All items (16 January 1962 = 100)	All items except food	Food
1970		140.2	140.2	140.1
1971		153.4	153.5	155.6
1972		164.3	164.1	169.4
	17 Oct	168.7	168.7	172.8
	14 Nov	169.3	169.1	174.3
	12 Dec	170.2	169.7	176.9
1973	16 Jan	171.3	170.8	180.4
	20 Feb	172.4	171.4	183.7
	20 Mar	173.4	171.9	187.1
	20 Apr	176.7	174.6	189.9
	22 May	178.0	175.5	193.3
	19 June	178.9	176.7	194.3
	17 July	179.7	177.8	194.6
	21 Aug	180.2	179.0	194.4
	18 Sep	181.8	180.4	198.5
	16 Oct	185.4	183.5	205.1
	13 Nov	186.8	184.9	207.0
	11 Dec	188.2	186.1	210.5
1974	15 Jan	191.8	189.4	216.7
		15 January 1974 = 100		
	19 Feb	101.7	101.9	100.9
	19 Mar	102.6	102.8	102.0

SOURCE: *Monthly Digest of Statistics* (July 1974).

TABLE 11.2

Components of price increases (annual rate, percentages)

	Wage and salary costs	Profits	Taxes	Import cost	Residual error	Output prices
Labour government						
Planning						
Oct 1964	+ 3.0	− 0.1	+ 0.8	+ 0.3	+ 0.1	+ 4.1
June 1966*	(+ 73)‡	(− 2)	(+ 20)	(+ 7)	(+ 2)	(100)
Freeze						
July 1966	+ 0.9	+ 0.8	+ 0.7	− 0.2	+ 0.7	+ 2.9
Sep 1967	(+ 31)	(+ 28)	(+ 24)	(− 7)	(+ 24)	(100)
Two years' 'hard slog'						
Oct 1967	+ 1.4	+ 0.7	+ 1.0	+ 1.4	+ 0.4	+ 4.9
July 1969	(+ 29)	(+ 14)	(+ 20)	(+ 29)	(+ 8)	(100)
Pre-Election						
July 1969	+ 4.4	+ 0.2	+ 0.9	+ 1.0	+ 0.1	+ 6.6
June 1970	(+ 67)	(+ 3)	(+ 14)	(+ 15)	(+ 2)	(100)
Conservative government						
July 1970	+ 4.6	+ 2.0	− 0.3	+ 0.5	+ 0.6	+ 7.4
Dec 1971†	(+ 62)	(+ 27)	(− 4)	(+ 7)	(+ 8)	(100)
Jan 1972	+ 4.9	+ 1.7	+ 0.7	+ 1.2	− 1.7	+ 6.8
Sep 1972	(+ 72)	(+ 25)	(+ 10)	(+ 18)	(− 25)	(100)
Freeze						
Oct 1972	+ 0.5	+ 1.0	+ 0.8	+ 5.1	− 0.1	+ 7.3
March 1973	(+ 7)	(+ 14)	(+ 11)	(+ 70)	(− 2)	(100)

*Based on quarterly figures and taken to the nearest date, e.g. two years' 'hard slog' followed devaluation in November 1967.

†The miners' strike in the first quarter of 1972 so distorted the figures that the changes are measured from the fourth quarter of 1971.

‡Figures in brackets are the percentage contribution to the total price increase in that period.

SOURCE: Data published in *The Economist* (8 - 14 Sep 1973).

it was about 24 per cent (see Table 11.1), demonstrating the striking influence of international factors in the inflationary process (see Table 11.2). Earnings (seasonally adjusted) during the 'freeze' period rose by just under 1 per cent. Wages rose much less rapidly during Phase I than before it, and also significantly less rapidly than prices (see Table 11.3).

In his budget speech (6 March 1973) Mr Anthony Barber, Chancellor of the Exchequer, reiterated the economic plans of the government:

(1) To maintain a faster rate of growth of national output; he aimed at a growth rate of about 5 per cent between the second half of 1972 and the first half of 1974,

with some slowing down in the later part of the period – around $3\frac{1}{2}$ per cent in 1974, broadly in line with the long-term rate of growth of productive potential.

(2) To attack inflation, and provide a stable economic base for the pursuit of growth; the Chancellor saw inflation as the biggest single threat to increasing prosperity and to improving standards of living because it reduced the competitiveness of exports, thereby endangering the stability of the pound sterling, it hampered investment and thus our rate of growth, and was, above all, socially unjust.

TABLE 11.3

Index of average earnings of all employees
(all industries and services covered: January 1970 = 100)

		Unadjusted	Seasonally adjusted
1970		107.2	
1971		119.4	
1972		134.8	
	Oct	141.4	140.5
	Nov	143.2	142.5
	Dec	141.3	143.1
1973	Jan	142.9	143.1
	Feb	144.5	144.4
	Mar	146.7	143.9
	Apr	145.8	146.6
	May	150.6	149.5
	Jun	155.2	151.9
	Jul	155.5	154.0
	Aug	153.5	154.0
	Sep	157.0	156.4
	Oct	159.1	158.2
	Nov	160.9	160.3
	Dec	159.7	161.4
1974	Jan*	153.9	154.1
	Feb*	156.9	156.8
	Mar	167.6	164.3

*The figures reflect temporary reductions in earnings while three-day working and other restrictions were in operation during January and February 1974.

SOURCE: *Monthly Digest of Statistics* (July 1974).

Phase II

Phase II of the government's counter-inflation programme came into operation on 1 April 1973. In its White Paper the government stressed the international aspects of inflation, stating that whilst governments could press home the attack on the domestic causes of rising prices, they could have virtually no influence on the movement of world commodity prices. It was mainly these uncontrollable prices – of raw materials and food, e.g. meat, grain, wool and metals, of which we are heavy importers – which rose most sharply under Phase I, and thus pushed up the general price index. Under Phase II the prices of certain products were exempt from control. These were fresh food and other imported products subject to fluctuations from external or seasonal causes, and goods and services whose prices were regulated as a result of international agreements or arrangements. All other prices were subject to control.

Strict limitations on profit margins from sales in the home market were imposed, net profit margins as a percentage of sales being restricted to the average level in the best two of the previous five years.

Two new agencies, a Price Commission and a Pay Board, were established, and they became responsible for operating the statutory price and pay code. (The major reports of the Pay Board are considered below.)

Pay

The pay code under Phase II was especially designed to favour the lower-paid workers and to bring about a more equitable distribution of income. Let us here note that as the Conservative government's incomes policy proceeded, increasing attention was given to the distribution of income. This tends to be a general characteristic of incomes policy; with the duration of the policy the question of equity necessarily becomes more and more important for its success. For that reason the allowable increase was not expressed as a single percentage limit. Wages and salaries negotiated after 6 November were increased at the average annual *per capita* rate of £1 per week plus 4 per cent. Those increases which were agreed on or before 6 November were allowed to take effect in full. The Phase II pay limit of £1 plus 4 per cent was related to the group, not to the individual, permitting increases in pay to be weighted in favour of the lower paid. Within this pay limit no individual would receive an increase of more than £250.

A rent-rebate scheme was introduced and control of dividends was continued under Phase II.

Prices rose during Phase II from 173.4 (March) to 185.4 (October), a rate of price increase of 7 per cent for the seven-month period. The price index for food increased from 194.4 (August) to 205.1 (October), an increase of 5.5 per cent in two months. The behaviour of the price index for basic materials was equally disturbing. It rose $4\frac{1}{4}$ per cent between September and October after persistent increases in the earlier months of 1973, making materials and fuel 42 per cent

more expensive than in October 1972. It has been estimated that the September –
October increase in materials and fuel prices had an impact of $1\frac{1}{2}$ per cent on the
cost of manufactured goods. It can be seen from Table 11.3 that average earnings
rose under Phase II from 143.9 (March) to 158.2 (October), a rate of increase of
10 per cent over the seven-month period, well in excess of the increase in retail
prices. Between November 1972 and October 1973, prices increased by 9.5 per
cent, earnings by 11 per cent. Although prices increased less rapidly than earnings,
they rose more quickly throughout the Phase I and Phase II period than during
the previous twelve months. Particularly alarming were the increases in food and
raw-material prices. Earnings rose at a slower rate under Phases I and II than
during the previous twelve months. Clearly, this control of earnings, together with
the expansion of production this permitted, helped to prevent piling a full-scale
domestic inflation on top of an imported one. The restraint of pay increases, and
the healthy increase in production, kept down costs of production with benefit
to domestic and export prices. Thus, importantly in spite of the increase in world
commodity prices, Phases I and II enabled a high rate of economic growth to be
continued.

Phase III

The Price and Pay Code for Stage III, A Consultative Document was in two parts.
The first described the government's proposals, and related them to the stage that
had been reached in the counter-inflation programme and to the expected economic background of the next stage. The second part explained the proposed amendments to the Price and Pay Code, and contained a draft of the revised code. The
document stated that the objectives of the counter-inflation programme were
unchanged. They were as follows: to maintain a high rate of growth and to
improve real incomes; to improve the position of the low paid and pensioners; and
to moderate the rate of cost and price inflation. Phase III became operative at the
beginning of November 1973 and lasted until the summer of 1974. (In this case
study, we only consider the operation of Phase III up to the time of the General
Election of February 1974.)

Prices

The government proposed to continue its strict control of dividends, prices and
profits. In recognition of the influence of international factors in the domestic
inflation process, the Price Code provided for a safeguard against high price
increases in the form of a 'threshold' scheme (described immediately below) in
order to protect living standards. The aims of the proposals for the Price Code
were to enforce the control strictly and fairly so as to restrain price increases and
secure price reductions; and to protect and encourage investment. It was intended
that the Price Code for Stage III should have a heavier impact on manufacturers

than in Phase II, and thus the code limited the extent to which cost increases could be passed on as price increases. Various loopholes in the old system were to be tightened up; categories like 'allowable costs' and 'permitted price increases' were strictly defined so as to leave firms in no doubt. Control of profit margins was strengthened; gross profit margins expressed as a ratio of profits before tax to sales or turnover were restricted to 10 per cent. The government felt that it was right and fair that control of prices and profits should be strictly applied in order to prevent profits being made out of inflation. There was some evidence that this was the case under Phase II, since sub-division of enterprises had been used by some firms to avoid the restraint of the profit-margin control. It was emphasised that this should be discontinued under Phase III. The code was to be more strictly enforced for category II firms (in manufacturing, those with sales between £5 million and £50 million a year), and it was proposed to make an order requiring these companies to report price increases and their justification for making these increases to the Price Commission. In sum, the Price Code of Phase III was much more rigorous than it was under Phases I and II.

Pay

The aims of the government's pay policy for Stage III were to:

(1) be fair and to give special help for the low-paid;

(2) provide for greater flexibility in negotiations; and

(3) protect living standards against a high rate of increase in prices.

Provision was therefore proposed for:

(1) pay increases for the group up to 7 per cent, or if negotiators preferred, up to an average of £2.25 a week per head for the group, with an individual maximum of £350 a year;

(2) a flexibility margin of a further 1 per cent available to negotiators for use in settlements which removed anomalies and obstacles to the better use of manpower;

(3) extra payments under new efficiency schemes when such schemes achieved genuine savings and contributed to stabilising prices;

(4) bringing premium payments to those working 'unsocial' hours (in other words at night or weekends) up to a minimum standard;

(5) dealing with anomalies created by the standstill;

(6) further progress towards equal pay between men and women;

(7) increases in certain types of London allowances outside the pay limit;

(8) the threshold safeguard to enable pay to be increased up to 40p per week, if, in Stage III, the increase in the Retail Price Index reached 7 per cent above the figure for October 1973, and by up to another 40p a week for every further 1 per cent rise.

Thus the pay policy placed great emphasis on helping the low paid, by means of the straight cash limit of £2.25 and the threshold agreements at a flat cash rate regardless of the level of income.

Table 11.2 indicates that prices rose during Phase III (October – February 1974) by an annual rate of 14 per cent.* Food prices continued to increase more rapidly, by 17 per cent. Apart from food, the price of oil and petrol increased very substantially. Basic raw materials (70 per cent of which are imported into the United Kingdom) rose by 17 per cent between December and January, and were 65 per cent higher than in December 1972. About three-quarters of this rise was the result of the increase in crude oil prices.

Over the complete Phase I – Phase III period (November 1972 to March 1974) prices rose by just under 16 per cent whilst earnings increased by 15.3 per cent.

A few general points can be made on incomes policies between 1972 and 1974:

(1) One major difference between incomes policies under the Labour government and the post-1970 Conservative government was that the Conservatives did not attempt to limit increases in earnings to productivity growth rates. After 1968 inflation accelerated and increasingly became an international (hence imported) rather than a purely domestic phenomenon.

(2) It is possible that the increasing role of international factors in the upward movement of the retail price index has rendered the prolonged successful operation of domestic incomes policies impossible in their present form, though this judgement may have to be modified in view of the greater flexibility of exchange rates seen in recent years; some of these points are illustrated by Table 11.2. It is clear that in the 1972 – 4 Conservative incomes policy, very pronounced increases in world commodity prices continually undermined the successful operation of the incomes policy.

(3) Both the Labour government of 1964 – 70 and the post-1970 Conservative government paid attention to the plight of low-paid workers, though between 1972 and 1974 the burden of increased food and oil prices fell disproportionately on this group.

(4) Voluntary policies have proved to be relatively ineffective compared to statutory ones, particularly under Conservative governments, when it was difficult to obtain trade-union co-operation.

(5) The success of incomes policy in restraining wage and price rises has throughout all policies diminished with time. During both the 1966 – 8 policy and Phases I – III of the 1970 – 4 Conservative government, initial success in restraining wages, and to some extent prices, was recorded; but this was followed by a series of very inflationary wage demands, both in the second half of 1967 onwards, and under Phase III.

(6) Incomes policy has a tendency to become more and more complex through time as injustices and inequalities begin to dominate the short-run necessity of depressing rates of inflation. Inevitably governments are eventually forced to

*Roughly calculated, owing to the change in the index; this also applies to the rate of increase of food prices referred to in the next sentence.

recognise problems of income distribution and equity resulting from the implementation of the incomes policy, and objectives of equity and efficiency may
conflict.

The following reports of the Pay Board are intended to illustrate points (4)
to (6) above, drawing attention to the particular problem of reconciling objectives
of efficiency and equity.

Anomalies Report (September 1973)

The *Anomalies Report* was to serve as a basis for remedying anomalies, the
principle being that the over-all cost should be met within Phase III, which
explicitly allowed for the removal of anomalies. Particular consideration was given
to anomalies arising from the effect of the standstill on groups whose pay was
determined:

(1) by links with settlements made by other groups; and
(2) by formal procedures for making comparisons with the pay of other
groups.

Clearly, in either case, since such links or procedures tend to operate with a
lag, there could be disruption arising from the imposition of an across-the-board
standstill from a given date, generating 'feelings of unfairness'. The main problem
was the tight definition of anomalous cases, to distinguish them from the general
run of those who had pay restrained; hence the emphasis on the above two
categories as against the wider arguments relating to comparability used in most
pay negotiations.

Thus, to qualify as an anomalous case, a group had to meet two criteria:

(1) the link or formal procedure must have been broken by the standstill; and
(2) the link or formal procedure would have determined the pay of the group.

A number of detailed criteria were laid down to establish the second point, relying
on clear identifications of the pay group being followed and the predictability,
within narrow limits, of the resultant pay increase due in the standstill period.
(Agreements formally concluded before the standstill were of course simply
deferred and therefore did not give rise to anomalies.)

The largest case, which will serve to illustrate the nature of the problem, was
that of 400,000 non-industrial civil servants. These workers had a well-established
formal procedure designed to maintain parity with outside groups, based on an
elaborate pay-research system, which provided information accepted by both
sides and which therefore closely controlled the pay increases available within any
given two-year review. Such a review was due in January 1973 and was therefore
blocked by the standstill. (Apart from these major realignments the civil service
also received interim or 'central' increases in line with the general trend of earnings; these would not generate anomalies.) This case was particularly sensitive,

involving the government as both employer and implementer of a pay-restraint policy.

The Report estimated that the cost of correcting anomalies in Stage III would not exceed £145 million, benefiting $1\frac{1}{4}$ million employees at most. The government subsequently claimed that the recommendations were promptly implemented and turned to the greater problems discussed in the Relativities Report.

Relativities Report (January 1974)

The *Relativities Report* was introduced in a final attempt to settle the miners' dispute (discussed in Case 32) within the terms of Phase III. It considered in general terms, in the light of industrial unrest, problems of identifying and dealing with 'special cases'. Thus, the *Relativities Report* examined the wider and more complex problems of pay relativities not considered in the *Anomalies Report*.

Relativities were defined as pay differences between separate negotiating units, and were distinguished from differentials which referred to pay differences within single negotiating units. The Report considered that Phases II and III had given adequate scope for the adjustment of differentials, and thus concentrated on the extremely tricky and potentially explosive question of relativities.

Whilst the Report saw clearly that relativities emerge from the interplay over time of a variety of economic, social and institutional factors, and that it was difficult to establish *a priori* precise criteria for deciding which relationships should be changed, it nevertheless suggested that certain groups of workers might deserve special treatment. Special treatment, for example, would be merited where a group found that over a period it was persistently falling a long way short of the average rate of increase of earnings. It was also indicated that criteria for the selection of special cases would need to be modified over time to reflect changes in the economic and social environment. Thus, there might be a *prima facie* case for increasing the relative pay of workers in those industries suffering from (1) manpower shortage, or (2) low pay, in the sense of receiving less than some stipulated minimum income.

The Report concludes, if rather vaguely:

> In our view, consideration should be given mainly to claims for significant shifts in external relativities, that is, relationships between large groups of workers of importance to the community as a whole. Such cases are likely to be few and would involve claims for the restoration of a relative position that had been lost over a given period of time, or for a change in position for some other reason (para. 61).

This attempt to identify 'special cases' indicated the increasing preoccupation of the Conservative incomes policy with the whole question of income distribution. It is clear that the very success of the incomes policy depended crucially at this stage on some measures of consensus between the T.U.C., the C.B.I. and the government over the very sensitive question of pay relativities. Formal procedures were recommended: The Pay Board would examine each case publicly in the light of some prior agreement between the T.U.C. and the C.B.I. over its 'special case' status. However, whereas the Report offered a useful method for considering long-term relativity problems, it was of little assistance to the immediate problem of industrial unrest, the most serious manifestation of which was the miners' dispute which culminated in the miners' strike of early 1974. We turn to consider this dispute in detail in the following case study.

Exercises

(11.1) In what sense do the changes in price and pay codes through Phases I, II and III represent an attempt to move from short-term emergency measures towards a viable long-run policy on inflation?

(11.2) How did Phase III attempt to introduce considerations of equity into the pay code? What sort of problems might this create in the longer term?

(11.3) Carefully distinguish 'anomalies' from 'relativities', as defined in the appropriate Pay Board Reports. Why are the problems raised by 'relativities' more likely to undermine the effectiveness of an incomes policy than those raised by 'anomalies'?

CASE 32. INCOMES POLICY, 1972 – 4: THE MINERS' DISPUTE

In the early 1970s the miners argued that, after considerable co-operation with the National Coal Board throughout the 1960s in order to streamline the industry and improve its competitiveness, they qualified for 'special case' treatment and merited significant increases in wages. In common with other public-sector workers the miners felt that they had slipped badly in the earnings league table. A series of unofficial strikes commenced in late 1969 and continued into the 1970s, finally culminating in the miners' strike of the winter of 1971 – 2. An independent inquiry was set up under Lord Wilberforce, which recommended increases well in excess of the Coal Board's offer. Indeed, the resulting settlement of the dispute was not unrelated to the subsequent introduction of Phase I.

At their annual conference in July 1973 the miners adopted wage targets which proved to be well in excess of those proposed in Phase III. Once again the miners argued that they had a real grievance over pay, that since the _Wilberforce Report_ in February 1972 relative earnings in the mining industry had fallen behind those in manufacturing. Moreover, in the latter half of 1973 it became clear that the radical change in the price of alternative forms of energy had made coal a relatively cheap and vital source of fuel. In sum, the miners contended that their relative earnings position was significantly out of line with the economic importance of mining to the country. It was argued that coal production should be stimulated and would only be increased by both attracting men into the industry and preventing the exodus of men from the industry which the Wilberforce settlement had failed to halt. This necessitated increases in wages, and indeed, arguably, was dictated by the economic criteria of a free and efficient labour market. However, the government used its influence to restrain this public-sector industry since it feared that such wage increases would spread to other sectors of the economy, undermining Phase III. In effect, the government cautiously reiterated the principle of uniform treatment for all groups of workers; only minor amendments to this principle seemed practicable. Following prolonged negotiations the mine-workers were offered $16\frac{1}{2}$ per cent in October 1973; this offer, which was felt to be consistent with Phase III, proposed the following breakdown of increases – basic wage rates (7 per cent), unsocial hours payment (6 per cent), productivity allowance ($3\frac{1}{2}$ per cent). The offer was rejected by the miners.

It became increasingly apparent that the energy crisis and the miners' dispute challenged the basic conception of Phase III of containing the pay of all groups within certain defined limits. The government eventually recognised that the on-going implementation of an incomes policy inevitably produces 'special cases', those wider problems of relativities. In a last-minute attempt to avert a strike in the mining industry and make Phase III more flexible, the government issued its _Relativities Report_, but, as has already been indicated above, this Report lacked sufficient precision to deal with immediate short-run industrial problems. In the interests of keeping down the rate of inflation, and in a context of growing industrial unrest, the government was reluctant to risk any interference with the delicate structure of wage relativities. The miners went on strike and demonstrated to the country the power of a highly organised trade union. Phase III could not survive the challenge of the energy crisis and the miners' strike, and the Conservative government called a General Election (February 1974). At the election, the Labour Party secured more seats than the Conservatives and came into power as a minority government.

The Pay Board's *Special Report on the Relative Pay of Mine Workers* was published in March 1974, and coincided with the settlement agreed between the Coal Board and the miners. The settlement, reached by traditional collective bargaining, cost £103 million, only £3 million more than the figure recommended by the Report, and resulted in an average rise of about 30 per cent in wages in the mining industry. This increase was almost twice the original offer. The following criteria were used in the Report:

(1) that the coal industry was undergoing a change in its relative importance to the economy as a result of developments in the supply and price of oil;

(2) that it was in the national interest to meet this increased demand for coal, by halting the decline in the production of coal since the early 1950s;

(3) that this could not be done without recruiting more miners and retaining them in the industry (it was pointed out that colliery manpower had declined from 704,000 in 1957 to 268,000 in 1973 as the contraction of the industry had proceeded); and

(4) that the miners should be compensated in pay for the unique combination of 'threats to health' that they have to endure.

The Report drew a distinction, on the basis of these criteria, between those who worked underground and those who did not, and thus suggested a significant alteration in:

(*a*) internal relativities or differentials (between underground and surface workers), since it was felt that the relative earnings of underground workers had declined compared with those of surface workers; as well as

(*b*) external relativities (between the mining industry and other manufacturing industries), acknowledging the miners' complaint that the industry as a whole had lost ground compared with manufacturing – they estimated this as a fall of around 3 to 4 per cent per annum over the last eighteen months.

Thus the Report suggested the following increases in pay (total cost £100.5 million):

(1) original cost £34 million;

(2) to underground workers an allowance of £1.20 a shift for every shift worked underground, at a cost of £51 million;

(3) to surface workers who had previously served a qualifying period under-ground a personal allowance of 50 per cent (that is 60p) of the underground allowance for every shift worked, at a cost of £2.5 million; and

(4) to facilitate any necessary further adjustments of internal relativities, at a cost of an additional £4 million.

The miners' dispute revealed clearly the problems of implementing an incomes policy in a mixed economy. Too often governments have relied for the success of their incomes policies on restraint in the public-sector industries. Such policies, generating sectoral inequities, inevitably produce resentment, which finally cul-minates in industrial unrest, as governments fail to reconcile the two objectives of efficiency and equity. One important lesson of the post-1964 period is that no incomes policy can ignore the importance of 'fair' relativities. However, such is the power of the trade unions that any government attempt to select certain sectors for 'special treatment' on grounds of both equity *and* efficiency too often results in across-the-board increases in pay, thus completely undermining the incomes policy.

Exercise

(11.4) In the light of the reports on relativities, and in a society where 'equit-able' differentials can only be maintained by upward pay adjustment, can attempts to maintain such 'equity' be reconciled with effective long-run over-all restraints on pay increases?

Postscript

A Labour government came into office at the end of February 1974; though committed to the abolition of statutory incomes policies, its weak parliamentary position obliged it to allow Phase III to remain in operation until July. (As already noted, a settlement was reached with the miners which was very similar to that independently recommended by the Pay Board.) Though Phase III operated only until July, and the Pay Board was abolished, after that date the powers of the Price Commission, and dividend and rent control, continued in force. In addition food subsidies were introduced; these were massively costly – the March 1974 budget allowed £500 million per annum. For pay restraint the government sub-sequently relied on the 'Social Contract' with the trade unions; this entailed voluntary observance of guidelines for collective bargaining, endorsed in detail at the T.U.C. in September 1974. These guidelines were that the main objective of wage negotiations should be to maintain real incomes, that major rises should be twelve months apart, and that there were certain exclusions – productivity deals, pay-structure reforms, rises for those earning less than £30 per week, elimination of lower pay for women, and job-security improvements. Subsequent experience showed that real incomes were more than maintained, many claims broke the

twelve-month provision, and the exclusion clauses were widely exploited. In
return for the unions' acceptance of the guidelines the government's side of the
'contract' involved such features as higher pensions and tax reform. As a consequence of the unions' interpretation of their side of the contract, basic wage
rates rose more rapidly than even the disturbingly fast increase in retail prices.
For the twelve-month period of up to end-March 1975 prices rose by 21 per
cent. In his budget speech of 15 April 1975, Chancellor Denis Healey, commenting on the fact that 'pay has been running about 8 per cent or 9 per cent ahead
of prices', said that 'I do not believe that anyone would claim that the T.U.C.
guidelines were intended to permit this result.' Against a background of mounting
crisis, the government announced plans for a sharp reduction in the rate of
inflation. These were published in a White Paper on 11 July 1975 (*The Attack on
Inflation*) and involved a limit of £6 per week on pay increases, over the period to
1 August 1976, with no increase at all for those earning in excess of £8500 per
annum. Some transitional arrangements were made. This was a partial compromise with proposals put forward by some trade-union leaders. There were no
direct statutory controls on pay. Firms were not allowed to pass on excessive pay
settlements in higher prices; a 10 per cent limit on increases in dividends was
imposed; local authority rent increases were further limited; and government
expenditure was to be sharply controlled. There was the possibility of the government taking additional powers if the policy was not adhered to. A bill was
introduced in mid-July, relieving employers of certain contractual obligations
and providing for the amendment of the existing price code; this was enacted two
weeks later.

Supplementary exercises

(11.5) It has been suggested that 'statutory' policies tend to be more effective
than 'voluntary' policies, at least in the short run, yet even the former cannot
apparently succeed for a reasonably long period without trade-union co-operation.
Discuss the dilemma that this creates for policy-makers.

(11.6) Is it possible to devise a viable, long-run prices and incomes policy in
an economy which is as 'open' as Britain's?

(11.7) Many of the devices which are used as short-run expedients in prices
and incomes policies are likely to create greater problems in the long run; consider,
for example, subsidies and restraint on nationalised-industry prices. Discuss why
this is so, and suggest reasons why governments none the less use such devices.

Sources and References

A Programme for Controlling Inflation: The First Stage, Cmnd. 5125 (London:
      H.M.S.O., Nov 1972).
A Programme for Controlling Inflation: The Second Stage, Cmnd. 5205 (London:
      H.M.S.O., Jan 1973).

K. HAWKINS, 'The Miners and Incomes Policy 1972 – 5', *Industrial Relations* (1975).

J. HUGHES and R. MOORE (eds), *A Special Case?* (Harmondsworth: Penguin, 1972).

Pay Board Advisory Report 1, Anomalies, Cmnd. 5429 (London: H.M.S.O., Sep 1973).

Pay Board Advisory Report 2, Relativities, Cmnd. 5535 (London: H.M.S.O., Jan 1974).

Special Report, Relative Pay of Mineworkers, Cmnd. 5567 (London: H.M.S.O., Mar 1974).

The Attack on Inflation, Cmnd. 6151 (London: H.M.S.O., July 1975).

The Economist (8 – 14 Sep 1973).

The Price and Pay Code for Stage 3, A Consultative Document, Cmnd. 5444 (London: H.M.S.O., Oct 1973).

CHAPTER 12

Indicative Planning

C.T. Sandford

Summary of Background Material

Meaning and Aims of Indicative Planning

Indicative planning is a form of national economic planning in which a target is set for the growth of national output over a series of years, usually about five. Quantitative estimates are made of what might happen to particular industries and sectors of the economy (e.g. private consumption, public consumption, invest-ment) if the global expansion is achieved. The figures are accompanied by a list of policy measures intended to help fulfil the plan. The figures are thus an 'indica-tion' of how the economy is expected to develop. The policy measures may include incentives or disincentives (such as subsidies or taxes) to promote the desired expansion, but these are not tied to the targets of the plan and there are no sanctions against industries or firms failing to achieve the output figures of the plan.

The introduction of indicative planning in Britain in the 1960s was an attempt to increase the rate of growth of national output, which had lagged behind that of most advanced industrial countries. The development owed something to the French example. The desirability of attempting indicative planning is a very controversial issue.

Advantages Claimed by Supporters

(1) Effect on demand expectations

The main argument for indicative planning is that it creates the expectation of economic growth which will itself promote growth. Enterprise, innovation and particularly investment by private industry, rest to a significant extent on expectations of future demand. If businessmen believe that incomes and demand will expand in accordance with the planned rate, this will encourage investment. and help to achieve the desired growth.

Moreover, an indicative plan might have a stabilising effect, in that if business-men were convinced of the attainability of the five-year target, they would not cut investment so heavily in response to any short-term reductions in demand, but would 'stick to trend'.

(2) Co-ordination of output decisions

The figures in the plan arise from a process of consultation between 'industry' and the planning body. They embody the views of representatives of the main industries about what expansion is likely in their industry in the context of an assumed global expansion. The planning process irons out inconsistencies and enables the various plans – of individual industries and of the public sector – to be co-ordinated. Both government and individual industries can plan on the basis of fuller knowledge of what each intends and in the light of the planned rate of global expansion. This fuller knowledge makes for better planning of each sector of the economy and reduces wasteful duplication of output or investment.

(3) Highlighting of obstacles to growth

The planning process throws into relief the likely obstacles to growth (e.g. shortage of skilled labour or inadequate expansion in a raw-material supply) and thus enables policies to be formulated to overcome these obstacles.

Obstacles could be indicated and the necessary policies outlined without all the statistical apparatus of the plan; but it is argued that the necessary policies are given increased urgency and reality by being presented in the context of a detailed quantitative forecast and that, in this form, they are more likely to be heeded by the public and applied by businessmen and trade unions.

(4) Economic education

More broadly, the consultation between government, industrialists and trade unionists in preparing the plan and in seeking to apply the policy recommendations is a useful form of education in the realities of economic life, and in understanding each others' point of view; publication of the plan helps to create an informed and educated public.

Disadvantages Claimed by Opponents

(1) Unsound statistics

The statistical basis of indicative plans is alleged to be unsound, highly speculative and with a built-in bias to over-optimism about growth rates. For example:

(*a*) estimates of output and investment five years ahead are required from firms and industries assuming a certain global growth rate for the economy. But many unknowns affect output, e.g. changes in price, technology and taste; again, one firm's estimate of its own growth in output depends in part on the output and pricing policy of its competitors. Investment, which in any case takes considerable time to affect production, is particularly difficult to forecast. In general, experience has shown wide discrepancies between such forecasts and actual production.

(*b*) Estimates of output by firms are as likely to express hopes as realistic assessments. No firm is likely to admit that it expects its market share to diminish, even if its managing director secretly fears this. Similarly, firms are likely to over-estimate exports.

(c) A crucial estimate is that of the growth of productivity for the economy as a whole; yet this is outstandingly difficult both to measure and forecast.

(2) Misdirection of effort and resources

The compilation of a national plan occupies the time of much skilled labour in government service and industry which could be more usefully employed in other ways than on a gigantic and detailed but essentially unreal statistical exercise. Worse still, the preparation of the plan diverts attention from the crucial issues of policy.

(3) Evils resulting from over-optimistic growth expectations

If a plan fosters over-optimistic expectations of growth in the economy, positive harm may result. For example:

(a) A growth rate for public expenditure determined on the basis of the target growth rate for the economy as a whole may be maintained when the actual growth rate for the economy falls short of the target. If the relative rate of growth of public to private consumption in the plan accurately reflected the community's wishes, it is highly unlikely that the relative rates of growth which actually result, with all the shortfall concentrated on private consumption, also reflects the community's wishes, and the disproportionate increase in public expenditure growth is likely to accentuate inflationary pressures.

(b) Cost inflation may be stimulated by wage demands based on over-optimistic estimates of growth rates and productivity increases.

(c) Some industries may be led into wasteful over-investment by acceptance of the global growth rates of the plan. (Sir Ronald Edwards, then Chairman of the Electricity Council, mainly attributed the increase in electricity tariffs in 1967 to over-investment for this reason. Electricity is a very capital-intensive industry and surplus capacity raises unit costs. Sir Ronald argued that the capital investment programme of the industry was accelerated in line with the global growth rate of the N.E.D.C. study and of the National Plan; then actual national growth fell short of planned growth, leaving over-capacity in electrical generating plant.)*

(4) The expectation boomerang

The main argument for the indicative plan is the effect of expectations in promoting growth. But any continuing validity of this argument depends on the expectations of growth being fulfilled. It is an argument concerned with the psychology of businessmen. If the 'planned' growth does not materialise, then the 'confidence trick' fails. Worse, if a government has set its seal on a growth rate

*See 'Financing Electricity Supply', *Lloyds Bank Review* (July 1967).

which an economy fails to obtain by a large margin, not only will future plans fail to inspire in businessmen the necessary confidence, but the credibility of government economic policy in general will be undermined.

Illustration by Case Studies

The three main plans or 'planning documents' which have been published in the United Kingdom in the 1960s are considered within the context of one 'case', 'An Experiment in Indicative Planning; the United Kingdom, 1961 - 9', showing the evolution and transformation in indicative planning during the period.

CASE 33. AN EXPERIMENT IN INDICATIVE PLANNING: THE UNITED KINGDOM, 1961 – 9

National Economic Development Council (N.E.D.C.)

Formation and terms of reference

N.E.D.C. was set up by the Conservative government initially as an advisory body to the Chancellor of the Exchequer, then Mr Selwyn Lloyd. It met for the first time in March 1962. Its objects were:

(1) to examine the economic performance of the nation with particular concern for plans for the future in both the private and the public sectors of industry;

(2) to consider together what are the obstacles to quicker growth, what can be done to improve efficiency and whether the best use is being made of our resources;

(3) to seek agreement upon ways of improving economic performance, competitive power and efficiency – in other words, to increase the rate of sound growth.

The organisation consisted of an office (N.E.D.O.) headed by a Director-General (initially Sir Robert Shone) and divided into an economic and an industrial department; and a Council originally of twenty members; the Chancellor of the Exchequer in the chair; two other Ministers; the Director-General; six industrialists from private industry and two from nationalised industries; six trade unionists; and two academics. The trade unionists joined only on conditions, notably that their presence did not imply acceptance of the government's wages policy and that they were free to report back to the T.U.C. economic committee and to criticise. The other Council members were present not as representatives but as individuals.

The study of 4 per cent growth

The Council decided that its first main task should be the preparation of a report studying the implications of an average annual rate of growth of 4 per cent for the period 1961 – 6. A specific figure was selected to give concreteness, and 4 per cent, whilst higher than our previous rate of growth, was not felt to be impossibly high. 1961 was chosen as the base date (even though the Council met for the first time in 1962 and did not publish its report until 1963) to provide a reliable statistical starting-point for the projections.

This feasability study (*the 4 per cent case*) was published early in 1963 (*Growth of the United Kingdom Economy, 1961 – 1966*). The report falls into two parts, reflecting a dual approach:

(1) *An industrial inquiry*, with a representative cross-section of public and private industry, to assess the impact and feasibility to them of a growth rate of

4 per cent per annum. Seventeen industries were included in the industrial survey, together covering nearly a half of industrial production, two-fifths of G.N.P., two-fifths of exports and a half of fixed investment other than dwellings.

Information was sought from each industry on existing plans and expectations; implications for the industry of a 4 per cent growth in G.D.P. during 1961 – 6; and in particular, problems which might impede expansion.

The industries were asked for forecasts of output, exports, imports, employment and capacity on the basis both of present plans and of *the 4 per cent case.* Estimates were also sought for gross fixed capital formation at home for each year from 1961 to 1966; industries were asked to make their estimates in terms of 1961 prices. Comments were invited on particular points industries might have on manpower, training facilities, finance, and research and development trends in each industry (*Growth of the U.K. Economy, 1961 – 66*, p. 2).

The results showed the industries as falling into three broad groups on the basis of a global 4 per cent growth rate:

(*a*) Most rapid growth rates: chemicals, electricity and electronics, petroleum, motor-cars, heavy electrical machinery and machine-tools (estimated necessary growth rates, 7 – 13 per cent per annum).

(*b*) Intermediate growth rates: Post Office, distribution, building, iron and steel, agriculture (approximately 3 – 6 per cent).

(*c*) Slowest growth rates: coal, gas, wool textiles, sugar confectionery (under 3 per cent).

The industries, individually, saw no insuperable difficulties in obtaining the manpower, equipment and finance for investment to achieve the growth rate appropriate to a national 4 per cent rate. The remainder of the economy would not need to expand as fast as the seventeen industries taken together.

(2) *A macroeconomic study* to consider the implications of a 4 per cent growth rate on the economy as a whole.

It was assumed that effective employment would rise by 0.8 per cent per annum during 1961 – 6. This estimate took into account natural increase in the relevant age groups; changes in unemployment (which was expected to decline from the 1962 level); an anticipated increase in activity rates following measures to encourage the employment of married women and older workers; and likely trends in working hours, holidays and net immigration.

An increase of 0.8 per cent in the labour force implied an increase in productivity (output per head) of *3.2 per cent* per annum to attain a 4 per cent growth rate. Average productivity increase for 1955 – 61 was estimated to have been 2.5 per cent per annum, but on a rising trend because of increased productive investment and rising expenditure on research and development. A 3.2 per cent per annum average increase was therefore considered to be attainable for 1961 – 6, but it was recognised that productivity would not suddenly leap ahead; hence an average of 3.2 implied a rather lower level in the earlier years, rising to a higher level in the later years.

The estimated growth for the main output/expenditure components in 1966 as compared with 1961 is summarised in Table 12.1.

TABLE 12.1

Resources available	Percentage increase in real terms	
	1966 over 1961	*per annum*
Output (G.D.P.)	22	4.0
Imports	22	4.0
		4.0
Use of resources		
Consumers'		
expenditure	19	3.5
Public consumption	19	3.5
Investment	30	5.3
Exports	28	5.0
		4.0

SOURCE: *Growth of the U.K. Economy, 1961 - 1966*, table 9.

The output figures (G.D.P.) followed from the 4 per cent case being considered. The level of imports was based on an estimate of the community's propensity to import at these output levels.

Turning to the estimates under 'use of resources', the figure for exports was that increase required to produce a balance-of-payments surplus of £300 million, on the basis of the previously estimated import level. The investment figure included estimates of stocks necessary to attain the higher output levels; public investment in education, hospitals and roads; dwellings; and private productive investment, which needed to rise considerably to achieve the desired productivity increase. Public consumption represented the government's forecast of current expenditure on defence, the social services, etc., on the basis of 4 per cent growth. Private consumption was largely a residual figure.

The results of the two parts of the report, the industrial study and the macro-study, dovetailed. Thus, for example, data collected from the seventeen industries informed the estimates of investment in the macro assessment; and the estimates of the over-all growth in the labour supply confirmed the view that the industries could obtain the total labour necessary for expansion compatible with a global growth rate of 4 per cent per annum, although there might be difficulties in the supply of skilled labour.

The report was sprinkled with suggestions, in general terms, of measures to overcome obstacles to growth. A further N.E.D.C. publication in 1963, *Conditions Favourable to Faster Growth*, extended this discussion, sometimes introducing novel ideas.

Another aspect of the work of the N.E.D.C. was the setting-up of Economic Development Committees (E.D.C.s) for a number of individual industries.

The outcome of the N.E.D.C. study

The 4 per cent growth of the N.E.D.C. feasibility study was approved by its Council, and that rate came to be looked upon as a target, although the Chancellor, by then Mr Maudling, never explicitly adopted it as government policy. In March 1964 N.E.D.C. issued a follow-up report assessing the way in which the programme was working out. By the time of the General Election in October 1964 it was clear that, whilst growth had been slow in 1961 – 3, the rate of growth had accelerated in 1963 – 4. But serious balance-of-payments difficulties had arisen; imports had grown more and exports less than predicted in the study.

The Department of Economic Affairs and the National Plan

The new Labour government immediately made important changes in the planning machinery. A Department of Economic Affairs (D.E.A.) was established, initially under Mr George Brown as First Secretary of State, with responsibility for drawing up a national plan. Many of the staff of N.E.D.C. were transferred to the D.E.A., and the activities of the N.E.D.C. organisation were channelled more on industrial lines, with the establishment of E.D.C.s for a growing number of industries. The Council continued to discuss planning documents, but these were prepared by the D.E.A. and not its own office. Some changes took place in the composition of the Council, notably that the Secretary of State for Economic Affairs replaced the Chancellor of the Exchequer as Chairman. Two points arising from these changes are particularly noteworthy:

(1) When planning became the responsibility of a government department, it carried the seal of government policy. If the main point of indicative planning is to promote growth by creating the expectation of it, a plan which automatically carries a government commitment ought to be more credible than that produced by a more independent body. On the other hand, an independent body is better able to criticise aspects of government policy which may impede growth.

(2) Although the Council still considered plans concerned with demand expectations and growth of the economy, the member of the government primarily concerned with demand management, that is the Chancellor of the Exchequer, whom the Council had originally been set up to advise, ceased to be a member of it.

The National Plan was hurriedly prepared by the D.E.A. and published in September 1965. The Foreword, by the First Secretary of State for Economic

Affairs, introduced the plan as a 'major advance in economic policy-making in the United Kingdom' and categorically stated: 'The plan for the first time represents a statement of Government policy and a commitment to action by the Government.'

The National Plan followed the same lines of approach as the N.E.D.C. study, with an industrial inquiry, a survey of the implications of the target growth rate for the economy as a whole and suggestions for overcoming obstacles to growth. We shall not attempt a comprehensive review of its contents, but rather compare it with the N.E.D.C. study to indicate important differences and similarities.

(1) *The target.* A global 25 per cent increase in national output between 1964 and 1970 was the target – an average annual rate of *3.8* per cent. Expression in aggregate terms over the six years had the advantage of providing a round figure, easier to remember and fire the imagination than the new annual rate; so expressed, the target was also compatible with variation in the annual rate within the six-year period – in fact, the planners expected a slower rate of growth in the earlier years than the later.

Ostensibly the target was less ambitious than the 4 per cent annual rate of the N.E.D.C. study; in fact it was more so. Projections for the labour force suggested an average growth of only about *0.25* per cent over the period of the plan; the estimate of productivity increase to achieve the target was therefore about *3.4* per cent, more than that of the N.E.D.C. study.

(2) *The scope.* The scope of the National Plan was very much wider than the N.E.D.C. study. (The published document ran to almost 500 closely printed pages.) Government expenditure on the various services was set out in detail, and the industrial inquiry covered a much wider range of industries and other economic activities. Much of the information for the industrial inquiry was collected through the E.D.C.s for the various industries instead of the trade associations, which had been the main agents for the N.E.D.C. industrial estimates.

(3) *Check list for action.* Distributed throughout the National Plan were suggested policies for removing obstacles to growth, as in the N.E.D.C. report, but in the plan these suggestions were also assembled near the beginning of the document as a *'Check List for Action Required'*.

(4) *Regional planning.* A separate chapter of the plan was devoted to regional planning. Although this contained little that was new, it reflected the government's intention to make regional planning 'an integral part of national planning'.

Earlier in 1965 the government had divided the country into planning regions, one each for Scotland and Wales and eight for England; each region had a Regional Planning Board (of civil servants) and an advisory council with the following terms of reference:

(*a*) to help in the formulation of a regional plan, having regard to the best use of the region's resources;

(*b*) to advise on the steps necessary for implementing the regional plan on the basis of information and assessments provided by the Economic Planning Board;

and

(*c*) to advise on the regional implications of national economic policies.

(5) *Balance-of-payments policy.* The National Plan had one unfortunate similarity with the N.E.D.C. study, namely that action proposed to remedy the large balance-of-payments deficit consisted of a series of palliatives rather than any major policy change. Defence expenditure overseas was to be reduced; aid to developing countries cut; private investment abroad limited; beyond that, proposed measures consisted of little more than the promotion of studies by E.D.C.s and other bodies to promote exports and save imports.

The outcome of the Plan

Within a year of the publication of the plan, the government had adopted measures to try to improve the balance of payments by cutting domestic demand, which made the growth objectives unattainable.

A marked disillusionment with indicative planning followed.

The Task Ahead: Economic Assessment to 1972

Britain devalued sterling in November 1967, and the third 'plan' in the series, setting forth a post-devaluation strategy, was prepared by the D.E.A. and published in February 1969. This document, entitled *The Task Ahead*, differed considerably from its predecessors.

(1) A non-plan

The first words of the first chapter of the National Plan proclaimed 'This is a plan.' *The Task Ahead* began not with a proclamation but a disclaimer: 'This is a planning document, not a plan.' It was a Green Paper, that is a document for discussion, rather than, as its immediate predecessor, a White Paper stating government policy. Its approach was cautious and defensive; it frequently explained that the economic assessment put forward was 'highly provisional' and stressed the limitations of forward planning.

(2) Scope

The scope of the document was much narrower than that of the National Plan (reflected in its much smaller size). *The Task Ahead* contained no detailed industrial survey. It offered a broad macroeconomic view of the prospects of the economy over the four years to 1972; some details were included of estimated public expenditure and of the nationalised industries, but there was no industrial survey. Rather, *The Task Ahead* was intended to provide a framework for discussion with the representatives of individual industries through their E.D.C.s or some other body. It was envisaged that a process of 'consultative planning' would lead to a series of documents setting out the view of the government, the results of 'the collaborative study of the situation' and the action that was needed.

(3) *The 'wedge' approach*

A significant change from the earlier plans lay in the 'wedge' approach. Instead of a single figure of say, the rate of growth of output, a range of possible out-turns from the current trends of the economy were indicated. A 'basic rate' of $3\frac{1}{4}$ per cent output growth was accompanied by figures representing possible higher or lower growth rates. The document stressed: 'The figure of $3\frac{1}{4}$ per cent a year is not a forecast of what will happen; the outcome could be worse, but the Government believe that, if all concerned pursue the right policies with determination, it could be much better, and the aim must certainly be to do better.' (A pious platitude with which it is difficult to disagree.)

(4) *The balance of payments*

The need for a substantial balance-of-payments surplus occupied a central place in the document, and the implications of the necessary transfer of resources to exports and import saving were discussed. The method adopted well demonstrates the new 'wedge' approach. The document considers the possible effect on exports and imports of three rates of growth (see Table 12.2).

TABLE 12.2

| | Per cent per annum (volume) | | |
	Basic	Higher	Lower
Estimated growth in output	$3\frac{1}{4}$	4	3
Assumed rise in imports	4	$4\frac{3}{4}$	$3\frac{3}{4}$
Required growth in exports	$5\frac{3}{4}$	6	$5\frac{1}{4}$

End of the D.E.A.

Thus three indicative plans or 'planning documents' emerged in the United Kingdom in the 1960s with significant differences in their purpose, scope and methods, and in the constitutional and political framework in which they were presented. Planning reached its high-water mark with the National Plan of the autumn of 1965, but with its failure fell quickly into disrepute. This was reflected in the fate of the D.E.A. In October 1969, as part of the reorganisation of the machinery of government, the D.E.A. ceased to exist. The Treasury acquired responsibility for medium-term planning and resumed its former link with N.E.D.C. with the Chancellor as Chairman. The regional economic planning boards remained, central responsibility for them passing to the Ministry of Housing and Local Government, which was itself absorbed into the Department of the Environment when the Conservatives came to power in 1970.

As provided in *The Task Ahead,* discussions with industry duly took place, and reports from the E.D.C.s and other consultative bodies were considered at meetings of the N.E.D.C.; but no new indicative plan was prepared for the economy.

Revival of Indicative Planning?

With the end of the D.E.A. indicative planning appeared to be not only dead but buried. However, there have been signs of its gradual revival, largely unannounced and in a more modest form than hitherto. In December 1969 the government began the publication of annual White Papers on public expenditure giving information on its own expenditure plans looking five years ahead. This public expenditure survey was necessarily based on an assessment of the growth of the economy as a whole over that period but the assessment was not at first published. Then, in December 1972, after pressure from the House of Commons Expenditure Committee, this medium-term projection for the economy started to be included in summary form in the Public Expenditure White Papers. Interestingly, the wedge approach, which appeared in *The Task Ahead,* was adopted, the implications of alternative growth rates being considered.

Subsequently, in October 1973, the N.E.D.C. published *Industrial Review to 1977.* The review covered agriculture and ten manufacturing industries, currently accounting for about 60 per cent of U.K. manufacturing output. In the style of the industrial section of the first two indicative plans, it explored the implications of growth over the next few years for these industries, on the basis of the two growth rates used in the 1972 Public Expenditure White Paper. The general conclusion was reached 'that these industries can achieve growth rates consistent with an annual rate of growth of $3\frac{1}{2}$ per cent or somewhat higher, by the economy as a whole up to 1977', subject to quick action on certain constraints which the assessment had identified.

With the return of a Labour government in 1974, the move towards some form of indicative planning continued. A White Paper on *The Regeneration of British Industry* called for a more positive relationship between government and industry and proposed a system of Planning Agreements and a National Enterprise Board, subsequently embodied in the *Industry Act** of 1975. At the end of 1975, after discussion in the N.E.D.C., the government published a further White Paper, *An Approach to Industrial Strategy* (Cmnd. 6315), outlining a procedure by which the E.D.C.s would analyse the prospects of a number of important sectors of industry in the context of the government's medium-term growth projections; the N.E.D.C. would then consider industrial policy in general in the light of the E.D.C.'s discussions and highlight areas for action and improvement.

The new 'strategy' does not attempt to provide a set of mutually consistent growth forecasts, so that one advantage claimed for the full indicative plan – its self-fulfilling nature resulting from its effect on demand expectations – has been

*See above, Chapter 5, pp. 100–1.

sacrificed. The new strategy is more modest, too, in that it concentrates on certain sectors of industry only. But it is clear that many of the characteristics of indicative planning have re-emerged.

Exercises

(12.1) (i) What is the difference between production and productivity?

(ii) Make a list of the more important factors affecting productivity.

(12.2) What factors would you take into account in attempting to forecast the supply of labour to the economy as a whole, three years hence?

(12.3) Suppose that you were the managing director of a firm making 'widgets', a comparatively new consumer product. Outline some of the difficulties you would have in answering the kind of questions put to industries and firms (as part of the industrial inquiries of the N.E.D.C. study and the National Plan) on expected output, exports, imports, employment and investment over the next five years, assuming, say, a 4 per cent growth for the economy as a whole.

(12.4) 'A national plan may achieve something and can do no harm.' Assess this verdict in the light of the National Plan published in September 1965.

(12.5) What evidence is there of a revival of indicative planning in the early 1970s?

Supplementary exercises

(12.6) 'The value of N.E.D.C. is that its backroom staff is still acting as a forcing house of original ideas and suggestions. The test should be whether the Government will take them up and act on them, not whether N.E.D.C.'s superfluous top Council of trade union and managerial dignitaries will sign pieces of paper about them' (*The Economist,* 8 Feb 1964). Comment.

(12.7) 'The National Plan was sacrificed on the altar of the exchange rate.' Explain and comment.

(12.8) Under a leading article headed 'End of the Road for the D.E.A.?', *The Times* (28 April 1969) stated: 'Mr. Shore's *Task Ahead* is no more than a pious statement of objectives, with at best a useful exercise in consultation with industry appended. The real national plan is contained in the Budget and the financial statement published with it.' Comment.

(12.9) Does indicative planning support or negate the market economy?

Sources and References

T. BALOGH, *Planning for Progress*, Fabian Tract 346 (Fabian Society, 1963).

JOHN BRUNNER, *The National Plan*, Eaton Paper 4, 2nd edn (London: Institute of Economic Affairs, 1965). Primarily a critique of the questionnaire used in the industrial inquiry for the National Plan.

D.E.A., *The National Plan*, Cmnd. 2764 (London: H.M.S.O., Sep 1965).

The Task Ahead: Economic Assessment to 1972 (London: H.M.S.O., 1969).

Public Expenditure to 1976 - 77, Cmnd. 5178 (London: H.M.S.O. Dec 1972).

SIR ROY HARROD, 'Are Monetary and Fiscal Policies Enough?', *Economic Journal* (Dec 1964).

J. JEWKES, 'The Perils of Planning', *Three Banks Review*, no. 66 (June 1965).

N.E.D.C., *Growth of the United Kingdom Economy to 1966* (London: H.M.S.O., 1963).

——, *The Growth of the Economy* (London: H.M.S.O., Mar 1964).

——, *Conditions Favourable to Faster Growth* (London: H.M.S.O., 1963).

——, *Industrial Review to 1977* (London: H.M.S.O., Oct 1972).

GEORGE POLANYI, *Planning in Britain: The Experience of the 1960s*, Research Monograph 11 (London: Institute of Economic Affairs, 1967).

P.E.P., 'The National Plan: Its Contribution to Growth', *Planning*, xxxi, 493 (Nov 1965).

——, 'Inquest on Planning in Britain', *Planning*, xxxiii, 499 (Jan 1967).

SIR ROBERT SHONE, 'Problems of Planning for Economic Growth in a Mixed Economy', *Economic Journal* (Mar 1965).

Part 4

Developing Countries and World Trade

Introduction

Edward Horesh

Characteristics of Developing Countries

The main characteristic of the 'developing countries' is their poverty. Therefore,
the chief underlying policy aims of governments in this group of countries,
which contain almost three-quarters of the world's population and embrace just
under two-thirds of its land mass, should be to raise the standard of living of
their peoples and, meanwhile, to make the fact of poverty as bearable as possible.
Developing countries are often defined as those whose measured *per capita* income
falls short of that of the world at large, so that the distinction between 'developed'
and 'developing' nations is defined in terms of a property (national income) which
is not logically connected with development itself. This definition takes in all the
countries of the world except for North America, Western Europe, the Eastern
European Communist countries and Australia and New Zealand (as well as certain
oil-producing countries in the Middle East). Nevertheless, poor countries do share
a number of other characteristics which can be associated with the development
concept.

With few exceptions these countries are agricultural; over half of their labour
force works on the land. Food production for domestic use is overwhelmingly
organised along peasant modes. Peasant economy is prevalent, so that producer and
consumer units are not clearly differentiated and families tend to cater for their
own food needs. Production techniques are primitive and there is little use of
modern methods – fertiliser application, irrigation, improved seeds and mechan-
isation. So labour productivity is low. But agricultural production is not confined
to domestic foodstuffs; a significant section is often devoted to exports, e.g.
cotton, coffee, cocoa, sugar, jute. The export sector may well be organised on
capitalistic lines within privately or socially owned plantations, but it may also
derive from a peasantry which has fully entered the cash economy. In such cases,
techniques will not differ greatly from the traditional.

Capitalistic techniques are, however, almost invariably used in mining, another
important activity in many developing countries. Mining products, ores and min-
eral oil again tend to be exported in the absence of significant markets at home,
for industries in these countries are generally sparse; to a large extent they are
small-scale and traditional. In most developing countries, the modern industrial
system which has been part of Western European culture for well over a century
is a new component of urban life.

Almost all developing countries have had a colonial or quasi-colonial past. This
means that until fairly recently their infrastructural development has been organ-

ised by foreign governments who have seen their economies as adjuncts of the economies of the industrialised West. Thus ports, railways and roads have been positioned and built with foreign capital and in the interest of foreign firms. Capitalist enterprises – plantations, mining and manufacturing – have been (and often still are) owned and controlled by foreigners and directed to particular foreign markets. Where the peasantry has been responsible for growing cash crops, marketing has been carried out by foreign buyers. The present consequences of this historical pattern have been various (depending on the extent of foreign control, and to some degree on the size of the country), but certainly, it has led to an overly rigid pattern of trade and capital movements so that the exports and imports of a particular developing country are often heavily concentrated within the trade of one Western partner. Also, the large international oligopolies of the West tend to occupy a dominating trading position in the economies of these countries, which their governments find hard to control.

The Need to Industrialise

If living standards are to improve, a poor country must eventually industrialise. This is true, not because industrialisation is itself desirable, but because, given the preponderance of the labour force on the land, a general rise in real income can only come about through increased agricultural productivity; higher agricultural incomes will increase the demand for non-food consumer goods. Eventually increased production will cause redundancy. Industry can absorb this manpower as well as helping to satisfy the demand for manufactures. Furthermore, local industry will increasingly be required to satisfy agricultural demand for fertilisers and other inputs as well as the processing of its output.

Now it may be argued that industrialisation is not necessary to sustain income growth – that an increasing food surplus could be exported and that the production of those primary products in which the developing countries enjoy a natural comparative advantage could be further developed. But if all countries were able to expand food production beyond self-sufficiency, there would be no more export outlets; as for continuing to concentrate on other primary products, the case studies will indicate that this is a very dangerous strategy. True, industrialisation will not always be an easy process, particularly in view of the limited size of many national markets. Almost certainly it can only come about after careful preparation and planning at the level of regional groupings of countries.

Development and the Balance of Payments

Typically, then, economic growth will require increased imports to sustain agricultural productivity, to develop manufacturing industry and to satisfy the burgeoning demand for consumer goods. Economic aid and commercial loans can only supply some of the necessary finance; the greater part must come from exports.

And most developing countries will have to rely, at first at any rate, on the revenues from the sale of primary goods. Many people would regard this as a counsel of despair, and with some reason. For it is often said that the markets for primary products are inherently unstable, and that this instability is transmitted through the exporting economies, making prosperity precarious and planning insecure. Second, it is argued that the terms of trade are inexorably moving against the primary products, and therefore reliance on these goods is bound, in the long run, to be misplaced. The extent to which these arguments are correct depends on the damage done by commodity market instability to the over-all economy of an exporting country, the extent to which this instability or its effect can be damped by national and/or international policies, and finally, the extent to which the developed countries will grow over the years and so afford the exporting countries a growing market for their products.

CHAPTER 13

Primary Products, Trade and Stability

Edward Horesh

Summary of Background Material

Table 13.1 outlines the relevant structure of world trade. Note that trade in manufactured goods predominates and that, although the developing countries trade almost exclusively in primary products, the industrialised countries export about the same quantities of these goods, and that the trade of the developing countries is mainly with the developed countries.

A list of the main primary products (including metal ores, which are classified under manufactured goods in Table 13.1) is given in Table 13.2. The list is divided into three parts according to whether the exports originate mainly in the developed countries (Group 1), the developing countries (Group 2) or whether they are competitive as between the two (Group 3). The value of Group 2 (non-competing exports) amounts to about one-fifth of all the primary product exports from the developing countries; the remainder are subject to competition from the developed countries. This means that any international policy agreement to aid the developing countries by supporting primary goods in general will benefit the industrialised primary producers as well. Table 13.3 lists the eleven most important money-spinners for the developing countries; only four are out of competition with the industrialised countries.

The table also shows how concentrated this export trade is with respect to its range; out of 140 commodity groups, fifteen accounted for just under two-thirds of its trade. Moreover, item by item, production and trade tend to be concentrated in a few countries. For example, world production of *crude petroleum* (which has been top of the list for many years and the predominance of which has been much increased by the rise in oil prices since 1973) was 2268 million metric tons in 1970; of this the five big Middle Eastern producers, Iran, Saudi Arabia, Libya, Kuwait and Iraq produced 742 million; Venezuela 194 million, so that these six producers account for 41 per cent of world production. [The United States and the Soviet Union account for 37 per cent.] In *coffee* five countries – Brazil, Columbia, Ivory Coast, Uganda and Angola – produced half the world total output in 1970. Likewise, Chile, Zambia, Zaire, Peru and the Phillipines accounted for one-third of world production of *copper,* whereas the United States, the Soviet Union and Canada produced a further 50 per cent of world output in 1970. These facts have some implications for international trade policies. At first

TABLE 13.1
World Exports, 1973*

			$000m. (f.o.b.)
A.	Total world exports		575
	(i) of which:	Primary products	199
		Manufactured goods	365
	(ii) from:	Capitalist developed countries	392
		non-socialist developing countries	109
		Socialist countries	58
B.	Exports of primary products		
	from:	Capitalist developed countries	89
		Non-socialist developing countries	80
		(of which fuel	43)
		Socialist countries	18
C.	Exports of manufactured goods		
	from:	Capitalist developed countries	296
		Non-socialist developing countries	28
		Socialist countries	37
D.	Exports from capitalist developed countries		
	to:	Other capitalist developed countries	293
		Non-socialist developing countries	70
		Socialist countries	19
E.	Exports from non-socialist developing countries		
	to:	Capitalist developed countries	81
		Other non-socialist developing countries	22
		Socialist countries	5

* Owing to certain discrepancies, as well as rounding of figures, the sum of individual items does not add up to the totals as shown.

SOURCE: *GATT: International Trade 1974/5* (Geneva, 1975).

TABLE 13.2

Group 1	Group 2	Group 3
Meat and livestock	Coffee	Citrus fruits
Fish	Cocoa	Sugar
Grains (not rice)	Tea	Rice
Dairy produce	Bananas	Cotton
Apples and pears	Natural rubber	Tobacco
Canned fruit and juices	Jute and jute goods	Vegetable oils and
Wool	Sisal	oilseeds
Lead	Tin	Hides and skins
Aluminium		Petroleum
Timber		Iron
		Copper
		Zinc

sight of Table 13.3, it would seem that if action were restricted to the few primary products which accounted for a large proportion of the developing countries' exports, this would be easier and more helpful than dealing with every product. But in so far as these countries may be competing with the industrial countries, the latter may be unwilling to make concessions, not merely because they are unwilling to give an advantage to their less well-endowed competitors, but more particularly because they would be unwilling to advantage other industrial producers. Second, while action directed to the large revenue-earning commodities would significantly affect the aggregate earnings of the developing countries, it would necessarily be selective; those countries who export a large slice of these goods would benefit much more than the others. On the other hand, action on the less important items in international trade might be less costly to the developed countries but have disproportionate significance to particular producers. For another aspect of primary trade is the way in which producing countries have specialised in the production of particular goods. Table 13.4 gives some examples of this type of concentration.

Stability and Primary Production

It is commonly argued that the dependence of most developing countries on the export of primary products creates special problems of instability. Prices of primary goods are more unstable than those of manufactures because the former are subject to low short-run supply elasticities; in general, operating costs on the farms and in the mines are low compared with overheads, and because of the time taken for new plantings of tree crops to bear fruit, short-run responses are difficult. Also,

TABLE 13.3

Main exports of primary products from the non-socialist developing countries, 1970

Commodity	Value of exports from these countries ($000 f.o.b.)	Item as a percentage of exports from all sources	Percentage of all exports from these countries
Crude petroleum	14.2	95	26
Petroleum products	3.9	51	7
Coffee	3.0	94	5
Copper	2.5	60*	4
Sugar	1.9	76	3
Cotton	1.6	76	3
Rubber (including synthetic)	1.5	71	3
Iron ore	1.1	46	2
Fresh fruit	1.0	41	2
Cocoa	1.0	86	2
Animal feed	0.9	41	2
Rough wood	0.8	55	1
Uncooked meat	0.6	20	1
Oil seeds, nuts, kernels	0.5	26	1
Tea	0.5	89	1
Total of above	35.2	68	63
Total exports of primary products	55.3	45	100

* estimated.

SOURCE: *UN: Yearbook of International Trade Statistics 1974*, vol. II. 'Trade by Commodity'(New York, 1975).

weather conditions are an important determinant of agricultural output. Thus these markets exhibit the classical conditions for 'cobweb' instability. Price fluctuations create instability in export proceeds, making it difficult to plan imports and government spending, since a large part of public revenue is collected on exports. It is also argued that export instability is inflationary because when export incomes rise, increased aggregate demand causes prices to rise. But although prices are 'flexible upwards' they do not come down when exports are depressed; thus there is an inflationary ratchet effect.

These arguments have been subjected to scrutiny in recent years, particularly by J. D. Coppock and A. I. MacBean. Coppock used an instability index obtained by averaging the proportional year-to-year changes of the statistics, after adjusting

TABLE 13.4

Concentration of exports, 1970, selected countries

Country	Value of all exports ($ m.)	Principal exports	
		Commodity	Percentage of all exports
Bolivia	193	Tin	52
		Other metals	42
Brazil	2739	Coffee	34
		Iron ore	8
		Cotton	6
Colombia	788	Coffee	59
		Petroleum	7
Cyprus	102	Copper	22
		Citrus fruit	17
		Potatoes	15
		Iron	6
Egypt (1969)	735	Cotton	41
Uganda	261	Coffee	54
		Cotton	19
		Copper	9
		Tea	5
Nigeria	1248	Petroleum	58
		Cocoa	15
		Vegetable oil and oilseeds	10
Ghana	424	Cocoa	69
		Wood	9
		Gold	6
Malaysia	1619	Rubber	29
		Tin	18
		Wood	17
		Palm oil	8
Turkey	588	Cotton	29
		Hazelnuts	15
		Tobacco	11
		Raisins	4

SOURCE: *I.M.F., Balance of Payments Yearbook.*

for trend. The period under study was 1948 – 58. Although the methods and results of these scholars have been the subject of some criticism (e.g. by P. Ady),
they are still rather disturbing to general opinion. On the argument that primary
products were less stable than manufactures, Table 13.5 summarises Coppock's
findings. In other words, although prices of primary goods are rather less stable
than manufactures, export proceeds are significantly more stable. This aggregate
comparison, surprising and interesting as it is, can conceal all manner of variations.
MacBean compares the average instability indices of a number of developing and
developed countries (Table 13.6). Once more there are less stable prices for the
developing countries, and in this study their proceeds are also less stable, but not
greatly so. The values for the developing countries vary a great deal, and half of the
forty-five are less than 23 – the developed countries' average.

TABLE 13.5

| Exports | Instability indices | |
	Primary goods	Manufactured goods
Proceeds	3.8	6.8
Volume	4.7	7.1
Price	8.4	7.6

TABLE 13.6

| Exports (1946 – 58) | Mean instability indices | |
	45 developing countries	18 developed countries
Proceeds	23.1	17.6
Volume	19.4	14.0
Prices	17.6	10.7

What caused export instability, where it existed? MacBean was unable to dis-
cover any general economic explanation; there is little or no correlation between
instability and *per capita* income, or the proportion of exports in primary goods,
or the degree of commodity concentration. Nevertheless, the conventional theory
outlined earlier does help to explain particular cases. MacBean examined the
twelve developing countries which experienced greatest instability (in descending
order: Iran, main export: petroleum; Indonesia: rubber, petroleum; Malaya: rubber,
tin; Argentina: meat, wheat, wool; Sudan: cotton, cottonseed; South Korea: tungsten, talc, fish; South Vietnam: rubber, rice; Pakistan: jute, cotton; Ghana: cocoa,

wood; Iraq: petroleum; Bolivia: tin, lead, tungsten; Haiti: coffee, sisal) and concludes (pp. 55 – 6)

> that in four of them – Argentina, Iran, Korea and Vietnam – high export instability was largely caused by political factors or war. In a further three – Indonesia, Iraq and Malaya – politics and war again played a part, but a less vital one. In the remaining five – Bolivia, Ghana, Haiti, Pakistan and Sudan – export instability is more evidently the result of basic supply and demand characteristics of the products they export. Apart from Haiti, each of these countries specialised in the export of commodities which were of average or more than average instability . . . . In other words, they specialised not merely in primary products but on specially unstable primary products. In the case of Haiti, variations in supply appear to account for export instability, since coffee markets in the post-war world do not seem to have been subject to very sharp short-period fluctuations.

It appears that the experience of highly volatile exports does not necessarily derive from economic factors, although it might. Diversification does not necessarily alleviate instability, although it might; for the new product (if at all subject to instability) may be either compensatory or additive in its effect. Evidently the theory outlined at the beginning of this section was too general.

Instability and Development

But what of the effect of export instability on growth and development? MacBean found, contrary to expectations, that there is no significant relationship between export fluctuations and fixed investment or economic growth. Neither are export fluctuations associated with fluctuations in national income. There is a relationship with inflation, but it is not clear whether the fluctuations cause inflation or vice versa. There are a number of hypotheses which might explain this rather astounding result. First, the size of the subsistence sector as a proportion of national income may cushion the economy as a whole; this implies that as the economy becomes increasingly monetised, instability may increase. An additional cushion may derive from the foreign-owned sector, which may suffer fluctuations in remitted profits – in which case, as this sector diminishes in significance, domestic instability may increase. In the domestic monetised sector, there is likely to be a high marginal propensity to import, dampening the 'multiplier effect' of changes in investment or exports. This implies that instability will increase with industrialisation.

Some conclusions can be drawn from this summary. First, that in so far as international trade policy is directed towards redressing the balance between the developed (rich) and developing (poor) countries, a generalised attention to primary products may misfire; it should be more selective in terms of those products which are relatively more important to the poor countries in aggregate as well as to individual countries. Second, the problem of market instability is perhaps exaggerated both in its extent and its effect, though it may be present in particular cases; and it may become more evident if countries succeed in certain of their development aims. In the meantime, costly stabilising programmes may be misplaced; indeed a *price*-stabilising policy may succeed in destabilising *income* if variations in *supply* are the cause of the price fluctuations.

Export Growth and Primary Production

The main inhibitions to increasing export revenues from primary production lie in the markets of the developed countries. While the continued growth of the developed countries is essential to the economic health of primary producers, it cannot be assumed that *pro rata* benefits will be passed on to them. The income elasticity of demand for foodstuffs is low, and industrial raw materials are more and more being placed in competition with synthetics. The institutional framework of trade often approximates a model where oligopolistic buyers are dealing with competitive sellers. All this leads to a situation where much of the benefits of cost-reducing technical change in production are passed on to buyers.

The developed countries often levy protective duties on processed primary products, so inhibiting the growth of these industries in the developing countries. Any international discussion on commodity policy has to take these facts, some of which are reversible, into account. The United Nations Conference on Trade and Development (UNCTAD), which was set up on the initiative of some developing countries, exists as a pressure group to attempt to change the institutional framework in the interests of the poor nations. Successful in this or not, their immediate prosperity lies in the thrall of the rich countries. The only way out is to reduce dependence on primary exports, and, ironically, the only way to do this is to increase earnings from these products. This, as we have seen, is difficult but possible. And success will breed success, for as the developing countries industrialise, they will provide new markets for their own products.

Illustration by Case Studies

The case study in this chapter illustrates attempts to lessen the internal effects of instability arising from commodity trade and to use this trade for development. The study describes the working of two West African marketing boards in their attempt to insulate the Ghanaian and Western Nigerian economies from the instabilities of the world cocoa market and to use the cocoa revenue for development purposes.

CASE 34. THE WEST AFRICAN COCOA
MARKETING BOARDS, 1948 – 62

The Purpose of the Boards

The West African marketing boards were conceived as cushions to protect the
peasant producer of exportable agricultural products from world market fluctuations. During the last war and immediately after, the British Ministry of Food
undertook the marketing of products from the West African colonies, but in 1947
marketing boards were set up under the control of the local colonial governments.
We shall discuss the activities of the Ghanaian* and Nigerian boards dealing in
cocoa. Although the Ghana Cocoa Marketing Board has retained its identity since
its inception, there is a discontinuity in the Nigerian case. Until 1954 the marketing of all Nigerian cocoa was undertaken by the Nigerian Marketing Board, but with
the setting-up of regional governments, regional marketing boards replaced the old
national one-commodity boards. Cocoa was the main crop of the Western Region;
very little cocoa is grown elsewhere in Nigeria, and attention in this case study will
be concerned with that crop. More will be said about the world cocoa market, but
at present it will be noted that MacBean gives cocoa a high rating for market instability; that Ghana was the principal producer throughout the period; and that Nigeria
was third largest in 1948 but moved to second in 1960 when its production over-
took Brazil's.

The purposes of the boards were set out in two White Papers published in 1944
and 1946. Each board would set a price for the season 'in advance of the sale of
the crop'. The crop would be bought on behalf of the board by licensed buying
agents at this pre-set 'producer price'; it would then sell the crop on the world
market. Some years it would make a profit, others a loss. The White Paper stated:
'Profits will be used *primarily* to maintain the maximum possible stability in the
price paid to the producer' and 'there will be no question of [the boards] making
a profit at the expense of West African cocoa producers'. The point of the scheme,
then, was to insulate the producer from short-term price fluctuations, both intra-
seasonal and over a period of years, but not to cut him off from any trend, either
upward or downward of world prices. In this way, the farmer would know what
price he could expect from his crop during the ensuing season, even if the world
price was fluctuating – and these fluctuations would not be transmitted through the
domestic economy. As well as this stabilising role, the boards had the duty 'to
assist in the development by all possible means of the cocoa industry'.

In the first few years of their operation the boards amassed quite large surpluses, and at the same time the producer price was changed considerably from

* The country was officially called Gold Coast until independence in 1957; to
avoid confusion, the present name will be used throughout.

season to season (Table 13.7). Professors Bauer and Paish argued in the *Economic Journal* that, far from stabilising, the boards were actually destabilising prices and that the accumulating surpluses were an inequitable and inefficient form of taxation. They saw the boards as an institutional device bound to act in this way, and in so far as a large proportion of the world market price was withheld from the producer, the progress of the West African cocoa industry would suffer relatively to other producing areas. They also argued that the boards' instructions were unclear as to the purpose and meaning of stability, and that price stability may cause income instability – as we have already noticed.

The Operation of the Boards

How has the subsequent practice of the boards measured up to these prognostications? Table 13.7 shows the movements of producer prices and the average export prices received by the boards. The rather erratic movements of prices noted by the critics did not continue beyond the early 1950s. But the difference between producer and export prices throughout the period is striking. This was not entirely due to marketing board policy; the greater part of the difference was paid by the boards to the government in taxes on behalf of the producers. In the whole of the period, the Nigerian board made a surplus of £43 million but paid an additional £52 million in taxes; the Ghanaian surplus was £87 million and £236 million was paid in taxes. Because of this, although the producer price was below the export price throughout, both boards experienced deficits in 1955 – 6, 1956 – 7 and 1960 – 1 – all years when the world price was very depressed. But after allowing for the effect of taxes, it is clear that the boards did not take their original mandate 'not to make a profit' too seriously, for their accumulated surpluses over the period were not insignificant; the marketing boards were being used as instruments of taxation, and both governments declared that surpluses should be used for development purposes. Inspection of Table 13.7 shows that this policy bore more heavily on the Ghanaian than the Western Nigerian farmer. Indeed, on publication of the Second Development Plan in March 1959, the United Ghana Farmers' Council – a wing of the ruling political party – announced that the farmers were thenceforth to make a 'voluntary contribution' of 12s. a load (60 lb.) or £22 a ton (see the producer price for 1959 – 60 and 1960 – 1). The extent to which cocoa incomes were withheld by the combined effect of board surpluses and taxes is shown in Table 13.8. Here, 'producer income' is the money actually paid to farmers (and middle-men). 'Potential income' is the money received by the boards after deducting marketing expenses but before taxes. Of course, this is only an approximation of potential income, for we do not know what the world price would have been without the influence of the monopolistic boards. Also, higher prices paid to farmers may have increased supply, and earnings would then have differed by an amount determined by the elasticities of supply and demand for cocoa. Nor do we know what proportion of the world price would have reached the farmer in the absence of a marketing board. For almost certainly he would have had to sell his crop through a merchant with greater market power and information than himself, and would thus be prone to monopsonistic exploitation. The figures for 'potential' income only give an idea of what might have been. During the period, Western Nigerian cocoa producers received 68 per cent of potential income; of the rest, 13 per cent was withheld by the boards and 19 per cent was taxed. In Ghana, producers got 55 per cent, 30 per cent was taxed, 2 per cent went as a 'voluntary contribution' and 11 per cent was kept by the board.

TABLE   13.7

Cocoa producer prices and average export prices: Ghana and Nigeria,
1947 - 8 to 1960 - 1 (£ per ton)

	1947-8	1948-9	1949-50	1950-1	1951-2	1952-3	1953-4
GHANA							
Producer	75	121	84	131	149	131	134
Export	201	137	178	269	245	231	358
NIGERIA							
Producer	63	120	106	120	170	170	166
Export	185	126	180	266	233	212	348

	1954-5	1955-6	1956-7	1957-8	1958-9	1959-60	1960-1
GHANA							
Producer	134	149	149	134	134	112	112
Export	353	222	189	304	280	226	175
NIGERIA							
Producer	196	196	146	146	146	156	148
Export	317	191	168	271	265	202	153

*Up to and including 1953 - 4, Nigerian figures refer to all Nigeria; from 1954 - 5 they refer to the Western Region only.

SOURCE: Ghana: T. Killick, 'The Economics of Cocoa', in *A Study of Contemporary Ghana,* ed. T. Killick, W. Birmingham, I. Neustadt and E. N. Omaboe (London: Allen & Unwin, 1966) ch. 15. Nigeria: G. K. Helleiner, *Peasant Agriculture, Government and Economic Growth in Nigeria* (Homewood, Ill.: Irwin, 1967).

Effect on Stability

To what extent did the boards fulfil their original purpose of price stability, and did this lead to income stability? As far as intra-seasonal prices are concerned, there is no problem; in only one year (in Nigeria) was the producer price changed during the season – the boards must have achieved their object in this respect. Inter-

TABLE 13.8

Cocoa producer and 'potential' incomes: Ghana and Nigeria,
1947 - 8 to 1960 - 1 (£ m.)

	1947 - 8	1948 - 9	1949 - 50	1950 - 1	1951 - 2	1952 - 3	1953 - 4
GHANA							
Producer	15.4	21.2	21.2	34.2	31.4	32.5	28.0
'Potential'	39.6	35.4	42.1	66.6	48.1	53.1	71.1
NIGERIA							
Producer	4.4	12.6	10.8	14.3	18.2	18.4	16.4
'Potential'	13.9	13.7	17.9	29.3	18.4	23.0	23.9

	1954 - 5	1955 - 6	1956 - 7	1957 - 8	1958 - 9	1959 - 60	1960 - 1
GHANA							
Producer	29.5	35.0	39.9	27.7	33.4	34.7	45.9
'Potential'	73.8	47.8	44.4	58.4	65.0	63.1	60.6
NIGERIA							
Producer	15.5	20.1	19.2	10.6	19.1	22.5	27.0
'Potential'	26.5	20.2	21.7	19.9	35.0	29.6	27.9

SOURCE: as Table 13.7.

seasonal stability is more difficult to assess. G. K. Helleiner has used two measures of instability in an attempt to answer these questions. The first (I_1 in Table 13.9) simply averages the percentage change in value from one year to the next, always expressing the percentage in terms of the higher of the two observations. The second measure (I_2) averages deviations from a five-year moving average and thus corrects for any trend.*

We have calculated these indices for the period 1947 - 8 to 1960 - 1,[†] and the results for both countries are displayed in Table 13.9. The figures mean that in Ghana, for example, the yearly change in producer prices was on average about 13 per cent compared with an average yearly change of about 22 per cent in export prices. Export prices deviated from trend by about 22 per cent a year as well, while the average deviation of producer prices was only 8 per cent. It will be seen that on both measures the board's pricing policies achieved greater producer price stability than would have been obtained if producers had been paid world prices.

*We have now noted three different methods of measuring instability, including the Coppock measure. This is one of the difficulties of empirical work, where one often has to choose between a number of alternative and unsatisfactory methods of describing in mathematical language what seems to be precisely described in words.

[†]Helleiner's Nigerian calculations, for the period 1947 - 8 to 1961 - 2, were recalculated in order to make them comparable with the Ghanaian data.

As for the smoothing of 'potential' incomes, which in any case were rather more stable than world prices, the record is less clear. The Ghanaians had some success in stabilising annual deviations from trend, but effected little when it came to year-to-year changes, which the Western Nigerians appear to have *destabilised*. We must conclude that the boards did enjoy some measure of success in price stability, but their record, in these years, was poor in the case of income smoothing. The Ghanaians were more successful on every count – but this is not surprising, for the lower the producer price in terms of the world price, the easier it is to maintain.

TABLE 13.9

Instability of cocoa prices and incomes: Ghana and
Western Nigeria, 1947-8 to 1960-1

	Ghana		Nigeria	
	I_1	I_2	I_1	I_2
Prices				
Producer	12.9	7.9	10.9	9.1
Average export	21.5	21.8	23.4	22.8
Incomes				
Producer	15.4	12.4	22.4	14.4
'Potential'	16.4	18.1	18.3	16.6

SOURCE: Calculated from Tables 13.7 and 13.8.

A Changing Role

It is clear that the role of the boards as agents of development had ousted their original stabilising role during the period under review. A large part of the boards' surpluses had been spent, in accordance with original instructions, on developing the cocoa industry. Grants were made to research institutes, university agricultural departments and demonstration programmes. Subsidies were paid for replanting in areas afflicted by disease and for insecticide spraying. The Ghana Cocoa Marketing Board built schools and feeder roads (which reduced transport costs) in the cocoa areas. There was misappropriation of funds and peculation, but unless it is thought that this is inevitable, it does not detract from the principle of the discussion. More and more, however, cocoa funds have been withdrawn from the cocoa sector. In Nigeria this trend began in earnest with the setting-up of regional boards in 1954, and in Ghana since the 'voluntary contribution' of 1959. In Nigeria, the flow of funds out of cocoa has moved partly into the public sector in the form of grants and loans to the federal and regional governments (before the *coup* of 1966) and partly into the private sector through loans and the purchase of equity. In Ghana, the funds have been turned over to the state. Doubtless, a great deal of productive and infrastructural investment in both countries is financed out of cocoa money. Two questions must be asked: Is this policy conducive to growth? If it is, is it an equitable policy? The answer to the first revolves around another. To what use would these funds be put, if the farmer was not taxed so heavily? Although the average propensity to consume of the West African peasant seems to be, not unnaturally, high, there is evidence to suggest that beyond a threshold income the marginal propensity to save is also high. This is partly because fluctuations give high incomes an unexpected flavour. It would appear that although these savings are partly hoarded and act as a personal stabilising fund, a significant proportion may be used for farm investment – clearing the bush for new planting, fertilisers, transport equipment, etc. Economists generally state that the bulk of the remainder finds its way into non-productive investment such as real property. In the absence of well-developed capital markets which channel personal savings along more productive lines, this pattern of disposal seems likely. If these impressions are correct, then a fair proportion of the cocoa money which is invested productively would otherwise have been spent on imported consumer goods or speculative property deals. It would be fair to state that the activities of the marketing boards have been conducive to growth and development, now conceived as their principal role. One might ask, however, why it is necessary to use the boards as a separate taxing authority. In the Nigerian case there is more justification, since, in so far as it can invest in the private sector, it has more latitude than a government. But the policy of the Ghana State Marketing Board seems to be firmly integrated with the government's, and its discretionary activity is confined to the sale of cocoa.

Our view of the justice of the policy as a whole must be coloured by our own ideological preconceptions. The out-and-out individualist would argue that the farmer should be in charge of his own affairs; he does not need a public authority to restrict his opportunity to spend and save money earned out of his own toil on the farm. If he does not wish to save for a rainy day, that is his business – and the operation of a stabilising fund is no part of government. That, put crudely, was the argument of Milton Friedman in the controversy initiated by Bauer and Paish referred to earlier. On the other hand, the collectivist (and this is the author's view) urges that in both countries the cocoa farmer is well favoured, for the crop is very specialised, and there is little wrong in subjecting him to heavy taxation in the interests of the nation at large. It is probably true that the cocoa farmer is taxed more than other citizens enjoying the same income, but with the paucity of taxation instruments open to the government of a developing country, this seems to be an injustice necessary to a nation wishing and needing to enjoy rapid growth and development.

Supply and the Producer Price

This general view should perhaps be qualified by a consideration of the effect of the overly low producer price that has recently been paid in both countries. Until 1966 this price was progressively reduced, and in that year it stood at £84 a ton in Ghana and £90 in Nigeria. Bauer and Paish had predicted that low prices would inhibit the progress of the cocoa industry; what evidence is there that this has happened? Cocoa farmers do seem to respond to price incentives in the long run; in the short run the price effect is less clear. The difficulties of establishing clear relationships are due to the complexity of the determinants of supply of crops from trees. Current output depends very much on weather conditions and disease as well as the number of trees in production, which depends on plantings seven or eight years previously. Since the life of a tree is well over thirty years and its yield varies with its age, first rising and then declining, the age structure of the tree and the time profile of planting are also important. Such information is exiguous in West Africa, and the verification of a rising long-run supply curve rests on the establishment of a relationship between price and *acreage under cocoa* rather than volume of output. Current planting will have its full effect many years later when the rising price trend which induced it is reversed. Since it is not possible to switch resources to other uses quickly, this is an element of cobweb instability, which of course it is the object of stabilisation policy to prevent. As for short-run responses, it has always been assumed that supply was inelastic since cultivation is cheap and current practices cannot be changed. This view may be increasingly anachronistic, as the growing use of fertilisers, spraying machines and other relatively sophisticated techniques may have given the farmer more scope to make decisions which can significantly affect current output. The poor West African crops in the late 1960s have convinced many commentators that there is a short-run response to price. Although these shortfalls may have been due to abnormally bad weather conditions, the goverments seem to have taken these warnings to heart (though they are doubtless also impressed by the relationship between low cocoa prices and *political* instability and have gradually increased the producer price. Subsidies for insecticides are also being increased. Ghana cocoa can still fetch a bigger price in the neighbouring countries of Ivory Coast and Togo; consequently smuggling is rife and the traveller on the roads leading out of Ghana is stopped more than once by police on the look-out for contraband cocoa. The present policy of price increases is probably necessary, but if it continues and the long-run response is too great, there is a danger than consequent surpluses may cause a collapse in the market and so do irreparable damage to the West African economy.

Exercises

(13.1) List the general characteristics of developing countries.

(13.2) Do most exports of primary goods originate from developed or developing countries? What do the figures suggest concerning the geographical pattern of *production* of primary goods?

(13.3) Explain what is meant by 'export stability'. Why are the prices of primary goods considered particularly unstable? Would you expect export proceeds to be more unstable than prices?

(13.4) How far do the researches of Coppock and MacBean validate the hypothesis (*a*) that developing countries experience greater export instability than developed countries, (*b*) that this instability hinders development?

(13.5) Why is increasing industrialisation of developing countries likely to magnify the multiplier effect of changes in investment and exports?

(13.6) Do you think that the cocoa marketing boards have been a help or a hindrance to the development of Ghana and Western Nigeria?

Supplementary exercises

(13.7) Distinguish between 'development' and 'growth'.

(13.8) Discuss the proposition that 'trade, not aid' should be the objective of international policies to help the developing countries.

Sources and References

These can be found at the end of Chapter 14 on 'International Commodity Agreements'.

CHAPTER 14

International Commodity Agreements

Edward Horesh

Summary of Background Material

The efforts of a government to stabilise the internal economy of its country's
primary production can be supplemented by international action to control or
regulate world markets. The fortunes of Ghanaian and Nigerian cocoa are obviously
affected by activity in competing countries, and co-operating policies could affect
the welfare of all producers. This is the purpose of international agreements, although importing countries also have an interest – manufacturers can be upset by
commodity fluctuations or prices that are kept high by control. Nor is it true that
all producers have the same interest: high-cost producers desire a higher maintained
price than low-cost producers; established producers have a greater interest in restricting production than new entrants.

Formerly, the contracting parties to these agreements were confined to producers, but after the last war, when the proposals of the Havana Charter with
regard to commodity agreements were adopted by the United Nations, it was laid
down that consumers shall be represented on any Commodity Council and have the
same voting powers as producers. Only in 'emergencies' do exporters have the
right to take unilateral action. Moreover, the Charter permits international commodity agreements only when it is thought that market forces cannot prevent
'burdensome surpluses' causing hardship to peasant producers or workers. A
number of commodity study groups have been set up by the U.N. and F.A.O.
which may recommend that conditions for an agreement exist, in which case the
U.N. can convene a conference to establish a control scheme. It is clear that the
writers of the Charter had in mind situations where the price was temporarily
depressed or was subject to violent fluctuations; they were not concerned to provide a long-term buttress for commodity prices.

U.N. attitudes have, however, been revised since 1947; spokesmen for the
developing nations take the view that their interests were not sufficiently represented in the post-war agreements, and UNCTAD has been formed to redress
this balance. During the Conference meetings in Geneva in 1964 and Delhi in
1968, it was resolved that commodity schemes should aim not merely at price
stabilisation but at support as well. Although member governments are not bound
by such resolutions, they do represent a political factor which cannot be ignored.
An importing country is represented at a Conference by a Minister and his officials,

flanked by advisers, many of whom are seconded by manufacturers and merchants. Although the negotiators' main concern will be these commercial interests, they cannot fail to be influenced by the prevailing international political climate.

Basically, there are three ways through which commodity control can be operated:

(1) A *multilateral agreement,* where each party contracts either to buy or sell agreed quantities of the commodity at prices which range between an agreed minimum and maximum. The market price can vary within these limits but never beyond them. An example of this type is the International Wheat Agreement.

(2) A *buffer stock,* as in the Tin Agreement. Here the stock manager controls the price by buying or selling the commodity in sufficient quantities. The process is similar to 'open-market operations', which are used by monetary authorities to control the price of securities. Success depends on the manager having sufficient funds or stocks when needed.

(3) Control can be exercised by imposing such limits on exports as are necessary to control prices within agreed limits. A basic *export quota* is allotted to each participating exporter at the beginning of the agreement, and current quotas are announced as a proportion of these.

Any scheme must be compounded of one or more of these elements.

Illustration by Case Studies

The following study illustrates an attempt to lessen the effects of external causes of instability. The difficulties of negotiating and operating a coffee agreement are described in the perspective both of the stability and the development of the developing countries.

CASE 35. THE INTERNATIONAL COFFEE AGREEMENT, 1962 – 72

Coffee production is dominated by Brazil, as Tables 14.1 and 14.2 show.

TABLE 14.1

World production of coffee, 1961 – 2 to 1970 – 1 (million bags)*

	1961 – 2	1962 – 3	1963 – 4	1964 – 5	1965 – 6	1966 – 7	1967 – 8	1968 – 9	1969 – 70	1970 – 71
Total	71	66	64	57	80	58	68	61	68	58
of which										
Brazil	36	29	23	18	34	18	23	17	21	11
Colombia	8	8	8	8	8	8	8	8	9	8

*One bag weighs 60 kg or 132 lb.

SOURCE: *Plantation Crops: A Review.*

TABLE 14.2

World production of coffee by regions, 1933 – 71 (million bags)

	Average of five seasons ending				
	1933 – 4	1938 – 9	1950 – 1	1960 – 1	1970 – 1
Brazil	24.0	22.5	16.8	28.5	18.0
Colombia	3.5	4.2	5.7	7.5	7.9
Other Central and South America	5.7	6.5	6.7	10.3	14.3
Africa	1.2	2.1	4.0	10.1	18.2
Asia	2.1	2.4	1.0	2.2	4.1

SOURCES: J. W. F. Rowe, *The World's Coffee* (London: H.M.S.O., 1963) p. 21 (for 1933/4 – 1960/1); *Plantation Crops: A Review*, derived from table 8 (for 1970/1).

It will be seen from Table 14.2, which presents five - year averages before and after the last war, that the small producing countries have increased their production considerably in recent years, while Brazilian production has been static and somewhat unstable. It will also be remembered that coffee is second only to petroleum as a foreign exchange earner and that many developing countries are dependent on it for this purpose. There are four different types of coffee, each with its own distinctive quality and flavour. They are listed in Table 14.3 in descending order of desirability together with the main producing countries of each.

TABLE 14.3

Coffee exports by type and country of origin, 1970 – 1 (thousand bags)

1. *Colombian mild Arabicas*	7943
of which	
Colombia	6331
Kenya	935
Tanzania	660
2. *Other mild Arabicas*	10373
of which	
El Salvador	1613
Mexico	1511
Guatemala	1563
Costa Rica	1070
3. *Unwashed Arabicas*	19466
of which	
Brazil	18068
Ethiopia	1332
4. *Robustas*	14210
of which	
O.A.M.C.A.F.*	5620
Uganda	3032
Angola	2822
Zaire	1145
Indonesia	1141
TOTAL	51992

*A union of French-speaking African states.

SOURCE: International Coffee Organisation.

Robusta coffee, the cheapest of the four, is plucked from a different variety of tree from the others; it has a less popular flavour (though it is apparently well liked in parts of Western Europe) and is the main ingredient of soluble (i.e. instant) coffee. Table 14.4 gives an indication of the behaviour of coffee prices over the past years.

TABLE 14.4
*Coffee: average annual spot prices of raw coffee on the New York
market, 1954–72 (cents per lb.)*

	1954	1955	1956	1957	1958	1959	1960
Brazil, Santos No. 4	79	57	58	57	48	37	37
Uganda, Washed Clean	58	38	34	35	38	29	20

	1961	1962	1963	1964	1965	1966	1967
Brazil, Santos No. 4	36	34	34	47	45	38	38
Uganda, Washed Clean	18	21	28	36	31	34	34

	1968	1969	1970	1971	1972
Brazil, Santos No. 4	37	41	55	45	51
Uganda, Washed Clean	34	33	42	42	44

SOURCE: 1954–62: Rowe, *The World's Coffee* p. 23; 1962–72: *Plantation
Crops: A Review* (1969–73).

TABLE 14.5
Imports and Consumption of coffee in selected countries in 1970

	Imports of raw coffee (thousand bags)	Estimated consumption per head (lb per annum)
United States	19.7	13.8
West Germany	5.2	10.6
France	4.0	10.4
Italy	2.6	6.8
Sweden	1.8	28.6
United Kingdom	1.5	4.4

SOURCE: *Plantation Crops: A Review.*

Nearly half the world's exports of coffee go the the United States, and almost all the rest to Europe. Table 14.5 indicates the six largest importers. There are strong signs, however, that these markets are becoming saturated, and *per capita* consumption is not rising significantly. The main hope for the coffee market lies in the poorer of the developed countries, where income elasticity of demand is relatively high, and in the Soviet Union and Eastern Europe, where *per capita* consumption is less than one-twentieth of that of the West.

The 1962 Agreement

The high prices of the early 1950s induced a wave of new planting, particularly in the Paraná state of Brazil and in Africa. When the trees began to bear in the latter part of the decade, the price plummeted, and Brazil with six other Latin American states signed a quota agreement in 1958; in 1959 eight other Latin American countries joined, and by 1961 all the main exporters except Ethiopia, Congo (now Zaire) and Indonesia were members. Meanwhile, a Coffee Study Group had been formed in 1958, and a draft agreement for a Coffee Conference had been prepared which recommended a gradual reduction in the price level, supported by a buffer stock. However, at the Alliance for Progress meeting in Punta del Este, the U.S. representative announced that his country was prepared to enter a long-term agreement which would stabilise the coffee price at its *current* level. This decision, which was political rather than commercial, set the tenor for the subsequent discussions. The other importing countries could hardly fail to follow the path of the largest of the importers and the leader of the Western Alliance.

The agreement, signed in 1963 but already effective in 1962, was to last five years and embraced over 90 per cent of the trade. It had six objectives:

(1) to provide adequate supplies at reasonable prices;
(2) to alleviate hardship from 'burdensome surpluses' and excessive price fluctuations;
(3) to contribute to the development of productive resources, employment and income of member countries;
(4) to assist in increasing the purchasing power of exporting countries;
(5) to encourage the consumption of coffee throughout the world; and
(6) to encourage international co-operation in the production, marketing and sales of coffee.

The basis of the agreement was the *export quota.*

Importers agreed to limit their purchases from non-members to an amount not greater than their average annual imports during the previous three years whenever the value of exports from member countries was less than 95 per cent of the 1961 value of world exports. Although this ensured that non-member exporters were able to continue in business, it did give them an incentive to join.

It effectively forced Kenya into the agreement, for with its small output of high-quality (albeit low-cost) coffee, it would have been unsure of its markets as a non-member.

Each exporting member was given a basic quota depending on estimated world demand and its own capacity. Effective annual quotas were allocated in terms of the 'basic,' but adjusted from one quarter to the next depending on movements in the market price. For example, at the beginning of the 1963 - 4 season the annual quota was 99 per cent of the basic, but owing to favourable price movements it was raised to 102.15 per cent in February 1964. Waivers were allowed to basic quotas if a country experienced particular hardships; when they have been granted, this has usually been conditional on the industry taking steps to curtail its capacity. Exports to certain scheduled countries, mainly the Communist bloc and Japan, which have low consumption rates, were excluded from the quota, provided that they did not import more than their domestic requirements. This allowed price discrimination - non-quota sales were cheaper - in order to encourage consumption in these countries. This practice, as the textbook writers would have predicted, gave rise to arbitrage dealings. Coffee was bought cheap in Eastern Europe and sold at a profit in the West. To prevent the movements of this 'tourist coffee', there were progressively stronger checks on certificates of origin and import controls.

But the main problem was over the level of prices and the export quota. Brazil has an interest in high prices to support her high-cost producers. Not all Brazilian coffee is produced at high cost, as about half now normally emanates from the relatively new plantings in Paraná; and even in the traditional growing areas, producers are paid well below market prices. In order to maintain the price above the 1962 level, exports had to be restricted. The African producers would be content with lower prices, as this would allow them to increase their output. The agreement encouraged diversification, and indeed the Brazilians were in 1962 already reducing their acreage under coffee, but for the new African producers this has meant not increasing their plantings. Before the agreement, the Brazilians and Colombians were maintaining the coffee price by withholding stocks, and the Africans were sheltering behind this policy; they enjoyed the relatively high price without being subjected to export controls. Now the cost of stockpiling had fallen on all producers. Since there is still little control over production, this had meant that whenever supply exceeded demand at the target price, all producers had to stockpile. In 1957 it was estimated that coffee stocks were about equivalent to four months of the world's needs; ten years later, in spite of a 40 per cent growth in consumption they were equivalent to fourteen months. Storing any crop is expensive, and after a time it may become unmarketable. In December 1968, 100,000 tons were burned or thrown into the sea in the Ivory Coast, Africa's largest producer, to obviate storage costs. Because of the resentment generated by the working of the agreement and because the different types of coffee have rather different market characteristics, a system of 'selective' quotas was introduced in December 1966 whereby the quotas for each country were adjusted according to the price movements of the coffee it exported. Hitherto, the indicator prices had been based on the average of each of the grades; but now 'floor' and 'ceiling' prices are quoted for each grade. For example, on the introduction of the selective system, the Robusta 'floor' price was 30.50 cents per lb. and its 'ceiling' 34.50 cents. If the price rose above this ceiling for fifteen consecutive days, the Robusta producers' quota was increased by 2.5 per cent. As a result of the selective system, Robusta quotas were increased more than once during that season whilst quotas for the other grades were reduced. In the ensuing season, at the insistence of the Latin American producers, the differentials between Robusta and the more expensive varieties were reduced. The selective system was retained in the new agreement.

In order to maintain their position, the Brazilians had set up an expanding processing industry and were exporting soluble coffee powder. This not only threatened the Robusta producers but reduced storage costs and angered the Americans. The export of this processed coffee was not then subject to the same export tax as the raw bean, and the American manufacturers saw this as a threat to their own industry. The extent of this activity can be measured from the figures shown in Table 14.6. In spite of these difficulties, the 1962 agreement

TABLE 14.6
American imports of soluble coffee from Latin America
(million lbs)

1962	1966	1967
3.8	10.7	27.4

was generally regarded as successful. The price was stabilised at a high level, and the Executive Director estimated that this earned for the producing countries over $500 million a year.

The 1968 Agreement

1968 saw the expiry of the first agreement and the renegotiation of a new one. It was expected that the International Coffee Agreement would continue in much the same way as before. As a concession to the Americans, producing countries were forbidden to discriminate in favour of exports of processed coffee. Accordingly, the Brazilian government imposed a tax on soluble coffee exports to the United States (but not to other countries). In spite of this, exports of soluble coffee to the United States increased by over 50 per cent of their 1967 level. An important innovation in the new agreement was the introduction of a fund to aid diversification. Hitherto, the only positive incentive to output reduction had been the offer of additional quotas on condition of diversification measures. Then there was a fund financed with the help of the World Bank and the U.S. government but mainly by a levy of sixty cents for each bag in excess of 100,000 exported to quota markets. This fund provided a fair amount of support to diversification policies in many countries.

During the first agreement, which had originated in a period of surpluses, conflict had centred on the question of quota-sharing within a relatively uncontroversial global total. This conflict was highlighted in the selectivity issue of 1966, when it was agreed that quotas for each country should be adjusted according to the price movement of the type of coffee it exported. This arrangement does not work so well in periods of shortage, when the consuming countries have a much stronger interest in the size of the global quota, and each producing country is trying to sell as much as it can at the prevailing high price. It soon became clear that the term of the second agreement (1968 – 73) was to be a period of shortage, partly due to the success of the diversification schemes but mainly to crop failures in Brazil (see Table 14.1) caused by frost in Paraná and the spread of the debilitating disease, coffee rust. At the start of the 1967 – 8 crop year, world stocks of coffee stood at 58 million bags, just under the previous year's production figure, whereas at the end of the 1972 – 3 year, stocks were estimated at 23 million bags, less than one-third of the year's production.

In spite of their relatively lower production, the Brazilian producers throughout this period breached the letter and spirit of the selective quota system by quoting very high prices but paying their customers discounts of as much as 25 per cent in the form of credit rates for further purchases. Thus the size of the 'Unwashed Arabicas' quota was increased since it was based on quoted prices.

Changes in the world economy also had disruptive effects on the working of the agreement. First, the American devaluations: since indicator prices were quoted in dollars, the producing countries called for an offsetting increase of four cents a pound during 1971 and 1972, and this request met with a denial from the United States. As a result, Brazil, Colombia, Ivory Coast and Portugal (on behalf of Angola), the four major producing countries, agreed not to accept an increase in quotas for the remainder of the year. During this period, the price of coffee rose on average by over two cents a pound, and whether this was due to collective market or normal market prices is arguable. At the annual conference in September 1972, there was argument over prices and the global quota; the consuming countries wished to restore the old relatively lower price by increasing export quotas. This disagreement found no compromise and no quotas were agreed, nor have been since; and it is on this issue that the renegotiation of a third agreement due to start in October 1973 foundered. Meanwhile, the producing countries increased their apparent solidarity, and under the leadership of Brazil set up a cartel which unilaterally restricts exports. This cartelisation is currently being strengthened by the setting up of a coffee marketing organisation in Brazil which is purchasing coffee from African producers in order to maintain the price.

The enlargement and strengthening of the E.E.C. and its associated territories in Africa has been another source of conflict. The associated territories enjoy a 7 per cent preference and this has been extended to every producing country in Africa (except Angola) and is now being offered by the new members of the E.E.C. The enlarged E.E.C. has created a market almost as large as that of the United States. In the abortive renegotiations of 1972 and 1973, the Latin American governments, with U. S. support, attempted to have the abolition of preferences written into the agreement.

Conclusion

The International Coffee Agreement enjoyed a five-year term of relative success but the conflicts experienced in its second period of operation have so far made it impossible to renegotiate for a third term. Politics provided the main impetus to its inception, and it is possible that the current U.S. lack of interest in the problems of the less developed countries has had some responsibility for the I.C.A.'s failure. Under the leadership of Brazil, the main producing countries are attempting to maintain prices in spite of the collapse of the agreement, but it is doubtful whether this is possible without the consuming countries policing any export-quota agreements. The Brazilian attempt to market coffee on behalf of other producers may prove too expensive a burden for one country to carry and in any case depends on the goodwill of its competitors, whose interests are not identical. The International Coffee Organisation is still in existence and may still succeed in bringing consumers and producers together.

In so far as the agreement has been or could again be successful in its intention to maintain prices, we should ask certain questions about this objective to maintain producers incomes by maintaining the price. This amounts to a transfer of income from consumers to producers; in other words, it might be described as a form of aid. But is this aid well directed? To qualify as a beneficiary, a country must be fortunate enough to participate in a commodity agreement; and even amongst the participants, the benefits are very unevenly spread. Brazil, a relatively rich country, has probably received most support from the Coffee Agreement, whilst Kenya's development may well have been inhibited. Neither is the aid collected on the basis of ability to pay, as it could be if its provenance derived from tax receipts of donor governments; rather its basis is the propensity to consume coffee. Seemingly, the income transfer would be more efficiently and equitably effected along another route.

Exercises

(14.1) What are the main objectives and features of international agreements on primary products?

(14.2) Compare the importance of coffee and cocoa as export earners for the developing countries.

(14.3) Why is it said that commodities with price elasticities greater than one are not suitable for international agreements? Will price support for a commodity whose demand is inelastic always help a producing country?

(14.4) Discuss the effect of the devaluation of the dollar on primary producers.

Supplementary exercises

(14.5) In what ways are the problems of (*a*) rubber, (*b*) sugar producers different from coffee and cocoa producers in respect to international agreements?

(14.6) Calculate the instability indices (I_1 and I_2) described in Chapter 13 for the New York spot prices of Brazilian Santos No. 4 coffee using the data for the years 1958 – 68 (Table 14.4). Comment on the results.

Sources and References

This covers Chapter 13 also.

A Special Correspondent, 'Cocoa Board Needs a More Positive Role', *Financial Times* (24 Feb 1969).

P. ADY, 'International Commodity Policy', in *Economic Development and Structural Change*, ed. I. G. Stewart (Edinburgh University Press, 1969).

S. CAINE, *Prices for Primary Producers*, Hobart Paper 24 (Institute of Economic Affairs, 1963).

Commonwealth Economic Committee, *Plantation Crops: A Review* (Commonwealth Economic Secretariat, annually).

J. D. COPPOCK, *International Economic Instability* (New York: McGraw-Hill, 1962).

B. S. FISHER, *The International Coffee Agreement: A Study in Coffee Diplomacy* (London: Pall Mall, 1972).

Food and Agricultural Organisation, *Commodity Review* (Rome: F.A.O., annually).

E. HORESH, 'Coffee's Conflicts', *West Africa* (27 Nov – 4 Dec 1972).

T. KILLICK, 'Commodity Agreements as International Aid', *Westminster Bank Review* (Feb 1967).

T. KILLICK, W. BIRMINGHAM, I. NEUSTADT and E. N. OMABOE (eds), *A Study of Contemporary Ghana*, I (London: Allen & Unwin, 1966).

A. I. MACBEAN, *Export Instability and Economic Development* (London: Allen & Unwin, 1966).

J. PINCUS, *Trade, Aid and Development* (New York: McGraw-Hill, 1967) ch. 7.

J. W. F. ROWE, *Primary Commodities in World Trade* (Cambridge University Press, 1965).

R. M. STERN, 'Determinants of Cocoa Supply in West Africa', in *African Primary Products and International Trade*, ed. I. G. Stewart and H. W. Ord (Edinburgh University Press, 1965).

Answers to Numerical Exercises

(2.1) Great Britain	Not applicable
North	− 0.8
Yorkshire and Humberside	− 0.9
East Midlands	+ 1.1
East Anglia	+ 4.8
South-east	− 0.3
South-west	+ 3.3
West Midlands	− 0.8
North-west	− 0.5
England	Not applicable
Wales	+ 0.2
Scotland	− 0.8
(2.3) Great Britain	28.7*
North	29.1
Yorkshire and Humberside	29.0
East Midlands	25.4
East Anglia	24.3
South-east	30.2
South-west	26.2
West Midlands	28.5
North-west	28.2
England	28.6*
Wales	24.1
Scotland	31.8

(4.1) (*a*) 86 per cent; (*b*) 90 per cent.

(6.1) £3 per ton.

(10.2) (*c*) £33$\frac{1}{3}$.

*Average migration within component regions, that is excludes migration be-
tween component regions.

Notes on Contributors

Joint Editors: C. T. SANDFORD and M. S. BRADBURY

Authors

M. S. BRADBURY.   Graduate of London University (B.Sc. 1964, M.Sc. 1971). Formerly a Senior Lecturer in Economics at the City of London Polytechnic and joint editor of *Economics,* journal of the Economics Association. Malcolm Bradbury became an Economic Adviser at the Ministry of Transport in 1969 and is now a Senior Economic Adviser in the Department of Industry.

EDWARD HORESH.   Graduated at the London School of Economics in 1952. After a period in industry, Mr Horesh held a lecturing post in Ghana until 1960, when he joined the staff of the Bristol College of Technology. Currently Senior Lecturer in Economics at Bath University, Edward Horesh was Visiting Lecturer at the University of Cape Coast, Ghana in 1974. Formerly an editor of *Economics.*

K. T. ROBINSON.   A Manchester graduate, Keith Robinson headed the Department of Economics and Political Studies, King Edward VII School, Sheffield, 1954 – 65. He then became Senior Lecturer in Economics and Modern Studies, Jordanhill College of Education, Glasgow, and now holds the post of Director of the Scottish Centre for Social Subjects. He is Secretary of the Scottish Branch of the Economics Association. His publications include *The Population of Britain* (London: Longmans, 1968).

T. K. SANDFORD.   Graduate of Manchester and London Universities. Since 1965 Cedric Sandford has been Professor of Political Economy at the University of Bath and he is also Director of a newly formed Centre for Fiscal Studies at Bath. He was a Visiting Professor, University of Delaware, U.S.A., in 1970. His publications include *Economics of Public Finance*, 2nd edn (Oxford: Pergamon, 1977), *Taxing Personal Wealth* (London: Allen & Unwin, 1971), *Hidden Costs of Taxation* (Institute for Fiscal Studies, 1973) and, with co-authors, *An Accessions Tax* (Institute for Fiscal Studies, 1973) and *An Annual Wealth Tax* (Institute for Fiscal Studies/ Heinemann, 1975).

M. J. SARGENT.   Graduate of Nottingham and London Universities after several years' experience in agriculture and horticulture. Since 1967 Malcolm Sargent has lectured at the University of Bath to students reading horticulture and economics. His published work includes *Economics in Horticulture* (London: Macmillan, 1973) and articles on economic aspects of horticulture.

CATHERINE WINNETT. Graduate of the University of East Anglia; subsequently engaged in post-graduate research at the University of Oxford. Since 1973 Lecturer in Economics at the University of Bath. Current research and teaching interests are in inflation and the international monetary system, capital and growth theory, and the history of economic thought.